Christmas Plates

& Other Commemoratives from Royal Copenhagen and Bing & Grøndahl

Lars Christoffersen

Schiffer Publishing Ltd
4880 Lower Valley Road, Atglen, PA 19310 USA

Acknowledgments

I extend thanks and gratitude to the following people for helping me with pictures and information for this book: Nic and Terri Birch for being the foundation in the beginning, until they left to do more interesting things; Paul Van Zwanenberg for editing the Royal Copenhagen Commemorative section; John Baremore for various pictures; Brian Strait for pictures of rare Bing & Grøndahl Christmas plates; Svend and Lisbeth Møller, George, Peter, Dennis, Egon, Dennis and Hans Otto for support and remarks; Jan Ringsmose (www.jamiri.dk) for pictures and help with the artist appendix; Ivar Ipsen, Frank Fagnano, Helle Fich-Olsen, Marie Louise Dunker-Nielsen, and Flemming Lindeløv from Royal Scandinavia in the USA and Denmark. Special thanks goes to Calista Firor, who is the "boss lady" at my store, for helping with sorting pictures and spelling. Also thanks to Laura Birch for help in editing the book.

Library of Congress Cataloging-in-Publication Data

Christoffersen, Lars.
Christmas plates & other commemoratives from Royal Copenhagen and Bing & Grondahl / by Lars Christoffersen.— 1st U.S. ed.
p. cm.
ISBN 0-7643-2089-0 (hardcover)
1. Royal Copenhagen A/S—Catalogs. 2. Bing & Grøndahl—Catalogs. 3. Christmas plates—Denmark—Copenhagen—Catalogs. 4. Christmas plates—Collectors and collecting—Catalogs. 5. Commemorative plates—Collectors and collecting—Catalogs. I. Title: Christmas plates and other commemoratives from Royal Copenhagen and Bing & Grondahl. II. Title.
NK4399.C6C48 2004
738.2'09489'13074—dc22

2004009410

Designed by Ellen J. (Sue) Taltoan
Type set in Allegro BT/Humanst521 BT

ISBN: 0-7643-2089-0
Printed in China
1 2 3 4

Published by Schiffer Publishing Ltd.
4880 Lower Valley Road
Atglen, PA 19310
Phone: (610) 593-1777; Fax: (610) 593-2002
E-mail: Info@schifferbooks.com

In Europe, Schiffer books are distributed by
Bushwood Books
6 Marksbury Ave.
Kew Gardens
Surrey TW9 4JF England
Phone: 44 (0) 20 8392-8585; Fax: 44 (0) 20 8392-9876
E-mail: info@bushwoodbooks.co.uk
Free postage in the U.K., Europe; air mail at cost.

Contents

Foreword

For over one hundred years, the famous Danish blue Christmas plates have been synonymous with holiday tradition in Denmark. Today the plates are collected and cherished the world over, along with the hand-painted figurines, collectors' items, and dinnerware by Royal Copenhagen.

We at Royal Copenhagen are pleased to be the focus of a comprehensive study of the collectibility of our products by Lars Christoffersen. We are confident that the recipient of this informative and enjoyable book will find it a useful tool now and in coming years.

Peter Lund
Managing Director
Royal Copenhagen, Denmark

Ivar M. Ipsen
President
Royal Copenhagen Porcelain USA

Preface

Danish Porcelain Imports

This book has been written to fill the void of information for collectors of Bing & Grøndahl and Royal Copenhagen plates. A great deal of useful information is presented concerning the major collector's series produced by Royal Copenhagen (RC), Bing & Grøndahl (B&G), Aluminia, and Anton Michelsen. Since this is a work in progress, rarity and uniqueness often make it impossible to catalog a flawless list of all items produced. I will happily accept any additional information that you, as a collector, might wish to bring to attention in order to make a future edition of this volume more complete. I would not have been able to gather all the rare and special issue plates without help from customers and dealers. It is the thrill of finding and seeing these treasures that has kept me going through the years.

I have collected the majority of data contained in this book through the daily operation of my company, Danish Porcelain Imports, where we specialize in buying and selling collectibles, dinnerware, and flatware by many Scandinavian producers.

Danish Porcelain Imports was established in 1998 and has grown to be one of Royal Copenhagen's largest international dealerships. Within a short time, we have become a full-line authorized dealer for Royal Scandinavia, which today includes the following companies: Royal Copenhagen, Bing & Grøndahl, Aluminia, Anton Michelsen, Holmegaard, Georg Jensen, Orrefors, and Kosta Boda. Once established with Royal Scandinavia, we branched out by adding: Arabia, Rorstrand, Hackman, Iittala, Waechtersbach, Hummel, Moody Glass, and many other smaller international companies. Collector items remain the core of the business. We also handle Flora Danica, unique artist signed items, Art Nouveau items, pre-1860 B&G and RC items, and discontinued dinnerware in Royal Copenhagen and Bing & Grøndahl.

It has been a pleasure writing this book. We hope you enjoy it and find it useful.

Lars Christoffersen
www.danishglass.com
www.danishporcelain.com

Chapter 1.

Introduction

The Factories

Bing & Grøndahl

Bing & Grøndahl was established in Copenhagen, Denmark, in 1853. The aspiring artist Frederick Wilhelm Grøndahl had left the Royal Copenhagen factory earlier that same year, reportedly because he felt that they were not fully supporting his creativity. He contacted the Bing brothers, Harald and Jacob, who owned a retail store in Copenhagen that sold art and much more. At that time, Grøndahl had plenty of design ideas but no financial security to back them. The Bings, on the other hand, held lucrative purses. From this initial contact, a great partnership bloomed. Unfortunately, Grøndahl died a mere two years later, leaving the lesser artistically inclined Bing brothers to make their way on their own.

After Grøndahl's death, the Bing & Grøndahl (B&G) company struggled forward without much success; however, the brothers refused to quit. In the mid-1880s, artists working at B&G learned how to produce an under-glazed product. This increased production and sales. The factory became world known in 1889 when, at the Paris World's Fair, they presented a new product by a relatively new artist. This breakthrough item was the Heron Dinnerware Service, which was designed by Pietro Krohn.

The next big success of the company came in the summer of 1895, when F. A. Hallin joined Bing & Grøndahl after leaving the Royal Copenhagen factory. He brought with him the art of relief painting, a revolutionary way of producing as well as painting plates. Because this process is an easier way to get a quality product every time, without detailed hand painting, it enabled artists to produce multiples of the same designs faster than ever before.

Using this new method, Harald Bing brought the world its first Christmas plate in 1895. Since then, many new series have been developed to complement different occasions. In 1908, B&G produced a large Christmas plate. Unfortunately, it was discontinued in 1911, due to lack of interest.

The second series that became popular was the Easter plates, which began in 1910 and ran until 1935. In 1915 a Jubilee, or Anniversary, plate was produced to commemorate the first Christmas plate from 1895. Since then a Jubilee plate has been produced every five years.

In 1969, B&G started the world's first Mother's Day plate series. It was so popular that initial sales were limited to only two plates per person. Since that time, many other plate series have been produced by B&G. Many of them can be found in this book.

Royal Copenhagen

F. H. Mueller founded the Royal Copenhagen Factory in 1775. In 1779, it was taken over by the King of Denmark, Christian the IV, due to a lack of financial stability. Because of a resolution the King made in 1848, the factory and almost everything else the Crown owned became owned by the state. The factory again came under private control in 1867, when the state sold it to A. Falch, with the right to retain the Royal Copenhagen name. In 1882, Philip Schou, who owned the faience factory Aluminia, bought Royal Copenhage and these two companies operated under his leadership.

The Royal Copenhagen (RC) factory produced its first collector plate in 1888 for the Scandinavian Fair, held in Copenhagen. These plates were painted through a stencil process, wherein an artist placed a stencil on top of a blank plate and dabbed it with a sponge dipped in paint. This was the only way to produce multiples of plates until seven years later, 1895, when both RC and B&G incorporated relief painting.

Aluminia

The Aluminia factory was founded in 1863, by August Schiøtt, in the center of Copenhagen, Denmark, not far from the Round Tower. In 1884, it was moved to its current location in Frederiksberg, where many of the original buildings still exist. The Aluminia factory has had many different logos during its history, beginning in 1863, with an oval logo which contained the words *Aluminia, Kjøbenhavn, AS*. In 1868 the words in the circle were changed to *Aluminia AS*, and in 1872 it became simply *Aluminia*. In 1903, the logo became what has been called the "beehive," a rounded "A" with three lines across the middle. This symbol was last used in the late 1960s on 2010 Series plaquettes and some stoneware.

The Aluminia factory produced two different Christmas plate series in 1904. The small series, that measured 16.5 cm, ended in 1938, while the large series, that measured 29 cm, ended eight years earlier, in 1930.

In 1909, Aluminia made the first Children's Help Day plate, followed closely by RC's first Children's Help Day plate the next year. The Aluminia series ran until 1930, with a couple of years having several different designs.

A. Michelsen

Anton Michelsen opened his first workshop in Denmark in 1841. He quickly became the leading designer in the gold and silver industry and was a significant influence on Danish jewelry design during the 19th and early 20th centuries. He became Crown Jeweler and Insignia Maker to the King in 1848. Producing insignia for the Crown involved the fine art of enameling, a specialty that the Michelsen company has refined over the years.

The idea of making an annual Christmas spoon and fork set, designed by a new artist each year, began in 1910. Every year since then, the company has commissioned a noted Danish artist, including members of the Michelsen family and the Queen herself, to create a new set in sterling silver, with 24-carat gold plating. These sets reflect a long and cherished tradition involving the finest artists of their time. The Commemorative spoons and forks were produced from 1910 to 1990. All but three of them commemorate special events with the Danish Royal family.

Anton's son, Carl Michelsen, first included enamel with sterling silver and gold. Carl's son, Poul Michelsen, designed several of the earliest sets, including those of 1912 and 1913. Shortages of enamels prevented their use during World War II. Poul's son, Jørgen Michelsen, created the 1956 set.

One of the most sought after sets today is the 75th set, produced in 1984, which Queen Margrete II of Denmark created. It was released with a specially printed red gift box.

Materials and Techniques

Denmark is one of the world's leading exclusive dinnerware producers, even though few of the materials used to make porcelain are found in Denmark. The quality of the craftsmanship, the relief technique, and the dedication to their work are the only ingredients that the Danes possess. The imported ingredients for porcelain include quartz, feldspar, and kaolin.

The relief technique used by Royal Copenhagen and Bing & Grøndahl is an exclusive Danish ingredient. It takes many hours of reverse molding work to prepare the first mold for use. Once the design for a New Year's plate has been chosen, the artist works closely with a master molder who skillfully carves out the design in plaster, producing the first mold. This initial mold is then used to fabricate other molds that are used to make the plates. Each mold is used for only twenty to thirty plates before it is discarded due to an excessive amount of water it absorbs from the drying porcelain. The plate is then painted by hand using an airbrush. After each layer of paint is applied, a sponge or cloth is used to wipe off excess paint to lighten or remove some of the color. At this point in the process, the blue color on the plate has a uniform shade. The plate is then inspected and taken to the glazing department where each piece is hand-dipped in a milky white substance. To completely harden the glaze that gives these plates their world-renowned shine, they must be baked in an oven at over 2700 degrees Fahrenheit (1400 degrees Celsius) for approximately forty-eight hours. As you can see, the manufacturing process takes several weeks, from the time the plate is poured into the mold until it is boxed after final inspection.

Investing in Seconds, Flawed and Repaired Items

Bing & Grøndahl

Bing & Grøndahl has never used the practice of marking collector plates as seconds. They thought such a practice would lessen the value of the product. Because of this, second quality pieces are always destroyed in the factory when they reach the quality control inspectors; therefore, if the plate left the factory it is first quality.

Generally, a reputable dealer will sell a plate at a reduced price if it has any major flaws that slipped through inspection or if an employee purchased the plate because it was flawed and later sold it. These flaws include, but are not limited to: bubbles in the glaze, cracks under the glaze, and parts of glaze missing on a plate. On earlier plates, it is common to find small black specks that came from using coal ovens to cure the glazing. These specks in no way lessen the value of the plate, as most, if not all, of the plates during these early years possess them.

Royal Copenhagen

A small percent of Royal Copenhagen items have been sold on the Danish market as seconds. An item is a second from Royal Copenhagen only if there is a perpendicular scratch in the glaze dissecting the wave mark on the bottom of the piece. Occasionally this mark cannot be seen, but it can always be detected by running a thumbnail across the logo.

The reasons for a plate being marked as second quality are numerous, ranging from pinholes in the glaze and large areas of missing glaze to cracks in the porcelain itself under the glaze. But most often, when the item is a plate, it is simply out-of-round, which means that it is not perfectly level if placed facedown on a hard, flat surface.

We see no reason not to recommend buying factory seconds to build a collection, since such plates are most often flawless in appearance and quality and can be obtained usually with a cost saving of ten to twenty percent.

Occasionally, an item has two, three, or even four scratches in the glaze through the factory mark's waves. These are third and fourth quality items that employees were allowed to purchase from the factory. They usually are first quality items that were marked as third and fourth quality when they left the factory to discourage the employees from reselling them. If you find an item marked in this manner, it is often more attractive than a second, as most have few, if any, flaws. If you have a plate that is marked as lower than second quality, that was not purchased by an employee, it will be easily recognized as it will be extremely out-of-round or have major flaws.

Value and Identification

Collector plates differ greatly in their values. There are plates that you can purchase for $5 and there are plates you will be lucky if you can obtain for $10,000. Whether they are expensive or not, they hold value to the collector. Adding to the monetary value of each piece is the story that generally accompanies it. For the collectors to safeguard themselves financially or to add monetary value to sentimental value, it is a good idea to get a professional appraisal and identification of the collection. If this is done and theft or breakage occurs, the precise item(s) can be replaced. In the case of a valuable collection, the insurance company will have information concerning what needs to be replaced from a reputable source. Be aware, though, that many insurance companies require a written estimation of value in order to insure the piece(s) in the first place, and that many insurance companies will not pay for pieces not specifically listed in the policy.

A professional plate dealer, specializing in Royal Copenhagen and Bing & Grøndahl items, should do such an appraisal, as most other appraisers will not be able to identify and place the correct value on the collection. Most appraisers will charge twenty to one hundred dollars for this service, depending on your collection and how much research must be done to get the correct prices. Appraisals are well worth the money spent if an accident or theft should occur.

Collecting Royal Copenhagen and Bing & Grøndahl

There are numerous ways to collect commemorative plates. You can acquire an entire series from one company, typically starting a series and continuing until all are found. Another style is collecting plates from sporadic years, such as specific years that have sentimental value from anniversary dates or birthdays. Some collectors simply enjoy the beauty of the plates and their collections usually include several from both companies' series, since they are harmonious in color and decoration.

There is no right or wrong way to collect plates, as long as they bring joy to the person in their home. These plates appeal to such a large group of people all over the world that they can be found in every country. This is also the reason why RC and B&G plates are the most widely collected Christmas plates in the world.

History of Royal Copenhagen and Bing & Grøndahl Collectors

In the early days, Danes were the primary collectors of these beautiful commemorative plates. They came from upper-class society and royalty, yet the appetite for the plates quickly spread to the rest of Europe. One of the most obvious clues to this phenomenon is found when one realizes that the Royal Copenhagen Christmas plate collection was produced in numerous languages besides Danish, including English, German, French, and Czechoslovakian.

Only after World War II did Christmas plate collecting take hold in the United States. American service men and women who served in Europe became acquainted with the blue, dated plates. They brought them home from Europe in the 1940s and '50s as presents, and soon thereafter a sizable market was established in the United States. This market has been a major factor in the increasing number of collectors throughout the world.

The earliest dealer's price list we are aware of was distributed in the United States in 1952, and it contained both Danish and English text and prices. All the brochures from the factory today are printed in several languages: Danish, English, German, Italian, and Japanese. This tradition has been followed in this book by including both English and Danish descriptions.

From the late 1960s through the late 1970s, the market for collectible plates exploded, and it is from this period forward that we find the largest number of plates produced. Due to demand, production was tremendously increased at the factory. Collectors today should realize that they are in good company; this market is currently at its highest volume ever.

Chapter 2.

Bing & Grøndahl Collections

Bing and Grøndahl Christmas Plates / BG

The Beginning of the Bing & Grøndahl Christmas Plate

Over the years, many differing stories regarding the beginning of the Christmas plate tradition have been told. It is entertaining to sort through these myths. The first such story claims that the tradition began a few hundred years ago as an annual gift to servants from their masters. It is said that these plates were often crudely made and used solely for the giving of cookies or candy, only to be discarded directly after use. After a while, it became more interesting as the servants bragged to their friends about who had received the nicest plate for Christmas. For this reason, the plates were made with better quality, evolving from wood to steel to bronze. The master who gave the nicest plate to their staff would be known as wealthier and kinder among their peers. In 1895 the Bing & Grondahl factory made the Christmas plate from porcelain so that each year it would be more memorable. None of this is true, nor does it have any historical value. People who did not know the history of Bing & Grondahl Christmas plates, but wanted to tell a story, made up this tall tale!.

The second story of how the Christmas plate came about is much simpler than the first and is, at least partially, correct. When Frederick Wilhelm Grøndahl died in 1855, his partners, the Bing brothers, decided to carry on the porcelain business. New artists were brought in to help the factory become more successful and to bring inspiration to the designs. One such artist was Peitro Krohn, who designed the Heron dinnerware which won much acclaim at the 1889 Paris exhibition. This is true. Nearly six years later, the factory had become so popular that it was in desperate need of expansion, so the company was moved to a new location. When they re-opened, Harold Bing and his brother needed something that would set B&G apart from all other porcelain manufacturers. In order to do so, they introduced a new and spectacular product at the opening ceremony; the world's first Christmas plate, "Behind the Frozen Window," by F. A. Hallin. (This is partially true, as Hallin did design the 1895 plate.) By doing so they not only created history but also a great new collectible series. Although closer to the truth, this story is still not what actually happened, although it is very entertaining.

The true story of what happened is not quite like the fairy tales mentioned previously. Actually, F. A. Hallin was working for Royal Copenhagen (from 1885 to the summer of 1895) as the main painter of most pieces designed or sketched by Arnold Krog. Hallin, however, was not credited for his work on these new and interesting pieces. He approached the president of Royal Copenhagen, Philip Schou, and asked for some credit. Mr. Schou did not appreciate his lack of respect for the master artist. Therefore, F. A. Hallin left the Royal Copenhagen factory unhappy and went to work at Bing & Grøndahl in the summer of 1895. Here he spoke to Harald Bing and presented him with the idea of relief painting for mass-producing plates. Bing, at the time, did not see any specific use for this new way of painting. Shortly thereafter, Harald Bing came up with the idea of making a Christmas plate to sell during the upcoming Christmas season. He knew that the Royal Copenhagen factory's earlier "commemorative" plates were well received, at least by the Danish upper class and royalty of the time. This version of the story is as close to the truth as one can discover, since all the people previously mentioned are now deceased.

Whether you believe the truth or you choose to believe one of the myths, one fact stands true; Bing & Grøndahl made the first Christmas plate in the world. It was also the first plate to be made using the innovative relief painting method. Up until this time, commemorative plates made by Royal Copenhagen were produced using stencils, dabbing the paint on to get the design. Each of the new-style plates is produced for only one year, after which the factory destroys the remaining molds. This keeps the plates interesting, highly collectible, and impossible to reproduce

Throughout the years, many other factories have attempted to produce comparable commemorative plates, but only Bing & Grøndahl and Royal Copenhagen have managed to keep their series running without interruption.

A small series of Christmas plates made with Icelandic inscriptions and a unique motif are the most rare of Bing and Grøndahl's Christmas plates (see the following section). These plates measure 7" in diameter, with the 1895 and 1896 ones being a tiny bit smaller.

BG-1895
Title / English: Behind the Frozen Window
Title / Danish: Bag den frosne rude
Designed by: F. A. Hallin
Price: $5000-7000

BG-1896
Title / English: New Moon Over Snow-covered Trees
Title / Danish: Nymåne over de snedækkede graner
Designed by: F. A. Hallin
Price: $1500-2500

BG-1897
Title / English: Christmas Meal of the Sparrows
Title / Danish: Spurvenes julemåltid
Designed by: F. A. Hallin
Price: $1000-1500

BG-1898
Title / English: Christmas Roses and Christmas Star
Title / Danish: Juleroser og julestjerner
Designed by: Fanny Garde
Price: $600-1000

BG-1899
Title / English: The Crows Enjoying Christmas
Title / Danish: Kragerne hygger sig
Designed by: Jens Peter Dahl Jensen
Price: $1100-1600

BG-1900
Title / English: Church Bells Chiming in Christmas
Title / Danish: Det kimer nu til julefest
Designed by: Jens Peter Dahl Jensen
Price: $900-1400

BG-1901
Title / English: The Three Wise Men from the East
Title / Danish: Vise mænd fra Østerland
Designed by: S. Sabra
Price: $375-550

BG-1902
Title / English: Interior of a Gothic Church
Title / Danish: Interiør fra en gotisk kirke
Designed by: Jens Peter Dahl Jensen
Price: $274-400

BG-1903
Title / English: Happy Expectation of the Children
Title / Danish: Børnenes forventning
Designed by: Margrethe Hyldahl
Price: $275-400

BG-1904
Title / English: View of Copenhagen from the Frederiksberg Hill
Title / Danish: Udsigt over København
Designed by: Cathinka Olsen
Price: $100-160

BG-1905
Title / English: Christmas Night Expectations
Title / Danish: Forventning til den kommende julenat
Designed by: Jens Peter Dahl Jensen
Price: $100-160

BG-1906
Title / English: Sleighing to Church on Christmas Eve
Title / Danish: Kanefart til kirken
Designed by: Jens Peter Dahl Jensen
Price: $60-90

BG-1907
Title / English: The Little Match Girl
Title / Danish: Den lille pige med svovlstikkerne
Designed by: E. Plockross
Price: $90-125

BG-1908
Title / English: St. Petri Church of Copenhagen
Title / Danish: Juletræet hentes
Designed by: Poul Jørgensen
Price: $60-80

BG-1909
Title / English: Happiness over the Yule Tree
Title / Danish: Glæde over juletræet
Designed by: Aarestrup
Price: $60-80

BG-1910
Title / English: The Old Organist
Title / Danish: Den gamle organist
Designed by: C. Ersgaard
Price: $60-80

BG-1911
Title / English: First it was Sung by the Angels to the Shepherds in the Field
Title / Danish: Englene sang den først
Designed by: H. Moltke
Price: $60-80

BG-1912
Title / English: Going to Church on Christmas Eve
Title / Danish: På vej til kirke juleaften
Designed by: Einar Hansen
Price: $60-80

BG-1913
Title / English: Bringing Home the Yule Tree
Title / Danish: Juletræet hentes
Designed by: Th. Larsen
Price: $60-80

BG-1914
Title / English: The Royal Castle Amalienborg, Copenhagen
Title / Danish: Amalienborg
Designed by: Th. Larsen
Price: $60-80

BG-1915
Title / English: Chained Dog getting Double Meal
Title / Danish: Lænkehunden selv får dobbelt sul
Designed by: Dahl Jensen
Price: $90-130

BG-1916
Title / English: Christmas Prayer of the Sparrows
Title / Danish: Spurvenes andagt
Designed by: J. Block Jørgensen
Price: $60-80

BG-1917
Title / English: Arrival of the Christmas Boat
Title / Danish: Juleskibet ankommer
Designed by: Johannes Achton Friis
Price: $60-80

BG-1918
Title / English: The Fishing Boat Returning Home for Christmas
Title / Danish: Fiskerbåden vender hjem
Designed by: Johannes Achton Friis
Price: $60-80

BG-1919
Title / English: Outside the Lighted Window (from *The Little Match Girl*)
Title / Danish: Uden for det oplyste vindue
Designed by: Johannes Achton Friis
Price: $50-70

BG-1920
Title / English: Hare in the Snow
Title / Danish: Harer i sneen
Designed by: Johannes Achton Friis
Price: $50-70

BG-1921
Title / English: Pigeons in the Castle Court
Title / Danish: Duer på slotspladsen
Designed by: Johannes Achton Friis
Price: $50-70

BG-1922
Title / English: Star of Bethlehem
Title / Danish: Stjerne ved Bethlehem
Designed by: Johannes Achton Friis
Price: $50-70

BG-1923
Title / English: The Royal Hunting Castle, the Ermitage
Title / Danish: Eremitagen
Designed by: Johannes Achton Friis
Price: $50-70

BG-1924
Title / English: Lighthouse in Danish Waters
Title / Danish: Fyrtårn i dansk farvand
Designed by: Johannes Achton Friis
Price: $50-70

BG-1925
Title / English: The Child's Christmas
Title / Danish: Barnets jul
Designed by: Johannes Achton Friis
Price: $50-70

BG-1926
Title / English: Churchgoers on Christmas Day
Title / Danish: På vej til kirke
Designed by: Johannes Achton Friis
Price: $50-70

BG-1927
Title / English: Skating Couple
Title / Danish: Skøjteløberpar
Designed by: Johannes Achton Friis
Price: $60-80

BG-1928
Title / English: Greenlanders Looking at Village Church
Title / Danish: Grønlændere ved landsby kirke
Designed by: Johannes Achton Friis
Price: $50-70

BG-1929
Title / English: Fox Outside Farm on Christmas Eve
Title / Danish: Ræv uden for bondegård
Designed by: Johannes Achton Friis
Price: $50-70

BG-1930
Title / English: Yule Tree in Town Hall Square
Title / Danish: Julestræet på Rådhuspladsen
Designed by: H. Flügenring
Price: $60-80

BG-1931
Title / English: Arrival of the Christmas Train
Title / Danish: Juletogets ankomst
Designed by: Johannes Achton Friis
Price: $60-80

BG-1932
Title / English: The Lifeboat
Title / Danish: Redningsbåden
Designed by: H. Flügenring
Price: $50-70

BG-1933
Title / English: The Korsor-Nyborg Ferry
Title / Danish: Korsør-Nyborg
Designed by: H. Flügenring
Price: $50-70

BG-1934
Title / English: Church Bell In Tower
Title / Danish: Kirkeklokke I tårn
Designed by: Immanuel Tjerne
Price: $50-70

BG-1935
Title / English: Lillebelt Bridge
Title / Danish: Lillebæltsbroen
Designed by: Ove Larsen
Price: $50-70

BG-1936
Title / English: Royal Guard Outside Amalienborg Castle in Copenhagen
Title / Danish: Den kgl garde uden for Amalienborg Slot
Designed by: Ove Larsen
Price: $60-80

BG-1937
Title / English: Arrival of Christmas Guests
Title / Danish: Julegæsternes ankomst
Designed by: Ove Larsen
Price: $80-110

BG-1938
Title / English: Lighting the Candles
Title / Danish: Lysene tændes
Designed by: Immanuel Tjerne
Price: $90-130

BG-1939
Title / English: Ole Lock-Eye, the Sandman
Title / Danish: Ole Lukøje
Designed by: Immanuel Tjerne
Price: $90-130

BG-1940
Title / English: Delivering Christmas Letters
Title / Danish: Postbud med juleposten
Designed by: Ove Larsen
Price: $140-200

BG-1941
Title / English: Horses Enjoying Christmas Meal in Stable
Title / Danish: Heste I stalden nyder julemåltidet
Designed by: Ove Larsen
Price: $140-200

BG-1942
Title / English: Danish Farm on Christmas Night
Title / Danish: Bondegård julenat
Designed by: Ove Larsen
Price: $140-200

BG-1943
Title / English: The Ribe Cathedral
Title / Danish: Ribe Domkirke
Designed by: Ove Larsen
Price: $140-200

BG-1944
Title / English: Sorgenfri Castle
Title / Danish: Sorgenfri slot
Designed by: Ove Larsen
Price: $70-100

BG-1945
Title / English: The Old Water Mill
Title / Danish: Den gamle vandmølle
Designed by: Ove Larsen
Price: $90-120

BG-1946
Title / English: Commemoration Cross
Title / Danish: Korset i Nyhavn
Designed by: Margrethe Hyldahl
Price: $50-70

BG-1947
Title / English: Dybbøl Mill
Title / Danish: Dybbøl Mølle
Designed by: Margrethe Hyldahl
Price: $70-90

BG-1948
Title / English: Watchman Sculpture
Title / Danish: Vægteren på rådhuset
Designed by: Margrethe Hyldahl
Price: $50-70

BG-1949
Title / English: Peasant Soldier
Title / Danish: Landsoldaten, Fredericia
Designed by: Margrethe Hyldahl
Price: $50-70c

BG-1950
Title / English: Kronborg Castle at Elsinore
Title / Danish: Kronborg, Helsingør
Designed by: Margrethe Hyldahl
Price: $60-80

BG-1951
Title / English: Jens Bang, Passenger Boat
Title / Danish: M/S Jens Bang
Designed by: Margrethe Hyldahl
Price: $60-80

BG-1952
Title / English: Old Copenhagen Canals at Wintertime
Title / Danish: Thorvaldsens Museum
Designed by: Børge Pramvig
Price: $50-70

BG-1953
Title / English: Royal Boat in Greenland Waters
Title / Danish: Kongeskibet ved Grønland
Designed by: Kjeld Bonfils
Price: $50-70c

BG-1954
Title / English: Birthplace of Hans Christian Andersen
Title / Danish: H. C. Andersens hus, Odense
Designed by: Børge Pramvig
Price: $50-70

BG-1955
Title / English: Kalundborg Church
Title / Danish: Kalundborg Kirke
Designed by: Kjeld Bonfils
Price: $50-70

BG-1956
Title / English: Christmas in Copenhagen
Title / Danish: Byens jul
Designed by: Kjeld Bonfils
Price: $70-100

BG-1957
Title / English: Christmas Candles
Title / Danish: Juletræet med lys
Designed by: Kjeld Bonfils
Price: $70-100

BG-1958
Title / English: Santa Claus
Title / Danish: Julemanden
Designed by: Kjeld Bonfils
Price: $70-100

BG-1959
Title / English: Christmas Eve
Title / Danish: Julestemning
Designed by: Kjeld Bonfils
Price: $60-80

BG-1960
Title / English: Danish Village Church
Title / Danish: Østerlars Kirke
Designed by: Kjeld Bonfils
Price: $60-80

BG-1961
Title / English: Winter Harmony
Title / Danish: Lille egern sad
Designed by: Kjeld Bonfils
Price: $60-80

BG-1962
Title / English: Winter Night
Title / Danish: Oltidsminde
Designed by: Kjeld Bonfils
Price: $30-50

BG-1963
Title / English: The Christmas Elf
Title / Danish: Julenissen på grøden venter
Designed by: Henry Thelander
Price: $60-80

BG-1964
Title / English: The Fir Tree and Hare
Title / Danish: Grantræet
Designed by: Henry Thelander
Price: $30-50

BG-1965
Title / English: Bringing Home the Christmas Tree
Title / Danish: I skoven før jul
Designed by: Henry Thelander
Price: $30-50

BG-1966
Title / English: Home for Christmas
Title / Danish: Hjem til jul
Designed by: Henry Thelander
Price: $30-50

BG-1967
Title / English: Sharing the Joy
Title / Danish: Fuglenese jul
Designed by: Henry Thelander
Price: $30-50

BG-1968
Title / English: Christmas in Church
Title / Danish: I kirke juleaften
Designed by: Henry Thelander
Price: $30-50

BG-1969
Title / English: Arrival of Christmas Guests
Title / Danish: Jul i præstegården
Designed by: Henry Thelander
Price: $30-50

BG-1970
Title / English: Pheasants in the Snow at Christmas
Title / Danish: Fasan I vintersne
Designed by: Henry Thelander
Price: $20-40

BG-1971
Title / English: Christmas at Home
Title / Danish: Jul i hjemmet
Designed by: Henry Thelander
Price: $20-40c

BG-1972
Title / English: Christmas in Greenland
Title / Danish: Jul i Grønland
Designed by: Henry Thelander
Price: $20-40

BG-1973
Title / English: Country Christmas
Title / Danish: Jul på landet
Designed by: Henry Thelander
Price: $20-40

BG-1974
Title / English: Christmas in the Village
Title / Danish: Jul lilandsbyen
Designed by: Henry Thelander
Price: $20-40

BG-1975
Title / English: The Old Water Mill
Title / Danish: Jul ved den gamle mølle
Designed by: Henry Thelander
Price: $20-40

BG-1976
Title / English: Christmas Welcome
Title / Danish: Julevelkomst. Hjem til jul
Designed by: Henry Thelander
Price: $20-40

BG-1977
Title / English: Copenhagen Christmas
Title / Danish: Jul i København
Designed by: Henry Thelander
Price: $20-40

BG-1978
Title / English: A Christmas Tale
Title / Danish: Julefortælling
Designed by: Henry Thelander
Price: $20-40

BG-1979
Title / English: White Christmas
Title / Danish: Hvid jul
Designed by: Henry Thelander
Price: $20-40

BG-1980
Title / English: Christmas in the Woods
Title / Danish: Jul Iiskoven
Designed by: Henry Thelander
Price: $20-40

BG-1981
Title / English: Christmas Peace
Title / Danish: Juleneget
Designed by: Henry Thelander
Price: $20-40

BG-1982
Title / English: The Christmas Tree
Title / Danish: Juletræet
Designed by: Henry Thelander
Price: $20-40

BG-1983
Title / English: Christmas in the Old Town
Title / Danish: Jul i den gamle by
Designed by: Edvard Jensen
Price: $20-40

BG-1984
Title / English: The Christmas Letter
Title / Danish: Juleposten sendes
Designed by: Edvard Jensen
Price: $20-40

BG-1985
Title / English: Christmas Eve at the Farmhouse
Title / Danish: Jul i den gamle Gård
Designed by: Edvard Jensen
Price: $20-40

BG-1986
Title / English: Silent Night, Holy Night
Title / Danish: Søllerød Kirke
Designed by: Edvard Jensen
Price: $20-40

BG-1987
Title / English: Snowman's Christmas Eve
Title / Danish: Børnenes julegæst
Designed by: Edvard Jensen
Price: $30-50

BG-1988
Title / English: In King's Garden
Title / Danish: Den Gamle digters jul
Designed by: Edvard Jensen
Price: $30-50

BG-1989
Title / English: Christmas Anchorage
Title / Danish: Juleaften i Nyhavn
Designed by: Edvard Jensen
Price: $50-70

BG-1990
Title / English: Changing of the Guards
Title / Danish: Vagtskifte på Fredensborg
Designed by: Edvard Jensen
Price: $50-70

BG-1991
Title / English: Copenhagen Stock Exchange
Title / Danish: Børsen ved Juletid
Designed by: Edvard Jensen
Price: $50-70

BG-1992
Title / English: Pastor's Christmas
Title / Danish: Nødebo Præstegård
Designed by: Jørgen Nielsen
Price: $50-70

BG-1993
Title / English: Father Christmas
Title / Danish: Julemanden på Amagertorv
Designed by: Jørgen Nielsen
Price: $50-70

BG-1994
Title / English: A Day at Deer Park
Title / Danish: Vinterdag Dyrehaven
Designed by: Jørgen Nielsen
Price: $50-70

BG-1995
Title / English: Towers of Copenhagen
Title / Danish: Københavns Tårne
Designed by: Jørgen Nielsen
Price: $50-70

BG-1996
Title / English: Winter at the Old Mill
Title / Danish: Møllebakken
Designed by: Jørgen Nielsen
Price: $50-70

BG-1997
Title / English: Country Christmas
Title / Danish: Skovens dyr
Designed by: Jørgen Nielsen
Price: $50-70

BG-1998
Title / English: Santa the Storyteller
Title / Danish: Julehistorier
Designed by: Jørgen Nielsen
Price: $50-70

BG-1999
Title / English: Dancing on Christmas Eve
Title / Danish: Rundt om juletræt
Designed by: Jørgen Nielsen
Price: $90-120

BG-2000
Title / English: Christmas at the Bell Tower
Title / Danish: Jul I klokketærnet
Designed by: Jørgen Nielsen
Price: $60-90

BG-2001
Title / English: Playing in the Snow
Title / Danish: Leg in sneen
Designed by: Jørgen Nielsen
Price: $50-70

BG-2002
Title / English: Christmas Eve
Title / Danish: Julen
Designed by: Jørgen Nielsen
Price: $50-70

BG-2003
Title / English: Frosty the Snowman
Title / Danish: Snemanden
Designed by: Jørgen Nielsen
Price: $72.50

BG-2004
Title / English: The Christmas Tree
Title / Danish: Juletræet fældes
Designed by: Jørgen Nielsen
Price: $72.50

BG-Mold-1
Title / English: The master mold for a Bing and Grøndahl Christmas plate from 1987. This is the mold that all the other forms were made after. It should not exist, as molds are destroyed each year. But, we were so lucky to get our hands on one and it is now in good hands in the Strait collection.

Bing and Grøndahl Icelandic Christmas Plates / BG-I

The Icelandic Christmas series was short-lived, only in production from 1928 to 1930, but there might also be one from 1931. They are the same size as the regular Christmas plates and done in the same relief style. Because the ones we have had are the only ones we have ever seen or heard about, our guess is that they were made as a special order. They are among, if not the, most costly of any plates produced.

BG-I-1928-A
Title / English: Family going to Chuch
Title / Danish: Familie paa vej til Kirke
Designed by: Unknown
Size: 7"
Price: $10,000-15,000

BG-I-1929-A
Title / English: Claimers on Mountain
Title / Danish: Folk klatre paa bjerg
Designed by: Unknown
Size: 7"
Price: $10,000-15,000

BG-I-1930-A
Title / English: Ship in the Fjord
Title / Danish: Skip i fjorden
Designed by: Unknown
Size: 7"
Price: $10,000-15,000

Bing and Grøndahl Large Christmas Plates / BG-L

The large Christmas series was only in production from 1908 to 1911. These plates were all 12-1/4" in diameter and hand-painted in relief in the cobalt blue color. The production amount of these plates is not really known, but the 1910 and 1911 were produced in fewer numbers than the first two, as interest dwindled. It is estimated that there were 1000 copies of the 1908 plate, 500 copies of the 1909 plate, and 100 to 200 copies of 1910 and 1911 plates.

BG-L1908
Title / English: Bethlehem
Title / Danish: Bethlehem
Designed by: Frk. Guldberg
Size: 12 1/4"
Price: $500-700

BG-L1909
Title / English: Poor sparrow fly down from the roof
Title / Danish: Fugl flyv ned fra taget
Designed by: Frederik August Hallin
Size: 12 1/4"
Price: $900-1200

BG-L1910
Title / English: A Child is born in Bethlehem
Title / Danish: Et barn er født i Bethlehem
Designed by: Jens Peter Dahl-Jensen
Size: 12 1/4"
Price: $2000-2500

BG-L1911
Title / English: Christmas Star
Title / Danish: Julestjerne
Designed by: Poul Jørgensen
Size: 12 1/4"
Price: $2000-2500

Bing and Grøndahl Christmas Jubilee Plates / BG-J

The first Christmas Jubilee plate was produced in 1915 to commemorate the production of the first Christmas plate. They are made every five years, are about 10" in diameter, and each feature a motif from a previous year. The jubilee plates from 1940 were made in a very limited edition. It is estimated that there may be fewer of them than of the Christmas plate from 1895.

BG-J1915
Title / English: Behind the Frozen Window from 1895
Title / Danish: Bag den frosne rude
Designed by: Frederik August Hallin
Price: $150-180

BG-J1920
Title / English: Church Bells 1900
Title / Danish: Det kimer nu til julefest
Designed by: Jens Peter Dahl Jensen
Price: $60-75

BG-J1925
Title / English: Dog Outside Window 1915
Title / Danish: Lænkehunden selv får dobbelt sul
Designed by: Jens Peter Dahl Jensen
Price: $120-145

BG-J1930
Title / English: The Old Organist 1910
Title / Danish: Den gamle organist
Designed by: C. Ersgaard
Price: $150-180

BG-J1935
Title / English: Little Match Girl 1907
Title / Danish: Den lille pige med svovlstikkerne
Designed by: E. Plockross
Price: $700-850

BG-J1940
Title / English: Three Wise Men 1901
Title / Danish: Vise mænd fra Østerland
Designed by: S. Sabra
Price: $2000-2400

BG-J1945
Title / English: Royal Guard 1936
Title / Danish: Den kgl garde uden for Amalienborg Slot
Designed by: Ove Larsen
Price: $150-180

BG-J1950
Title / English: Greenlanders Looking at Village Church 1928
Title / Danish: Grønlændere ved landsby kirke
Designed by: Johannes Achton Friis
Price: $150-180

BG-J1955
Title / English: Dybbol Mill 1947
Title / Danish: Dybbøl Mølle
Designed by: Margrethe Hyldahl
Price: $150-180

BG-J1960
Title / English: Kronborg Castle 1950
Title / Danish: Kronborg Slot, Helsingør
Designed by: Margrethe Hyldahl
Price: $140-170

BG-J1965
Title / English: Church Goers 1926
Title / Danish: På vej til kirke
Designed by: Johannes Achton Friis
Price: $70-85

BG-J1970
Title / English: Amalienborg Castle 1914
Title / Danish: Amalienborg
Designed by: Th. Larsen
Price: $15-20

BG-J1985
Title / English: Lifeboats at Work 1932
Title / Danish: Redningsbåden
Designed by: H. Flügenring
Price: $55-65

BG-J1995
Title / English: Home for Christmas 1966
Title / Danish: Hjem til jul
Designed by: Henry Thelander
Price: $60-75

BG-J1975
Title / English: Horses Enjoying a Meal 1941
Title / Danish: Heste i stalden nyder julemåltidet
Designed by: Ove Larsen
Price: $35-45

BG-J1990
Title / English: Royal Boat 1953
Title / Danish: Kongeskibet ved Grønland
Designed by: Kjeld Bonfils
Price: $70-85

BG-J2000
Title / English: Star of Bethlehem 1922
Title / Danish: Stjerne ved Bethlehem
Designed by: Johannes Achton Friis
Price: $85-100

BG-J1980
Title / English: Happiness over the Yule Tree 1909
Title / Danish: Glæde over juletræet
Designed by: Aarestrup
Price: $35-45

Bing and Grøndahl Mother's Day Plates / BG-MD

A new plate in this series has been issued by Bing & Grøndahl every year since 1969 when the first Mother's Day plate was produced. They are 6" in diameter and are hand-painted under the glaze in the traditional cobalt blue that has made Bing & Grøndahl famous around the world. The artist's initials are found on the reverse of each plate. The plate from 1969 really rocketed the plate mania; its value went up 100-fold within months of its release.

BG-MD1971
Title / English: Cat with Kitten
Title / Danish: Kat med killinger
Designed by: Henry Thelander
Price: $15-25

BG-MD1973
Title / English: Duck with Ducklings
Title / Danish: And med Ællinger
Designed by: Henry Thelander
Price: $15-25

BG-MD1969
Title / English: Cocker Spaniel with Puppies
Title / Danish: Cocker spaniel med hvalpe
Designed by: Henry Thelander
Price: $300-400

BG-MD1972
Title / English: Mare with Foal
Title / Danish: Hest med føl
Designed by: Henry Thelander
Price: $15-25

BG-MD1974
Title / English: Polar Bear with Cubs
Title / Danish: Isbjørn med unger
Designed by: Henry Thelander
Price: $15-25

BG-MD1970
Title / English: Sparrow with Chicks
Title / Danish: Spurv med unger
Designed by: Henry Thelander
Price: $15-25

BG-MD1975
Title / English: Doe with Fawns
Title / Danish: Hjort med kid
Designed by: Henry Thelander
Price: $15-25

BG-MD1976
Title / English: Swan with Cygnets
Title / Danish: Svane med unger
Designed by: Henry Thelander
Price: $15-25

BG-MD1977
Title / English: Squirrel with Young
Title / Danish: Egern med unge
Designed by: Henry Thelander
Price: $15-25

BG-MD1978
Title / English: Grebe with Chicks
Title / Danish: Lappedykker med unger
Designed by: Henry Thelander
Price: $15-25

BG-MD1979
Title / English: Vixen with Cubs
Title / Danish: Ræv med unger
Designed by: Henry Thelander
Price: $15-25

BG-MD1980
Title / English: Woodpecker with Chicks
Title / Danish: Flagspætte med unger
Designed by: Henry Thelander
Price: $20-30

BG-MD1981
Title / English: Hare with Leverets
Title / Danish: Hare med killing
Designed by: Henry Thelander
Price: $20-30

BG-MD1982
Title / English: Lioness with Cubs
Title / Danish: Løve med unger
Designed by: Henry Thelander
Price: $20-30

BG-MD1983
Title / English: Raccoon with Cubs
Title / Danish: Vaskebjørn med unger
Designed by: Henry Thelander
Price: $20-30

BG-MD1984
Title / English: Stork with Chicks
Title / Danish: Stork med unger
Designed by: Henry Thelander
Price: $20-30

BG-MD1985
Title / English: Bear with Cubs
Title / Danish: Bjørn med unger
Designed by: Henry Thelander
Price: $20-30

BG-MD1986
Title / English: Elephant with Children
Title / Danish: Elefant med unger
Designed by: Henry Thelander
Price: $20-30

BG-MD1987
Title / English: Ewe with Lamb
Title / Danish: Får med lam
Designed by: Henry Thelander
Price: $40-60

BG-MD1988
Title / English: Peewit with Chicks
Title / Danish: Vibe med unger
Designed by: Henry Thelander
Price: $40-60

BG-MD1989
Title / English: Cow with Calf
Title / Danish: Ko med kalv
Designed by: Henry Thelander
Price: $40-60

BG-MD1990
Title / English: Hen with Chicks
Title / Danish: Høne med kylling
Designed by: Henry Thelander
Price: $50-70

BG-MD1991
Title / English: Nanny-Goat with Kids
Title / Danish: Ged med kid
Designed by: Henry Thelander
Price: $40-60

BG-MD1992
Title / English: Panda with Cubs
Title / Danish: Panda med unger
Designed by: Henry Thelander
Price: $50-70

BG-MD1993
Title / English: St. Bernard with Puppies
Title / Danish: Sct. Bernhard med hvalpe
Designed by: Allan Therkelsen
Price: $70-100

BG-MD1994
Title / English: Cat with Kittens
Title / Danish: Kat med killinger
Designed by: Allan Therkelsen
Price: $70-100

BG-MD1995
Title / English: Hedgehog with Kids
Title / Danish: Pindsvin med unger
Designed by: Allan Therkelsen
Price: $40-60

BG-MD1996
Title / English: Koala with Cubs
Title / Danish: Koala med unger
Designed by: Allan Therkelsen
Price: $40-60

BG-MD1997
Title / English: Goose with gosling
Title / Danish: Gås med gæslinger
Designed by: Allan Therkelsen
Price: $70-100

BG-MD1998
Title / English: Emperor Penguin with Young
Title / Danish: Pingvin med unger
Designed by: Pia Langelund
Price: $40-60

BG-MD1999
Title / English: Rabbit with young
Title / Danish: Kanin med unger
Designed by: Finn Clausen
Price: $40-60

BG-MD2000
Title / English: Dolphin with calf
Title / Danish: Delfin med unge
Designed by: Finn Clausen
Price: $40-60

BG-MD2001
Title / English: Seal with baby
Title / Danish: Sæl med unge
Designed by: Finn Clausen
Price: $40-60

BG-MD2002
Title / English: Kangaroo with Joey
Title / Danish: Kænguro med unge
Designed by: Finn Clausen
Price: $40-60

BG-MD2003
Title / English: Pig with Piglets
Title / Danish: So med pattegrise
Designed by: Finn Clausen
Price: $50-60

BG-MD2004
Title / English: Otter with Young
Title / Danish: Odder med unge
Designed by: Finn Clausen
Price: $50-60

Bing and Grøndahl Mother's Day Jubilee Plates / BG-MDJ

The Mother's Day Jubilee plate series premiered in 1979 with a picture of the now-famous 1969 Mother's Day plate on it. This series has been produced every five years since then. It is 9" in diameter.

BG-MDJ1979
Title / English: Cocker Spaniel with Puppies
Title / Danish: Cocker spaniel med hvalpe (first issued on the 1969 Mother's Day plate)
Designed by: Henry Thelander
Price: $20-30

BG-MDJ1984
Title / English: Swan with Cygnets
Title / Danish: Svane med unger (first issued on the 1976 Mother's Day plate)
Designed by: Henry Thelander
Price: $30-40

BG-MDJ1989
Title / English: Mare with Foal
Title / Danish: Hest med føl (first issued on the 1972 Mother's Day plate)
Designed by: Henry Thelander
Price: $60-80

BG-MDJ1994
Title / English: Woodpecker with Chicks
Title / Danish: Flagspætte med unger (first issued on the 1980 Mother's Day plate)
Designed by: Henry Thelander
Price: $60-80

BG-MDJ1999
Title / English: Panda with Cubs
Title / Danish: Panda med unger (first issued on the 1992 Mother's Day plate)
Designed by: Finn Clausen
Price: $60-80
No picture available

BG-MDJ2004
Title / English: St. Bernhard with Puppies
Title / Danish: Skt. Bernhardshund med hvalpe
Designed by: Allan Therkelsen
Price: $97.50

Bing and Grøndahl Easter Plates / BG-E

The Easter plate series was started in 1910 because of the great success of the Christmas plates. The Easter plates are concave and some feature religious scenes. The plates were designed by some of the top artists working for B&G, yet they never caught on as well as the Christmas plates. For this reason they were discontinued in 1935. These plates measure 7 3/8".

BG-E1910
Title / English: Marie Magdalene by the Grave
Title / Danish: Marie Magdalene ved graven
Designed by: Jens Peter Dahl Jensen
Price: $50-70

BG-E1911
Title / English: And the Angel Flew Down from Heaven
Title / Danish: Og englen for ned fra himlen
Designed by: Jens Peter Dahl Jensen
Price: $75-100

BG-E1912
Title / English: Golgatha
Title / Danish: Golgatha
Designed by: Jens Peter Dahl Jensen
Price: $50-70

BG-E1913
Title / English: When the Black Swallow Comes
Title / Danish: Når den sortblå svale kommer
Designed by: Jens Peter Dahl Jensen
Price: $50-70

BG-E1914
Title / English: Easter Morning
Title / Danish: Påskemorgen
Designed by: Jens Peter Dahl Jensen
Price: $50-70

BG-E1915
Title / English: Easter Lamb
Title / Danish: Påskelam
Designed by: Jens Peter Dahl Jensen
Price: $50-70

BG-E1916
Title / English: The Coming of Spring
Title / Danish: Første Forårsbebuder
Designed by: M. Hatting
Price: $50-70

BG-E1918
Title / English: Stork
Title / Danish: Storken
Designed by: Johannes Achton Friis
Price: $50-70

BG-E1920
Title / English: The Ancient Tomb
Title / Danish: Kæmpegrav
Designed by: Johannes Achton Friis
Price: $50-70

BG-E1919
Title / English: Black Bird
Title / Danish: Stæren
Designed by: Johannes Achton Friis
Price: $50-70

BG-E1917
Title / English: Easter Lilies
Title / Danish: Påskeliljer
Designed by: Jens Peter Dahl Jensen
Price: $50-70

BG-E1921
Title / English: Viber
Title / Danish: Viber
Designed by: Johannes Achton Friis
Price: $50-70

BG-E1922
Title / English: Flying Swans
Title / Danish: Flyvende svaner
Designed by: Johannes Achton Friis
Price: $50-70

BG-E1923
Title / English: Man Plowing
Title / Danish: Plovmand
Designed by: Johannes Achton Friis
Price: $50-70

BG-E1924
Title / English: Man Seeding
Title / Danish: Sædemand
Designed by: Johannes Achton Friis
Price: $75-100

BG-E1925
Title / English: Sheep on Meadow
Title / Danish: Får på heden
Designed by: Johannes Achton Friis
Price: $75-100

BG-E1926
Title / English: Farmer
Title / Danish: Bondemand
Designed by: Johannes Achton Friis
Price: $75-100

BG-E1927
Title / English: Rooster Crowing
Title / Danish: Hanegal
Designed by: Johannes Achton Friis
Price: $75-100

BG-E1928
Title / English: Easter Morning
Title / Danish: Påskemorgen
Designed by: Johannes Achton Friis
Price: $75-100

BG-E1929
Title / English: Shepherd
Title / Danish: Hyrdedreng
Designed by: Johannes Achton Friis
Price: $75-100

BG-E1930
Title / English: Wild Geese
Title / Danish: Vildgæs
Designed by: H. Flügenring
Price: $100-150

BG-E1931
Title / English: Storks
Title / Danish: Storke
Designed by: Johannes Achton Friis
Price: $100-150

BG-E1932
Title / English: Swans
Title / Danish: Svaner
Designed by: Johannes Achton Friis
Price: $100-150

BG-E1933
Title / English: Church at Frederiksberg Castle
Title / Danish: Frederiksberg Slotskirke
Designed by: Johannes Achton Friis
Price: $200-300

BG-E1934
Title / English: Frederiksberg Garden
Title / Danish: Frederiksberg Have
Designed by: Ove Larsen
Price: $300-400

BG-E1935
Title / English: Willow Tree with blooms
Title / Danish: Piletraeer med Gæslinger
Designed by: Ove Larsen
Price: $600-800

Bing and Grøndahl Children's Day Series / BG-Ch

The Children's Day series was designed in 1985 by Svend Vestergaard. They are all 5 1/4" in diameter and feature scenes of children enjoying themselves, as happy children should.

BG-CH1985
Title / English: The Magical Tea Party
Title / Danish: Den Magiske the fest
Price: $15-25

BG-CH1986
Title / English: A Joyful Flight
Title / Danish: En vidunderful Flyvetur
Price: $15-25

BG-CH1987
Title / English: The Little Gardeners
Title / Danish: De stolte Gartner
Price: $50-60

BG-CH1988
Title / English: Wash Day
Title / Danish: Den lille piges vaskedag
Price: $50-60

BG-CH1989
Title / English: Bedtime
Title / Danish: Sengetid
Price: $50-60

BG-CH1990
Title / English: My Favourite Dress
Title / Danish: Min bedste kjole
Price: $50-60

BG-CH1991
Title / English: Fun on the Beach
Title / Danish: Sjov på stranden
Price: $50-60

BG-CH1992
Title / English: Summer Day in the Meadows
Title / Danish: Sommer dag på marken
Price: $50-60
No picture available

BG-CH1993
Title / English: The Carousel
Title / Danish: Karrusellen
Price: $50-60

BG-CH1994
Title / English: The Little Fisherman
Title / Danish: Lille fiskermand
Price: $50-60

BG-CH1995
Title / English: My First Book
Title / Danish: Min første bog
Price: $50-60
No picture available

BG-CH1996
Title / English: The Little Racer
Title / Danish: Lille racer
Price: $50-60

BG-CH1997
Title / English: Bath Time
Title / Danish: Badetid
Price: $50-60
No picture available

BG-CH1998
Title / English: Little Vendors
Title / Danish: Små sælgere
Price: $50-60

BG-CH1999
Title / English: The Little Concert
Title / Danish: Lille Koncert
Price: $50-60

BG-CH2000
Title / English: Don't Tell
Title / Danish: Sig det ikke
Price: $50-60

BG-CH2001
Title / English: Be My Valentine
Title / Danish: Vær min valentine
Price: $35-45

BG-CH2002
Title / English: The Little Juggler
Title / Danish: Lille junglør
Price: $35-45

BG-CH2003
Title / English: At the Seashore
Title / Danish: På stranden
Price: $35-45
No picture available

BG-CH2004
Title / English: Dance Lesson
Title / Danish: Dansetime
Price: $49

Bing and Grøndahl Santa Series / BG-S

The Santa series was designed by Hans Henrik Hansen in 1989. They are all 7 3/4" in diameter and feature Santa getting ready and delivering Christmas presents.

BG-S1989
Title / English: Santa's Workshop
Title / Danish: Julemandens værksted
Price: $50-70

BG-S1990
Title / English: Santa's Sleigh
Title / Danish: Julemandes slæde
Price: $50-70

BG-S1991
Title / English: The Journey
Title / Danish: Rejsen
Price: $50-70

BG-S1992
Title / English: Santa on the Roof
Title / Danish: Julemanden på taget
Price: $50-70

BG-S1993
Title / English: Santa's gifts
Title / Danish: Julemandes gaver
Price: $50-70

BG-S1994
Title / English: Christmas Stories
Title / Danish: Jule historier
Price: $50-70

BG-S1996
Title / English: Santa in the Orient
Title / Danish: Julamanden I Orienten
Price: $50-70

Bing and Grøndahl Christmas Around the World Plates / BG-S cont.

The Christmas Around the World series is a continuation of the Santa series, also designed by Hans Henrik Hansen. They are all 7 3/4" in diameter and feature Santa traveling the world delivering presents.

BG-S1995
Title / English: Santa in Greenland
Title / Danish: Julemanden i Grønland
Price: $50-70

BG-S1997
Title / English: Santa in Russia
Title / Danish: Julemanden i Rusland
Price: $60-80
No picture available

BG-S1998
Title / English: Santa in Australia
Title / Danish: Julemanden i Australien
Price: $50-70

BG-S1999
Title / English: Santa in Europe
Title / Danish: Julemanden i Europa
Price: $60-90
No picture available

BG-S2000
Title / English: Santa in New York
Title / Danish: Julemanden i New York
Price: $75-100

Bing and Grøndahl Snow Fairies Christmas Series / BG-SF

Kirsten Seeberg designed the Snow Fairies Christmas series in 2001. This series will consist of five plates, each accompanied by a story about the Snow Fairies' Christmas written by Gitte Broksø. These plates measure 7 5/8".

BG-SF2001 "Snow Fairies"

BG-SF2002 "King Frost"

BG-SF2003 "The Fairy Palace"

BG-SF2004 "Queen Winter"

BG-SF2005 "Sleigh Ride"

Bing and Grøndahl Hans Christian Andersen Series / BG-HCA

The Hans Christian Andersen series was done in relief, full color, and limited edition. Designed by Jørgen Nielsen, it is one of many different H. C. Andersen plate series created by the B&G factory.

BG-HCA1
Title / English: The Little Mermaid
Title / Danish: Den Lille Havfrue
Price: $35-45

BG-HCA2
Title / English: Thumbelina
Title / Danish: Tommelise
Price: $35-45

BG-HCA3
Title / English: The Emporer's New Clothes
Title / Danish: Kejserens Nye Klæder
Price: $35-45

BG-HCA4
Title / English: The Flying Trunk
Title / Danish: Den Flyvende Kuffert
Price: $35-45

BG-HCA5
Title / English: The Tinder Box
Title / Danish: Fyrtøjet
Price: $35-45

BG-HCA6
Title / English: The Ugly Duckling
Title / Danish: Den Grimme ælling
Price: $35-45

Bing and Grøndahl Town Plates / BG-T

The Bing and Grøndahl Town plates are high quality plates that were produced in 1894 and 1895. Each of them measures 9 1/2" in diameter and, unlike the Christmas plates, each one is hand painted using a stencil and a sponge. The artists were free to paint what they wanted, within reason. Each artist left their unique signature on every plate rather than having a quality control number asigned to them, as was the case with production painters.

The idea for the Town plates originated with Effie Hagerman-Lindencrone, one of the foremost and beloved porcelain painters/designers of that time. Hegerman-Lindencrone used magazine articles featuring city seals as her inspiration for designing the plates. After hesitantly consenting to put the idea into production, the factory agreed to give 50% of the sale price of each plate to the artist as payment for their work.

The quantity produced of each plate is unknown, but the fact that they are hand painted by the best painters suggests that they were produced in a very limited quantity. The total number of different plates produced is also unknown, but it is believed that a plate was produced for each trade city. There are also a few plates picturing foreign cities. Over 70 different Town Plates are known at this time.

BG-T1
Town: Aarhus
Production #
Artist: Effie Hegerman-Lindencrone
Price: $300-500

BG-T2
Town: Aarhus 1672
Production #
Artist: Effie Hegerman-Lindencrone
Price: $300-500

BG-T3
Town: Aarhus
Production #376
Artist: CF
Price: $300-500
No picture available

BG-T4
Town: Aarhus
Production # 2356
Artist: J. Plockross Irminger
Price: $300-500
No picture available

BG-T5
Town: Aalborg
Production #2919
Artist: MDIJ
Price: $300-500

BG-T6
Town: Aalborg
Production #
Artist: Effie Hegerman-Lindencrone
Price: $300-500
No picture available

BG-T7
Town: Assens, 1535
Production #670
Artist: Effie Hegerman-Lindencrone
Price: $300-500

BG-T8
Town: Bogense, 1564
Production #2422
Artist: J. Plockross Irminger
Price: $300-500

BG-T9
Town: Bogense
Production #
Artist: Effie Hegerman-Lindencrone
Price: $300-500
No picture available

BG-T10
Town: Copenhagen 1662
Production #
Artist: Effie Hegerman-Lindencrone
Price: $300-500
No picture available

BG-T11
Town: Copenhagen North West
Production #
Artist: J. Plockross Irminger
Price: $300-500
No picture available

BG-T12
Town: Copenhagen Wholesale Trade
Production #
Artist: Effie Hegerman-Lindencrone
Price: $300-500
No picture available

BG-T13
Town: Fredericia
Production #
Artist: CF
Price: $300-500
No picture available

BG-T14
Town: Frederiksberg,
Production #3011
Artist: MDJ
Price: $300-500

BG-T15
Town: Frederikshavn
Production #
Artist: Effie Hegerman-Lindencrone
Price: $300-500
No picture available

BG-T16
Town: Haderslev
Production #
Artist: Effie Hegerman-Lindencrone
Price: $300-500
No picture available

BG-T17
Town: Helsingør / Elsinor
Production #292
Artist: Effie Hegerman-Lindencrone
Price: $300-500

BG-T18
Town: Hillerød
Production #1121
Artist: Effie Hegerman-Lindencrone
Price: $300-500

BG-T19
Town: Hobro
Production #2359
Artist: J. Plockross Irminger
Price: $300-500

BG-T20
Town: Holbæk
Production #279
Artist: Effie Hegerman-Lindencrone
Price: $300-500

BG-T21
Town: Holmiae
Production #
Artist: Effie Hegerman-Lindencrone
Price: $300-500

BG-T22
Town: Holsterbro
Production #
Artist: Effie Hegerman-Lindencrone
Price: $300-500
No picture available

BG-T23
Town: Horsens
Production #2151
Artist: Effie Hegerman-Lindencrone
Price: $300-500

BG-T24
Town: Hjørring
Production #2778
Artist: MDJ
Price: $300-500

BG-T25
Town: Kallunborg
Production #
Artist: Effie Hegerman-Lindencrone
Price: $300-500
No picture available

BG-T26
Town: Kierteminde, 1535
Production #1872
Artist: J. Plockross Irminger
Price: $300-500

BG-T27
Town: Kolding
Production #
Artist: J. Plockross Irminger
Price: $300-500

BG-T28
Town: Kolding
Production #288
Artist: Effie Hegerman-Lindencrone
Price: $300-500
No picture available

BG-T29
Town: Køge
Production #
Artist: Effie Hegerman-Lindencrone
Price: $300-500
No picture available

BG-T30
Town: København
Production #2275
Artist: J. Plockross Irminger
Price: $300-500
No picture available

BG-T31
Town: Lemvig
Production #
Artist: Effie Hegerman-Lindencrone
Price: $300-500
No picture available

BG-T32
Town: Mariager
Production #2507
Artist: J. Plockross Irminger
Price: $300-500

BG-T33
Town: Maribo, 1839
Production #
Artist: Effie Hegerman-Lindencrone
Price: $300-500

BG-T34
Town: Nakskov, 1889
Production #
Artist: Effie Hegerman-Lindencrone
Price: $300-500

BG-T35
Town: Nibe
Production #2512
Artist: J. Plockross Irminger
Price: $300-500

BG-T36
Town: Nibe
Production #
Artist: CF
Price: $300-500

BG-T37
Town: Nyborg
Production #
Artist: Effie Hegerman-Lindencrone
Price: $300-500

BG-T38
Town: Nyborg 1584
Production #1021
Artist: Effie Hegerman-Lindencrone
Price: $300-500
No picture available

BG-T39
Town: Nykoebing Mors
Production #
Artist: Effie Hegerman-Lindencrone
Price: $300-500
No picture available

BG-T40
Town: Næstved, 1519
Production #989
Artist: Effie Hegerman-Lindencrone
Price: $300-500

BG-T41
Town: Nørresundby
Production #
Artist: J. Plockross Irminger
Price: $300-500

BG-T42
Town: Nørresundby
Production #2934
Artist: MDJ
Price: $300-500
No picture available

BG-T43
Town: Odense 1535
Production #
Artist: Effie Hegerman-Lindencrone
Price: $300-500
No picture available

BG-T44
Town: Odense
Production #
Artist: J. Plockross Irminger
Price: $300-500
No picture available

BG-T45
Town: Odense, 1584
Production #345
Artist: Effie Hegerman-Lindencrone
Price: $300-500

BG-T46
Town: Raders
Production #
Artist: Effie Hegerman-Lindencrone
Price: $300-500
No picture available

BG-T47
Town: Randers
Production #2676
Artist: J. Plockross Irminger
Price: $300-500

BG-T48
Town: Ribe
Production #
Artist: MDI
Price: $300-500
No picture available

BG-T49
Town: Ringkøbing
Production #2175
Artist: Effie Hegerman-Lindencrone
Price: $300-500

BG-T50
Town: Ringsted
Production #2067
Artist: Effie Hegerman-Lindencrone
Price: $300-500

BG-T51
Town: Roskilde
Production #
Artist: CF
Price: $300-500
No picture available

BG-T52
Town: Skanderburg
Production #2489
Artist: J. Plockross Irminger
Price: $300-500

BG-T53
Town: Skive
Production #
Artist: Effie Hegerman-Lindencrone
Price: $300-500
No picture available

BG-T54
Town: Sorø
Production #
Artist: Effie Hegerman-Lindencrone
Price: $300-500
No picture available

BG-T55
Town: Stockholm
Production #44
Artist: Effie Hegerman-Lindencrone
Price: $300-500
No picture available

BG-T56
Town: Store Heddinge
Production #
Artist: Effie Hegerman-Lindencrone
Price: $300-500
No picture available

BG-T57
Town: Svendborg
Production #2242 (42 or 92)
Artist: DI
Price: $300-500

BG-T58
Town: Svendborg
Production #
Artist: Effie Hegerman-Lindencrone
Price: $300-500
No picture available

BG-T59
Town: Sæby
Production #
Artist: Effie Hegerman-Lindencrone
Price: $300-500
No picture available

BG-T60
Town: Varde
Production #
Artist: Effie Hegerman-Lindencrone
Price: $300-500
No picture available

BG-T61
Town: Vejle
Production #280
Artist: Effie Hegerman-Lindencrone
Price: $300-500

BG-T62
Town: Viborg
Production #
Artist: Effie Hegerman-Lindencrone
Price: $300-500
No picture available

Bing and Grøndahl Christmas In America – American Heritage Series / BG-AH

The Christmas In America, American Heritage series was started in 1986 and ended in 2004. It features scenes from the United States, they are all 5" in diameter. The Christmas In America plates were designed by American artist Jack Woodson. The American Heritage plates are designed by Christopher Magadini.

BG-AH1986
Title: Christmas in Williamsburg
Price: $85-100
No picture available

BG-AH1987
Title: Christmas at the White House
Price: $25-45
No picture available

BG-AH1988
Title: Christmas at Rockefeller Center
Price: $25-45

BG-AH1989
Title: Christmas in New England
Price: $25-45
No picture available

BG-AH1990
Title: Christmas Eve at the Capitol
Price: $25-45
No picture available

BG-AH1991
Title: Christmas Eve at Independence Hall
Price: $25-45
No picture available

BG-AH1992
Title: Christmas in San Francisco
Price: $25-45
No picture available

BG-AH1993
Title: Coming Home for Christmas
Price: $25-45
No picture available

BG-AH1994
Title: Christmas in Alaska
Price: $25-45
No picture available

BG-AH1995
Title: Christmas Eve on the Mississippi
Price: $25-45
No picture available

BG-AH1996
Title: Christmas Eve at the Statue of Liberty
Price: $25-45
No picture available

BG-AH1997
Title: Christmas Eve at the Lincoln Memorial
Price: $25-45
No picture available

BG-AH1998
Title: Christmas at the Chicago Watertower
Price: $25-45
No picture available

BG-AH1999
Title: Christmas Eve at Mt. Rushmore
Price: $25-45
No picture available

BG-AH2000
Title: Christmas Eve at the Alamo
Price: $25-45
No picture available

BG-AH2001
Title: Christmas at the White House
Price: $25-45

BG-AH2002
Title: Christmas at the Golden Gate Bridge
Price: $40

BG-AH2003
Title: Christmas Eve at Lincoln's Cabin
Price: $40
No picture available

Bing and Grøndahl Centennial Plates / BG-Cen

This Centennial Collection, consisting of only five plates, was created as a tribute to Harald Bing. Each hand-decorated plate was painted under the glaze and has a 24 karat gold border. The designs were replicated from separate Christmas plate designs. These plates measure 5 7/8".

BG-Cen1
Year: 1991
Title / English: Crows Enjoying Christmas
Title / Danish: Kragerne hygger sig
Designed by: Dahl Jensen (first issued on the 1899 Christmas plate)
Price: $30-50

BG-Cen2
Year: 1992
Title / English: Christmas Tree in Town Hall Square
Title / Danish: Julestræet på Rådhuspladsen
Designed by: H. Flügenring (first issued on the 1930 Christmas plate)
Price: $30-50

BG-Cen3
Year: 1993
Title / English: Christmas Elf
Title / Danish: Julenissen på grøden venter
Designed by: Henry Thelander (first issued on the 1963 Christmas plate)
Price: $30-50

BG-Cen4
Year: 1994
Title / English: Christmas Eve in Church
Title / Danish: I kirke juleaften
Designed by: Henry Thelander (first issued on the 1968 Christmas plate)
Price: $30-50

BG-Cen5
Year: 1995
Title / English: Behind the Frozen Window
Title / Danish: Bag den frosne rude
Designed by: F.A. Hallin (first issued on the 1895 Christmas plate)
Price: $30-50

Bing and Grøndahl Centennial Jubilee Miniature Plates / BG-CJ

The Centennial Jubilee collection of miniature plates was issued to commemorate the 100th Jubilee of the world's first Christmas Plate made by Bing and Grøndahl in 1895. They have a gold border with inscription.

BG-CJ1
Title / English: Behind the Frozen Window
Title / Danish: Bag den frosne rude
Designed by: F. A. Hallin (first issued on the 1895 Christmas plate)
Price: $25-35

BG-CJ2
Title / English: Christmas Night Expectations
Title / Danish: Forventining til den kommende julenat
Designed by: Dahl Jensen (first issued on the 1905 Christmas plate)
Price: $25-35

BG-CJ3
Title / English: Outside the Lighted Window (from *The Little Match Girl*)
Title / Danish: Uden for det oplyste vindue
Designed by: Johannes Achton Friis (first issued on the 1919 Christmas plate)
Price: $25-35

BG-CJ4
Title / English: Skating Couple
Title / Danish: Skøjteløberpar
Designed by: Johannes Achton Friis (first issued on the 1927 Christmas plate)
Price: $25-35

BG-CJ5
Title / English: The Lifeboat
Title / Danish: Redningsbåden
Designed by: H. Flügenring (first issued on the 1932 Christmas plate)
Price: $25-35

BG-CJ6
Title / English: The Old Water Mill
Title / Danish: Den gamle Vandmøllen
Designed by: Ove Larsen (first issued on the 1945 Christmas plate)
Price: $25-35

BG-CJ7
Title / English: Hans Christian Andersens House, Odense
Title / Danish: H. C. Andersens hus, Odense
Designed by: Børge Pramvig (first issued on the 1954 Christmas plate)
Price: $25-35

BG-CJ8
Title / English: Birds Christmas
Title / Danish: Fuglenese jul
Designed by: Henry Thelander (first issued on the 1967 Christmas plate)
Price: $25-35

BG-CJ9
Title / English: Christmas in the Country
Title / Danish: Jul I landsbyen
Designed by: Henry Thelander (first issued on the 1974 Christmas plate)
Price: $25-35

BG-CJ10
Title / English: Bringing Home the Christmas Tree
Title / Danish: Juletræet hentes
Designed by: Henry Thelander (first issued on the 1982 Christmas plate)
Price: $25-35

Bing and Grøndahl 100th Year Anniversary Items / BG-Ann

The 100th Anniversary plates are limited edition special production pieces made for the 100th Anniversary of the first Christmas plate; the last one was produced in full color, whereas the first plate and the vase are direct copies of the first Christmas plate by F. A. Hallin. The plates are both 7" in diameter.

BG-AnnPlate
Year: 1995
Title / English: Behind the Frozen Window
Title / Danish: Bag den frosne rude
Designed by: F. A. Hallin in 1895
Price: $100-150

BG-AnnVase
Year: 1995
Title / English: Behind the Frozen Window
Title / Danish: Bag den frosne rude
Designed by: F. A. Hallin in 1895
Price: $200-300

BG-AnnPlateColor
Year: 1995 produced in full color.
Title / English: Dawn over Copenhagen
Title / Danish: Solopgang over København
Designed by: Christopher Magadini
Price: $80-120

Bing and Grøndahl King Plates / BG-K

The King Plates series of Danish Monarch plates features pictures of some of the best-known and most important Rulers of Denmark. They are all 9 1/8" in diameter and are limited to a production of 5000 each.

BG-K1
Monarch: Queen Margrethe I
Ruled from: 1375-1412
Price: $50-70

BG-K2
Monarch: King Christian I
Ruled from: 1448-1481
Price: $50-70

BG-K3
Monarch: King Christian II
Ruled from: 1513-1523
Price: $50-70

BG-K4
Monarch: King Christian III
Ruled from: 1534-1559
Price: $50-70

BG-K5
Monarch: King Christian IV
Ruled from: 1588-1648
Price: $50-70

BG-K6
Monarch: King Frederik III
Ruled from: 1648-1670
Price: $50-70

BG-K7
Monarch: King Christian V
Ruled from: 1670-1699
Price: $50-70

BG-K8
Monarch: King Christian VI
Ruled from: 1730-1746
Price: $50-70

BG-K9
Monarch: King Christian VIII
Ruled from: 1839-1848
Price: $50-70

BG-K10
Monarch: King Frederik VII
Ruled from: 1848-1863
Price: $50-70

BG-K11
Monarch: King Christian IX
Ruled from: 1863-1906
Price: $50-70

BG-K12
Monarch: Frederik IX
Ruled from: 1947-1972
Price: $50-70

Bing and Grøndahl Windjammer Collection / BG-W

Six of the world's most famous sailing training ships are shown in this series, designed by American marine artist James E. Mitchell. Twenty-two colors were used. The plates have a pierced border with hand- applied, 24-carat gold. Limited to 10,000 worldwide, they were produced in 1980-81.b

BG-W1 (8866/633)

Inscription: DANMARK off Elsinore Castle, Denmark. This full rigged ship of 845 tons, built in 1933, is owned by the directorate of Maritime Education and is used as a training ship to prepare young Danes for seagoing careers. Measuring 252 feet 9 inches in overall length, she has a beam of 32 feet 10 inches and carries 17,610 feet of sail on her three masts.
Year: 1981 (#4)
Price: $100-200

BG-W2 (8867/633)

Inscription: EAGLE entering the Golden Gate, San Francisco. The three-masted barque "Eagle" of 1,727 tons was built in 1936 and is owned and operated by the U.S. Coast Guard Academy as a training ship for cadets. With an overall length of 294 feet 5 inches and a beam of 39 feet, she carries 21,345 square feet of sail.
Price: $100-200

BG-CM9
Year: 1897
Description / English: King Christian IX's 25th year as king.
Description / Danish: Kong Christian den IX's 25 regents aar.
Price: $200-300

BG-CM10
Year: 1898
Description / English: Roskilde County Exhibition in Holbaek
Description / Danish: Amts udstilling i Holbæk 1898
Designed by:
Size: 7", 18cm
Price: $130-170

BG-CM11
Year: 1898
Description / English: King Christian the IX's 35th year as king.
Description / Danish: Virtute Et Fidelitate 1863-1898
Designed by:
Size: 8", 20.50cm
Price: $130-170

BG-CM12
Year: 1899
Description / English: Paris coat of arms
Description / Danish: Paris' byvaaben
Designed by:
Size: 10.25", 26cm
Price: $1000

BG-CM13
Year: 1899
Description / English: Roskilde Cathedral
Description / Danish: Soli Deo Gloria
Designed by: Frederik August Hallin
Price: $130-170

BG-CM14
Year: 1901
Description / English: Business school
Description / Danish: Købmandsskolen
Designed by: Frederik August Hallin
No picture available

BG-CM15
Year: 1901
Description / English: Warburg Art Publishing Company
Description / Danish: Warburg Kunstforlag Kjøbenhavn
Designed by: Frederik August Hallin
Size: 5 1/2", 14cm
Price: $3000
No picture available

BG-CM16
Year: 1901
Description / English: 100 year anniversary of the Battle of the "Reden"
Description / Danish: Saa Kæmpe de helte hin 2 April 1801-1901.
Designed by: Aamodt
Size: 8 1/4', 21cm
Price: $130-170

BG-CM17
Year: 1901
Description / English: C.M. Hess, Vejle 25th jubilee
Description / Danish: C.M. Hess, Vejle 25-Års jubilaeum.
Designed by: Frederik August Hallin
Size: 7 1/10", 18cm
Price: $130-170

BG-CM18
Year: 1901
Description / English: Plate formed like a waterlilly, with a Royal Crown and the year 1901
Description / Danish:
Designed by:
Size: 6" x 5"
Price: $500
No picture available

BG-CM19
Year: 1902
Description / English: Advertising plate from Tuborg Brewery
Description / Danish: Reklame platte fra Tuborgs fabrikker
Designed by: Frederik August Hallin
Size: 8" x 6 1/2"
Price: $200

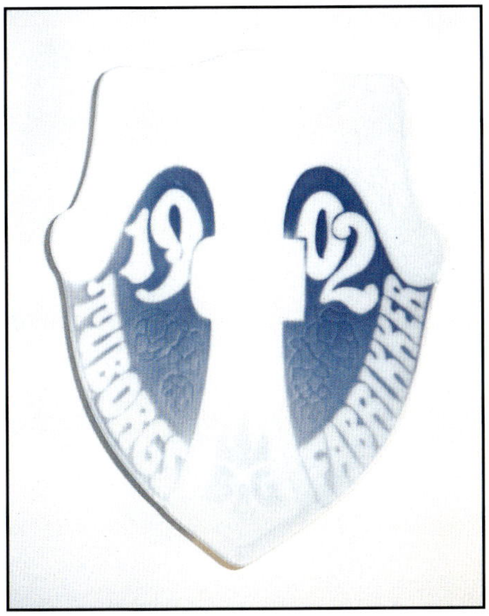

BG-CM20
Year: 1903
Description / English: Commemorating the erection of the town hall of Copenhagen
Description / Danish: Opførelsen af Københavns Raadhus
Designed by: Frederik August Hallin
Size: 9 1/4", 23.50cm
Price: $130-170

BG-CM21
Year: 1904
Description / English: 50th jubilee of the state-owned phone company
Description / Danish: 50 aars jubilæum for Dansk Stats telegraf
Designed by:
Size: 7 1/10", 18cm
Price: $130-170

BG-CM22
Year: 1906
Description / English: King Christian IX's memorial plate. King of Denmark from 1863 to 1906
Description / Danish: Med Gud for ære og Ret 1863-1906
Designed by: Jens Peter Dahl Jensen
Size: 8 1/4", 21cm
Price: $100

BG-CM23
Year: 1906
Description / English: Commemorating Her Majesty Queen Louise
Description / Danish: Til minde om Dronning Louise
Designed by: Jens Peter Dahl Jensen
Price:
No picture available

BG-CM24
Year: 1907
Description / English: The Royal Ship "Dannebrog" Iceland trip
Description / Danish: Kongeskibet, ved en Islands tur i 1907.
Designed by:
Size: 9", 23.cm
Price: $130-170

BG-CM25
Year: 1907
Description / English: Aarhus Cathedral
Description / Danish: Aarhus Domkirke
Designed by: Jens Peter Dahl Jensen
Size: 9", 23cm
Price: $130-170

BG-CM26
Year: 1907
Description / English: Commemorating the famous writer Henrik Ibsen
Description / Danish: Til minde om Henrik Ibsen
Designed by: Christian Krogh
Size: 8", 21cm
Price: $130-170

BG-CM27
Year: 1907
Description / English: Commemorating the restoration of Viborg Cathedral
Description / Danish: Til minde om restorationen af Viborg Domkirke
Designed by: Jens Peter Dahl Jensen
Size: 9", 23cm
Price: $130-170

BG-CM28
Year: 1908
Description / English: Ribe Cathedral
Description / Danish: Ribe Domkirke
Designed by: Jens Peter Dahl Jensen
Size: 9", 23cm
Price: $130-170

BG-CM29
Year: 1907
Description / English: 50th Jubilee for the city of Frederiksberg 1907
Description / Danish: Frederiksberg 50 aars jubilaeum som selvstaedig by i 1907.
Designed by: Jens Peter Dahl Jensen 9th of September 1908
Price: $130-170

BG-CM30
Year: 1908
Description / English: Valmuefesten 1st of April 1908
Description / Danish: Valmuefesten 1. April 1908
Designed by:
Size: 7", 18cm
Price: $130-170

BG-CM31
Year: 1908
Description / English: Commemorating Niels R. Finsen
Description / Danish: Til minde om Niels R. Finsen
Designed by: C. Mortensen
Price: $130-170

BG-CM32
Year: 1909
Description / English: Herlufsholm
Description / Danish: Herlufsholm
Designed by: Jens Peter Dahl Jensen
Size: 8 1/7", 20.5cm
Price: $130-170

BG-CM33
Year: 1909
Description / English: Klitgaard Soroe
Description / Danish: Klitgaard Sorø
Designed by:
Produced in 550 copies
Price: $130-170

BG-CM34
Year: 1909
Description / English: Tivoli
Description / Danish: Tivoli
Designed by: Jens Peter Dahl Jensen
Size: 8 1/7", 20.5cm

BG-CM35
Year: 1909
Description / English: Air Balloon
Description / Danish: Luftskipsplatte
Designed by: Jens Peter Dahl Jensen
Size:
Price: $130-170
No picture available

BG-CM36
Year: 1909
Description / English: Aarhus plate
Description / Danish: Aarhus platte
Designed by: Sternow
Size: 8 1/7", 20.5cm
Price: $130-170

BG-CM37
Year: 1909
Description / English: Politiken 1884-1909 1st October. Their 25th Jubilee
Description / Danish: Politikens 25års jubilæum
Designed by: Harald Moltke
Size: 9 1/4", 23.50cm
Price: $150-200

BG-CM38
Year: 1910
Description / English: Conquest of the North Pole
Description / Danish: Nordpolens Erobring
Designed by: Harald Moltke
Price: $200-250

BG-CM39
Year: 1910
Description / English: 25th jubilee of the Copenhagen Journalist Union
Description / Danish: 25-års jubilæum for Københavns Journalistforening
Designed by: Hans Tegner
Size: 8 1/7", 20.5cm
Price: $175-200

BG-CM40
Year: 1912
Description / English: Commemorating the death of Frederik VIII
Description / Danish: Til minde om Frederk d.8
Designed by: Jens Peter Dahl Jensen
Size: 8", 20cm
Price: $130-170

BG-CM41
Year: 1914
Description / English: The Baltic Exhibition in Malmo 1914
Description / Danish: Den Baltiske udstilling i Malmø i 1914
Designed by:
Size: 5 1/7", 13cm
No picture available

BG-CM42
Year: 1915
Description / English: Peace plate
Description / Danish: Fredsplatte
Designed by: Hans Tegner
Size: 8 1/7", 20.5cm
Price: $130-170

BG-CM43
Year: 1915
Description / English: Munke Mill
Description / Danish: Munke Mølle
Designed by:
Price:
No picture available

BG-CM44
Year: 1915
Description / English: Pro-Patria
Description / Danish: Pro-Patria
Designed by: Achton Friis
Price: $130-170

BG-CM45
Year: 1916
Description / English: 25th jubilee of the Credit Union "Øststifternes Kreditforening"
Description / Danish: 25-års jubilæum for Øststifternes Kreditforening
Designed by: Achton Friis
Price: $130-170

BG-CM46
Year: 1916
Description / English: Peace plate. Pigeon with Olive Leaves
Description / Danish: Fredsplatte. duer og olivenkrans
Designed by: Achton Friis
Size: 6" x 5"
No picture available

BG-CM47
Year: 1916
Description / English: Charity plate for The Red Cross
Description / Danish: Voltgørenshedsplatte for Røde Kors
Designed by: Achton Friis
Size: 8", 20cm

BG-CM48
Year: 1917
Description / English: 25th Jubilee of the 15th Battalion in the 1st regiment
Description / Danish: 25-års jubilæum for første regiments 15 battalion
Designed by: Achton Friis
Price: $130-170

BG-CM49
Year: 1917
Description / English: 100 year anniversery of Niels W. Gade 1817-22nd February, 1917
Description / Danish: 100-års jubilæum for Niels W. Gade
Designed by: Achton Friis
Size: 7", 17.5cm
Price: $130-170

BG-CM50
Year: 1918
Description / English: Military's 25th jubilee for the 1st regiments 1st battalion
Description / Danish: 25- Jubilæum for the 1. regiments 1. battallion
Designed by: Achton Friis
Size: 7", 17.5cm
Price: $130-170

BG-CM51
Year: 1907
Description / English: 750th jubilee of Koldinghus
Description / Danish: Koldinghus 750th jubilæum
Designed by:
Price: $130-170

BG-CM52
Year: 1919
Description / English: 700th jubilee of the Volmerbattle
Description / Danish: 700-årsdagen for Volmerslaget
Designed by: Achton Friis
Size: 10 1/3", 26cm
Price: $130-170

BG-CM53
Year: 1919
Description / English: The reunification of Southern Jutland with Denmark
Description / Danish: Sønderjyllands kommer tilbage under dansk flag
Designed by: Achton Friis
Size: 8 1/7", 20.5cm
Price: $130-170

BG-CM53A
Year: 1919
Description / English: The reunification of Southern Jutland with Denmark
Description / Danish: Sønderjyllands kommer tilbage under dansk flag
Designed by: Achton Friis
Size: 12 3/4", 32.5cm
Price: $600-800

BG-CM54
Year: 1920
Description / English: 50th Birthday of King Christian the 10th
Description / Danish: Til minde om Kong Christian d.10's fødselsdag
Designed by: Hans Tegner
Price: $200-250

BG-CM55
Year: 1921
Description / English: Sail ship in Greenland Fjord 1721-1922.
Description / Danish: Sejlskib i Grønlandsk fjord 1721-1922
Designed by: Achton Friis
Size: 7 1/3", 18cm
Price: $130-170

BG-CM56
Year: 1922
Description / English: Commemorating the 200th jubilee of the Danish Theater
Description / Danish: Den Danske Skueplads 200-år jubilæum
Designed by: Hans Tegner
Size: 8 1/7", 20.5cm
Price: $130-170

BG-CM57
Year: 1922
Description / English: 50th jubilee of the Copenhagen Glass & Porcelaln Dealer Union
Description / Danish: 50års jubilæum for Københavns glas og porcelains-handler forning
Designed by: Frederik August Hallin
Size: 6 1/3", 16cm

BG-CM58
Year: 1923
Description / English: King Christian the 10th and the Queen's Silver Wedding Anniversary
Description / Danish: Kong Christian d.10's og Dronningens Sølvbryllup
Designed by: Achton Friis
Size: 7 1/3", 18cm
Price: $130-170

BG-CM59
Year: 1923
Description / English: Marselisborg Castle
Description / Danish: Marselisborg Slot
Designed by: Achton Friis
Price: $130-170

BG-CM60
Year: 1923
Description / English: Sogenfri Castle
Description / Danish: Sogenfri Slot
Designed by: Achton Friis
Price: $130-170

BG-CM61
Year: 1924
Description / English: Scoresbysund 1924 Greenland
Description / Danish: Scoresbysund 1924 Grønland
Designed by: Frederik August Hallin
Size: 7 1/3", 18cm
Price: $130-170

BG-CM62
Year: 1924
Description / English: Jutland Bakery Masters Union 50th jubilee
Description / Danish: Jyllands Bagermesterforenings 50-års jubilæum
Designed by: Frederik August Hallin
Size: 9 1/2" x 8 1/8", 24 x 20.5cm

BG-CM63
Year: 1924
Description / English: Nielsen & Lydiche Jubilee plate
Description / Danish: Nielsen & Lydiche Jubilæumsplatte
Designed by: Hans Tegner
Size:
No picture available

BG-CM64
Year: 1931
Description / English: Gift from the male workers at Bing & Grøndahl to the Glass and Porcelain Dealers Union on their 25th jubilee. 1906-1931
Description / Danish: 25-års jubilæumsgave fra de mandlige arbejde på BG til glas og porcelænshandlerforeningen
Designed by: Ove Larsen
Copies: 1
Size: 14", 35cm
Price: $5000-6000

BG-CM65
Year: 1926
Description / English: Comm. first fight between Copenhagen and Tokyo by A.P. Botved
Description / Danish: A. P. Botveds flyvning mellem København og Tokyo
Designed by: Achton Friis
Size: 7 1/3", 18cm
Price: $130-170

BG-CM66
Year: 1930
Description / English: 125th Anniversary of H. C. Andersen's Birth
Description / Danish: 125-års dagen for H. C. Andersens sødsel
Designed by: I. Tjerne
Size: 9 1/4", 23.50cm
Price: $130-170

BG-CM67
Year: 1930
Description / English: 1000th year anniversary of the Icelandic parliament
Description / Danish: 1000-årsdagen for Islands Alting
Designed by: Achton Friis
Price: $200-250b

BG-CM68
Year: 1933
Description / English: Virgin Islands, USA
Description / Danish: De amerikanske Vestindiske øer
Designed by: I. Tjerne
Size: 5 1/3", 13.5cm

BG-CM69
Year: 1935
Description / English: The Little Belt Bridge
Description / Danish: Lillebæltsbroen
Designed by: Ove Larsen
Price: $50-100

BG-CM70
Year: 1936
Description /English: Craftsman Union
Description / Danish: Håndværkerforegningen
Designed by: Ove Larsen
Price:
No picture available

BG-CM71
Year: 1937
Description / English: Habor Mill in Aalborg
Description / Danish: Havnemøllen i Aalborg
Designed by: Ove Larsen
Size: 6" x 5"
No picture available

BG-CM72
Year: 1939
Description / English: Denmark San Francisco
Description / Danish: Danmark San Francisco
Designed by: Ove Larsen
Size: 7 1/3", 18cm
No picture available

BG-CM73
Year: 1957
Description / English: Odd Fellow on Iceland
Description / Danish: Odd Fellow ordenen på Island
Designed by:
Price: $1000

Bing and Grøndahl

Gentle Love Collection / GL

The Gentle Love Collection is a series of four plates made in 1985 by Addie Heesen Cooper. All the plates reflect the bond between a mother and a child. Each plate is made in a limited edition of 9500 copies.

BG-GL1
Year: 1985
Title / English: Joanna and John
Title / Danish: Joanna og John
Designed by: Addie Heesen Cooper
Price: $40-60

BG-GL2
Year: pre-1985
Title / English: Alexandra and Amy
Title / Danish: : Alexandra og Amy
Designed by: Addie Heesen Cooper
Price: $40-60

BG-GL3
Year: 1985
Title / English: Ingrid and Lisa
Title / Danish: Ingrid og Lisa
Designed by: Addie Heesen Cooper
Price: $40-60

BG-GL4
Year: 1985
Title / English: Elizabeth and David
Title / Danish: Elizabeth og David
Designed by: Addie Heesen Cooper
Price: $40-60

Bing and Grøndahl Dealer Signs / Sign

Dealer signs are found in numerous different designs, ages, and languages. The production of dealer signs started very early, but it was not until the late 19th century when the products were being marketed through a larger number of retail outlets in Denmark and across the world that there was wider use of them. The earlier signs can be found hand painted in overglaze and underglaze styles. Most of the newer signs are done as transferware.

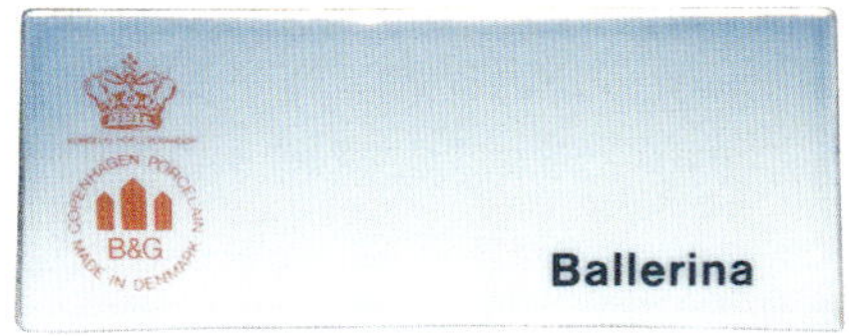

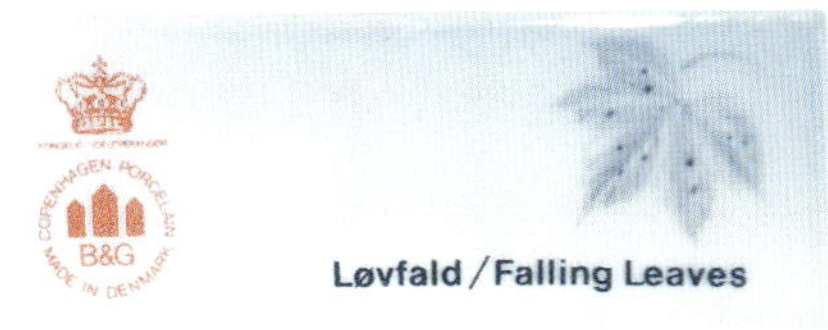

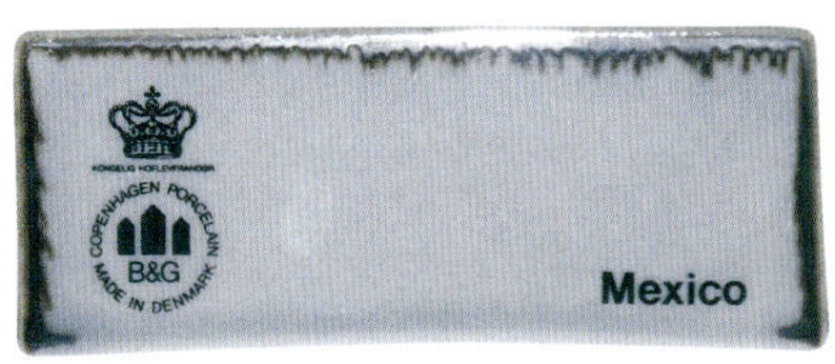

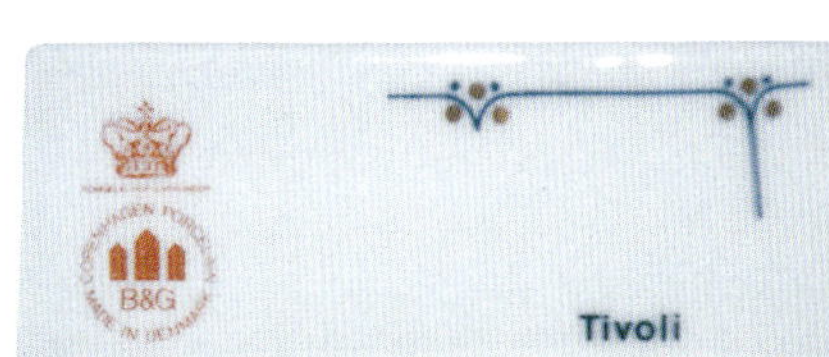

BG-O-6
Title / English: Artist signed Kronborg plate
Designed by: Amalie Schou

BG-O-8
Title / English: Artist signed landscape plate
Designed by: CMO

BG-O-7
Title / English: Artist signed charger
Designed by: CMO

BG-0-9
Title / English: Artist signed vase with gold
Designed by: Marie Smith

BG-O-10
Title / English: Christmas vase made from 1916 to 1932
Size: Varies

BG-O-12
Title / English: Commemorative vase. Made for different occasions
No picture available

BG-O-13
Title / English: Rotary Copenhagen bowl
Designed by: Unknown 1915-1947

BG-O-14
Title / English: Artist signed charger
Designed by: Henry Klyde

BG-O-15
Title / English: Mother's day vase. Made various years

Chapter 3.

Royal Copenhagen Collections

Royal Copenhagen Christmas Plates / RC

All Royal Copenhagen Christmas Plates are 7" in diameter, unless otherwise stated. Each plate made from 1908 to 1952 is inscribed with the year and "JUL" or "Julen," which means Christmas in the Danish language. From 1953 to the present, only the year is inscribed on the plate. Small quantities of the Royal Copenhagen Christmas plates were inscribed with a variety of different languages for the word "Christmas." *Weihnachten* is the German word for Christmas; plates with this word were produced from 1908 to 1944. *Noel* is the French word for Christmas; plates with this word were produced from 1909 to 1944. *Vanoce* is Czechoslovakian for Christmas; plates with this word were produced from 1909 to 1943. *Kerstmis* is Dutch for Christmas; plates with this word are said to have been produced in both 1931 and 1932, eventhough collectors have yet to see one from 1932. *Christmas* is English and plates with this word were produced from 1910 to 1941.

A smaller version of the 1911 Christmas plate was produced. It has become known as the "thief plate," as it is believed that this plate was never sold in stores since the regular 7" plate had already been produced. These rare plates were apparently "stolen" by the workers at Royal Copenhagen. We have also been told that the small 1911 plates were only shipped to the second largest city in Denmark, Aarhus, before the plate was withdrawn from production. That story seems credible, as most of the plates in the secondary trade originated from that area.

A small version of the 1927 plate, on which the motif is ducks, has also been produced in various languages. This plate is not included in this book, but the value, depending on the language, is $200-500.

Three years in a row, a special Royal Copenhagen Christmas plate was made for the General of the German Air force in Denmark. They were produced from 1941 to 1943 at the "request" of the German General. They all have the same inscription over the glaze on the bottom of the plate that reads, "General der luffwaffe in Denmark." They were produced in a very limited quantity, perhaps only two copies in any of the three years. For pictures of some of the rare special issue plates, see the photos after the Christmas plate section in this book.

RC-1908 (RC-CM87)
Title / English: Mary with Child – 6"
Title / Danish: Mary med barnet.
Designed by: Christian Thomsen
Price: $5000-6000

RC-1909 (RC-CM90)
Title / English: Snow Landscape – 6"
Title / Danish: Snelandskab
Designed by: Stephan Ussing
Price: $175-250

RC-1910 (RC-CM105)
Title / English: The Adoration of the Magi – 6"
Title / Danish: De hellige tre konger tilbedende barnet
Designed by: Christian Thomsen
Price: $150-200

RC-1911 (RC-CM112)
Title / English: Wooden Fence with Sheaf
Title / Danish: Gærde med neg
Designed by: Oluf Jensen
Price: $150-200

RC-1912 (RC-CM129)
Title / English: An Old Couple at a Table with a Small Christmas Tree
Title / Danish: To ældre folk ved bord med juletræ.
Designed by: Christian Thomsen
Price: $160-210

RC-1913 (RC-CM141)
Title / English: The Tower and Spire on the Marble Church in Copenhagen
Title / Danish: Spiret på Marmorkirkens kuppel og julestjerne over byens tage.
Designed by: Arthur Boesen
Price: $150-200

RC-1914 (RC-CM147)
Title / English: Sparrows in a Tree in Front of a Lit Church Window (the church of the Holy Ghost in Copenhagen)
Title / Danish: Spurve i træ foran oplyst vindue i Helligåndskirken i København.
Designed by: Arthur Boesen
Price: $150-200

RC-1915 (RC-CM152)
Title / English: Snow-covered Landscape with Spruce, Sledge and Church
Title / Danish: Snelandskab med gran, kane og kirke.
Designed by: Arnold Krog
Price: $150-200

RC-1916 (RC-CM161)
Title / English: Angel and Shepherd
Title / Danish: Engel og hyrde.
Designed by: Richard Bøcher
Price: $90-120

RC-1917 (RC-CM166)
Title / English: The Church of Our Savior in Copenhagen
Title / Danish: Vor Frelsers kirke i København.
Designed by: Oluf Jensen
Price: $90-120

RC-1918 (RC-CM174)
Title / English: Shepherds in a Meadow on Christmas Night
Title / Danish: Hyrder på marken julenat.
Designed by: Oluf Jensen
Price: $90-120

RC-1919 (RC-CM187)
Title / English: Birds in Snow-covered Garden
Title / Danish: Fugle i snedækket have.
Designed by: Oluf Jensen
Price: $90-120

RC-1920 (RC-CM191)
Title / English: The Virgin Mary with Christ the Child
Title / Danish: Maria med barnet.
Designed by: Gotfred Rode
Price: $80-110

RC-1921 (RC-CM198)
Title / English: Old Houses on the Town Square of Aabenraa
Title / Danish: Gavlhuse på torvet i Aabenraa.
Designed by: Oluf Jensen
Price: $60-80

RC-1922 (RC-CM204)
Title / English: Angels Singing
Title / Danish: Syngende engle.
Designed by: Ellinor Selchau
Price: $60-80

RC-1923 (RC-CM213)
Title / English: Snow-covered Landscape with Church
Title / Danish: Snelandskab med kirke.
Designed by: Oluf Jensen
Price: $60-80

RC-1924 (RC-CM222)
Title / English: Schooner at Sea Christmas Night
Title / Danish: Tomastet skonnert på havet julenat.
Designed by: Christian Benjamin-Olsen
Price: $90-120

RC-1925 (RC-CM231)
Title / English: Old Houses at Christianshavn
Title / Danish: Motiv med gamle huse på Christianshavn.
Designed by: Oluf Jensen
Price: $80-100

RC-1926 (RC-CM238)
Title / English: Old Warehouses at Christianshavns Canal in Copenhagen
Title / Danish: Parkhuse ved Christianshavns kanal.
Designed by: Richard Bøcher
Price: $80-100

RC-1927 (RC-CM247)
Title / English: Helmsman at the Wheel Christmas Night
Title / Danish: Rorvagt ombord julenat.
Designed by: Christian Benjamin-Olsen
Price: $100-130

RC-1928 (RC-CM251)
Title / English: Vicar on His Way to Church
Title / Danish: Præst på vej til kirke.
Designed by: Gotfred Rode
Price: $80-100

RC-1929 (RC-CM257)
Title / English: The West Front of Grundtvig Church
Title / Danish: Grundtvigskirkens tårn.
Designed by: Oluf Jensen
Price: $80-100

RC-1930 (RC-CM262)
Title / English: Fishing Vessels on their way towards Harbor
Title / Danish: Fiskerbåde på vej mod havn.
Designed by: Christian Benjamin-Olsen
Price: $100-130

RC-1931 (RC-CM265)
Title / English: Children at the Christmas Tree
Title / Danish: Børn ved juletræ.
Designed by: Gotfred Rode
Price: $100-130

RC-1932 (RC-CM268)
Title / English: The Statue of King Frederik VI (sculptor H. V. Bissen) in Frederiksberg Gardens, Copenhagen
Title / Danish: H. V. Bissens statue of Frederik VI in Frederiksberg Have.
Designed by: Oluf Jensen
Price: $100-130

RC-1933 (RC-CM273)
Title / English: The Ferry Odin Outside Nyborg Harbor
Title / Danish: Færgen Odin ud for Nyborg havn
Designed by: Christian Benjamin-Olsen
Price: $150-200

RC-1934 (RC-CM275)
Title / English: Scene from Deer Garden Outside Copenhagen with the Bunting Lodge Eremitagen
Title / Danish: Dyrehavemotiv med Eremitageslottet.
Designed by: Oluf Jensen
Price: $175-225

RC-1935 (RC-CM276)
Title / English: Fishing Boat, South of Elsinore Castle
Title / Danish: Fiskekutter syd for Kronborg
Designed by: Christian Benjamin-Olsen
Price: $200-250

RC-1936 (RC-CM277)
Title / English: The Cathedral in Roskilde
Title / Danish: Roskilde Domkirke
Designed by: Richard Bøcher
Price: $200-250

RC-1937 (RC-CM279)
Title / English: Christmas Scene from "Strøget," Shopping Street in Copenhagen
Title / Danish: Jul på Strøget
Designed by: Niels Thorsson
Price: $300-350

RC-1938 (RC-CM282)
Title / English: Osterlars Church in Bornholm
Title / Danish: Østerlars rundkirke på Bornholm
Designed by: Herne Nielsen
Price: $350-450

RC-1939 (RC-CM285)
Title / English: Ship in Heavy Ice near Greenland
Title / Danish: Skib i pakis ved Grønlands kyst
Designed by: Svend Nicolaj Nielsen
Price: $500-600

RC-1941 (RC-CM288)
Title / English: Nørre Herlev Church, Frederiksborg County
Title / Danish: Nørre Herlev kirke
Designed by: Theodor Kjølner
Price: $500-600

RC-1943 (RC-CM290)
Title / English: The Flight to Egypt
Title / Danish: Flugten til Ægypten
Designed by: Niels Thorsson
Price: $600-800

RC-1940 (RC-CM287)
Title / English: Shepherd in a Desert Landscape
Title / Danish: Hyrde i ørkenlandskab
Designed by: Kai Lange
Price: $500-600

RC-1942 (RC-CM289)
Title / English: Bell-frame on Church Roof
Title / Danish: Jysk klokkestabel på kirketag
Designed by: Niels Thorsson
Price: $500-600

RC-1944 (RC-CM291)
Title / English: Snow-covered Landscape with Church
Title / Danish: Snelandskab med kirke
Designed by: Viggo Olsen
Price: $275-375

RC-1945 (RC-CM292)
Title / English: Angel Looking at Christmas Rose
Title / Danish: Engel foran julerose
Designed by: Richard Bøcher
Price: $600-700

RC-1946 (RC-CM293)
Title / English: The Church at Farum Outside Copenhagen
Title / Danish: Farum kirke
Designed by: Niels Thorsson
Price: $180-280

RC-1947 (RC-CM294)
Title / English: Shepherd with His Flock
Title / Danish: Hyrde med får
Designed by: Kai Lange
Price: $300-375

RC-1948 (RC-CM295)
Title / English: The Church at Nøddebo, Frederiksborg County
Title / Danish: Nøddebo Kirke, Frederiksborg Amt.
Designed by: Theodor Kølner
Price: $180-280

RC-1949 (RC-CM296)
Title / English: The Cathedral of Copenhagen, the Church of Our Lady
Title / Danish: Vor Frue kirke i København.
Designed by: Hans Henrik Hansen
Price: $180-280

RC-1952 (RC-CM299)
Title / English: Feeding Place for the Deer Herd in Deer Garden Outside Copenhagen
Title / Danish: Foderhus i Dyrehaven
Designed by: Kai Lange
Price: $100-120

RC-1950 (RC-CM297)
Title / English: The Church at Boeslunde, Sorø County
Title / Danish: Boeslunde kirke, Sorø amt.
Designed by: Viggo Olsen
Price: $200-300

RC-1951 (RC-CM298)
Title / English: Angel Holding a Candle Opens a Door
Title / Danish: Engel med lys åbner dør
Designed by: Richard Bøcher
Price: $350-450

RC-1953 (RC-CM300)
Title / English: Frederiksborg Castle in Hillerød
Title / Danish: Frederiksborg Slot
Designed by: Theodor Kjølner
Price: $100-120

RC-1954 (RC-CM301)
Title / English: Amalienborg Palace with the Equestrian of King Frederik V
Title / Danish: Amalienborg med Frederik V.s statue
Designed by: Kai Lange
Price: $100-120

RC-1955 (RC-CM302)
Title / English: Small Girl in the Local Costume of Fanø Feeding Birds
Title / Danish: Fanøpige fodrer fugle
Designed by: Kai Lange
Price: $140-200

RC-1956 (RC-CM303)
Title / English: Rosenborg Castle in Copenhagen
Title / Danish: Rosenborg Slot
Designed by: Kai Lange
Price: $140-200

RC-1957 (RC-CM304)
Title / English: Shepherd with His Herd
Title / Danish: Hyrde med får
Designed by: Hans Henrik Hansen
Price: $100-120

RC-1958 (RC-CM305)
Title / English: Scenery from Greenland
Title / Danish: Grønlandsmotiv
Designed by: Hans Henrik Hansen
Price: $100-120

RC-1959 (RC-CM306)
Title / English: Angel Playing for the Animals in the Forest
Title / Danish: Engel spiller for skovens dyr
Designed by: Hans Henrik Hansen
Price: $130-180

RC-1960 (RC-CM307)
Title / English: Stag in the Forest
Title / Danish: Kronhjort
Designed by: Hans Henrik Hansen
Price: $100-130

RC-1961 (RC-CM309)
Title / English: The Sail Training Ship "Danmark"
Title / Danish: Skoleskibet Danmark
Designed by: Kai Lange
Price: $100-130

RC-1962 (RC-CM310)
Title / English: The Little Mermaid
Title / Danish: Den lille Havfrue
Sculptor: Edvard Eriksen, 1913
Designed by: Kai Lange
Price: $180-270

RC-1963 (RC-CM312)
Title / English: Old Windmill in Snow-covered Landscape
Title / Danish: Snelandskab med vindmølle
Designed by: Kai Lange
Price: $50-70

RC-1964 (RC-CM314)
Title / English: Horse-drawn Sled in Snow-covered Landscape
Title / Danish: Kane i snelandskab
Designed by: Kai Lange
Price: $50-70

RC-1965 (RC-CM315)
Title / English: Small Skaters
Title / Danish: Små skøjteløbere
Designed by: Kai Lange
Price: $50-70

RC-1966 (RC-CM316)
Title / English: Blackbird and Church
Title / Danish: Solsort ved snedækket kirke
Designed by: Kai Lange
Price: $40-60

RC-1967 (RC-CM317)
Title / English: "The Royal Oak" near Jægerspris (approximately 1.400 years old)
Title / Danish: Kongeegen ved Jægerspris i sne
Designed by: Kai Lange
Price: $40-60

RC-1969 (RC-CM322)
Title / English: Geese in Snow-covered Courtyard
Title / Danish: Gæs ved gård
Designed by: Kai Lange
Price: $40-60

RC-1971
Title / English: Hare in Winter
Title / Danish: Hare i vinterlandskab
Designed by: Kai Lange
Price: $30-40

RC-1968 (RC-CM319)
Title / English: The Last Umiak in Greenland (Umiak = boat rowed by women)
Title / Danish: Konebåd i grønlandsk farvand
Designed by: Kai Lange
Price: $40-60

RC-1970 (RC-CM326)
Title / English: Cat on a Windowsill with a Snow-covered Landscape
Title / Danish: Kat i vindueskarm, i baggrunden snelandskab
Designed by: Kai Lange
Price: $40-60

RC-1972
Title / English: In the Desert
Title / Danish: Østerland
Designed by: Kai Lange
Price: $30-40

RC-1973
Title / English: Going Home for Christmas
Title / Danish: Hjem til jul
Designed by: Kai Lange
Price: $30-40

RC-1974
Title / English: Winter Twilight
Title / Danish: Vinterskumring
Designed by: Kai Lange
Price: $30-40

RC-1975
Title / English: Marselisborg Palace
Title / Danish: Marselisbog Slot
Designed by: Kai Lange
Price: $30-40

RC-1976
Title / English: Vibaek Mill
Title / Danish: Vibæk Mølle
Designed by: Sven Vestergaard
Price: $30-40

RC-1977
Title / English: Immervad Bridge
Title / Danish: Immervad Bro
Designed by: Kai Lange
Price: $30-40

RC-1978
Title / English: Greenland Scenery
Title / Danish: Rast på slæderejse
Designed by: Kai Lange
Price: $30-40

RC-1979
Title / English: Choosing a Christmas Tree
Title / Danish: Juletræet vælges
Designed by: Kai Lange
Price: $40-50

RC-1980
Title / English: Bringing Home the Christmas Tree
Title / Danish: Juletræet bringes hjem
Designed by: Kai Lange
Price: $40-50

RC-1981
Title / English: Admiring the Christmas Tree
Title / Danish: Juletræet beundres
Designed by: Kai Lange
Price: $40-50

RC-1982
Title / English: Waiting for Christmas
Title / Danish: Julestemning
Designed by: Kai Lange
Price: $60-80

RC-1983
Title / English: Merry Christmas
Title / Danish: Glade Jul
Designed by: Kai Lange
Price: $40-50

RC-1984
Title / English: Jingle Bells
Title / Danish: Kanetur
Designed by: Kai Lange
Price: $40-50

RC-1985
Title / English: The Snowman
Title / Danish: Snemanden
Designed by: Kai Lange
Price: $50-70

RC-1986
Title / English: Christmas Vacation
Title / Danish: Juleferie
Designed by: Sven Vestergaard
Price: $40-60

RC-1987
Title / English: Winter Birds
Title / Danish: Vinterfugle
Designed by: Sven Vestergaard
Price: $60-80

RC-1988
Title / English: Christmas Eve in Copenhagen
Title / Danish: Den gamle digters jul
Designed by: Sven Vestergaard
Price: $60-80

RC-1990
Title / English: Christmas at Tivoli
Title / Danish: Jul i Tivoli
Designed by: Sven Vestergaard
Price: $100-150

RC-1993
Title / English: Christmas Guests
Title / Danish: Julegæsterne ankommer
Designed by: Sven Vestergaard
Price: $300-400

RC-1989
Title / English: The Old Skating Pond
Title / Danish: Vinterleg ved Kastellet
Designed by: Sven Vestergaard
Price: $70-100

RC-1991
Title / English: The Festival of Santa Lucia
Title / Danish: Skt. Lucia Fest
Designed by: Sven Vestergaard
Price: $80-100

RC-1992
Title / English: The Royal Coach
Title / Danish: Chr. VIII Karet
Designed by: Sven Vestergaard
Price: $60-80

RC-1994
Title / English: Christmas Shopping
Title / Danish: Med far på indkøb
Designed by: Sven Vestergaard
Price: $70-90

RC-1995
Title / English: Christmas at the Manor House
Title / Danish: Jul på slottet
Designed by: Sven Vestergaard
Price: $350-450

RC-1996
Title / English: Lighting the Street Lamps
Title / Danish: Lygtetændingstid
Designed by: Sven Vestergaard
Price: $70-90

RC-1997
Title / English: Roskilde Cathedral
Title / Danish: Roskilde Domkirke
Designed by: Sven Vestergaard
Price: $70-90

RC-1998
Title / English: Welcome Home
Title / Danish: Velkomstkomite
Designed by: Sven Vestergaard
Price: $150-250

RC-1999
Title / English: The Sleigh Ride
Title / Danish: Hjem med træet
Designed by: Sven Vestergaard
Price: $80-100

RC-2000
Title / English: Trimming the Tree
Title / Danish: Juletræet pyntes
Designed by: Sven Vestergaard
Price: $60-80

RC-2001
Title / English: Feeding the Birds
Title / Danish: Foddertræet
Designed by: Sven Vestergaard
Price: $60-80

RC-2002
Title / English: Winter in the Forest
Title / Danish: Vinter i skoven
Designed by: Sven Vestergaard
Price: $60-80

RC-2003
Title / English: Seasons Greetings
Title / Danish: Julegaven
Designed by: Sven Vestergaard
Price: $75

RC-2004
Title / English: Awaiting the Christmas Train
Title / Danish: Venter på Juletoget
Designed by: Sven Vestergaard
Price: $78.00

Royal Copenhagen Specialty Plates

A number of alternative plates were produced, including trial and proof plates for each issue. Here we show a small selection of what is available. These are among the most valuable plates in the world.

RC-1941GL
Title / English: Nørre Herlev Church
Title/Danish: Nørre Herlev Kirke
Special inscription: General of der Luffwaffer in Denemark
Designed by: Theodor Kjølner

RC-1920S
Title / English: The Virgin Mary with Christ the Child
Title / Danish: Maria med Barnet
Special border: It says 19 Jul 20, instead of Jul 1920, plus it has a slimmer border.
Designed by: Gotfred Rode

RC-1909T
Title / English: Snowy Landscape with Church
Title / Danish: Snelandskab med Kirke
Designed by: Steffan Ussing
Artist signed by: Oluf Jensen
Price: $10,000-15,000

RC-1910
Title / English: The Adoration of the Magi
Title / Danish: De Hellige 3 konger
Designed by: Christian Thomsen
Artist signed by: Oluf Jensen
Price: $10,000-15,000

RC-CM111
Title / English: Snow-covered Landscape with Lake
Title / Danish: Landskab med Sø og snedaekket trae, i baggrunden en kirke.
Designed by: Steffan Ussing
Copies: Approximately 120 along with the RC Icelandic plate, this plate is the most expensive of all collector plates in the world
Price: $10,000-15,000
Same picture as page 134.

RC-CM1A
Year: 1888
Description / English: The Scandinavian Exhibition in Copenhagen for Industry, Agriculture, and Art. Crown over three wavy lines.
Description / Danish: Den Nordiske Industri, Landbrugs-og Kunstundstilling i København
Designed by: Arnold Krog
Number of copies / size: 6 3/4", 17 1/2 cm
Price: $1000-1500
Same picture as page 151.

Royal Copenhagen Mother's Day Plates / RC-MD

This series began in 1971. They are all 5 1/2" in diameter.

RC-MD1971
Title / English: American Mother
Title / Danish: Amerikansk mor
Designed by: Kamma Svensson
Price: $15-25

RC-MD1972
Title / English: Oriental Mother
Title / Danish: Orientalsk mor
Designed by: Kamma Svensson
Price: $15-25

RC-MD1973
Title / English: Danish Mother
Title / Danish: Dansk mor
Designed by: Kamma Svensson
Price: $15-25

RC-MD1974
Title / English: Greenlandic Mother
Title / Danish: Grønlandsk mor
Designed by: Arne Ungermann
Price: $15-25

RC-MD1975
Title / English: Bird in Nest with Her Young One
Title / Danish: Fugl i rede med unger
Designed by: Arne Ungermann
Price: $15-25

RC-MD1976
Title / English: Mermaids
Title / Danish: Havfruer
Designed by: Arne Ungermann
Price: $15-25

RC-MD1977
Title / English: Children in Carriage
Title / Danish: Børn i barnevogn
Designed by: Arne Ungermann
Price: $15-25

RC-MD1978
Title / English: Mother with Child
Title / Danish: Mor med barn
Designed by: Ib Spang Olsen
Price: $15-25

RC-MD1979
Title / English: Mother with Child
Title / Danish: Mor med barn
Designed by: Ib Spang Olsen
Price: $15-25

RC-MD1980
Title / English: Mother on Bicycle with Child
Title / Danish: mor på cykel med barn
Designed by: Ib Spang Olsen
Price: $15-25

RC-MD1981
Title / English: Mother with Child
Title / Danish: Mor med barn
Designed by: Ib Spang Olsen
Price: $15-25

RC-MD1982
Title / English: Mother Reading for Children
Title / Danish: Mor læser for børnene
Designed by: Ib Spang Olsen
Price: $15-25

Royal Copenhagen Mother and Young Plates / RC-MY

This series with animals took over from the Mother's Day series. They are 5 1/2" in diameter.

RC-MY1982
Title / English: Mother Robin and Her Young One
Title / Danish: Rødkælk med unger
Designed by: Sven Vestergaard
Price: $30-50

RC-MY1983
Title / English: Mother Cat and Her Young One
Title / Danish: Kat med killing
Designed by: Sven Vestergaard
Price: $30-50

RC-MY1984
Title / English: Mother Horse and Her Young One
Title / Danish: Hoppe med føl
Designed by: Sven Vestergaard
Price: $30-50

RC-MY1985
Title / English: Mother Rabbit and Her Young One
Title / Danish: Kanin med unge
Designed by: Sven Vestergaard
Price: $30-50

RC-MY1986
Title / English: Mother Dog and Her Young Ones
Title / Danish: Hund med hvalpe
Designed by: Sven Vestergaard
Price: $30-50

RC-MY1987
Title / English: Mother Goat with Kid
Title / Danish: Ged med kid
Designed by: Sven Vestergaard
Price: $30-50

Royal Copenhagen Motherhood series / Mor og Barn / RC-MH

The Motherhood series was only produced in 1989. The motif was created by Sven Vestergaard and decorated in underglaze. This plate measures 6 1/8".

RC-MH1989
Title / English: Father's Homecoming
Title / Danish: Far kommer hjem
Designed by: Sven Vestergaard
Price: $30-50

Royal Copenhagen Nature's Children Series / Unger i Naturen / RC-NC

The Nature's Children series was produced from 1993 to 1998. Each plate is individually numbered and produced in a limited edition. The motifs were created by Jørgen Nielsen and decorated in the overglaze technique. These plates measure 6 1/2".

RC-NC1993
Title / English: The Robins
Title / Danish: Rødkælk
Designed by: Jørgen Nielsen
Price: $30-50

RC-NC1994
Title / English: The Fawn
Title / Danish: Rådyr
Designed by: Jørgen Nielsen
Price: $30-50

RC-NC1995
Title / English: The Mallards
Title / Danish: Gråand
Designed by: Jørgen Nielsen
Price: $30-50

RC-NC1996
Title / English: The Colt
Title / Danish: Hest
Designed by: Jørgen Nielsen
Price: $30-50

RC-NC1997
Title / English: The Swans
Title / Danish: Knopsvane
Designed by: Jørgen Nielsen
Price: $30-50

RC-NC1998
Title / English: The Rabbits
Title / Danish: Kanin
Designed by: Jørgen Nielsen
Price: $30-50

Royal Copenhagen Children's Help Day Series / RC-CH

The Children's Help Day series ran from 1910 to 1940 and was produced to raise money for the Children's Help Day Foundation (the Danish equivalence of the Help the Children Foundation). These plates are approximately 5" in diameter. The world's first Children's Help Day took place in Copenhagen on May 6th. 1904. The idea to start such a day came from County Doctor Johan Carlsen, who founded the Children's Help Day Foundation in early 1904 to raise money for the needy kids in Denmark, especially in the capital, Copenhagen. It turned out to be a grand celebration! Most of the famous actors and artists of the day took part. Even the Royal Family was seen on the streets of Copenhagen giving money to the collectors. On this one glorious day, 84.476 kr (with current exchange rates, around $12,000) were raised. The first company to produce a Children's Day plate was the faience factory, Alumina. Royal Copenhagenmsoon followed. These plates picture children playing and being happy.

RC-CH1910
Title / English: Child and Leaves
Title / Danish: Barn og bladhang
Designed by: Bent Helweg-Møller
Price: $75-120

RC-CH1911
Title / English: Child and Bird
Title / Danish: Barn og fugl
Designed by: Bent Helweg-Møller
Price: $75-120

RC-CH1912
Title / English: Child on Flower Horn
Title / Danish: Barn på blomster horn
Designed by: Bent Helweg-Møller
Price: $75-120

RC-CH1913
Title / English: Rocking Horse
Title / Danish: Gyngehest
Designed by: Bent Helweg-Møller
Price: $75-120

RC-CH1914
Title / English: Child by the Beach
Title / Danish: Barn på stranden
Designed by: Bent Helweg-Møller
Price: $75-120

RC-CH1915
Title / English: Girl Picking Flowers
Title / Danish: Pige plukker blomster
Designed by: Michael Pedersen
Price: $75-120

RC-CH1916
Title / English: Girl with Flowers
Title / Danish: Pige med blomster
Designed by: Christian Thomsen
Price: $75-120

RC-CH1917
Title / English: Boy with Flowers
Title / Danish: Dreng med blomster
Designed by: Christian Thomsen
Price: $75-120

RC-CH1918
Title / English: Boy with Hat and Coat
Title / Danish: Dreng med hat og jakke
Designed by: Christian Thomsen
Price: $75-120

RC-CH1919
Title / English: Chicken with Chicks
Title / Danish: Børn med kyllinger
Designed by: Oluf Jensen
Price: $75-120

RC-CH1920
Title / English: Girl Picking Flowers
Title / Danish: Pige plukker blomster
Designed by: Oluf Jensen
Price: $75-120

RC-CH1921
Title / English: Storks Nest
Title / Danish: Storkerede
Designed by: Oluf Jensen
Price: $75-120

RC-CH1922
Title / English: Girl Wading
Title / Danish: Pige sopper
Designed by: Oluf Jensen
Price: $75-120

RC-CH1923
Title / English: Girl with Dandelion
Title / Danish: Pige med Mælkebøtte
Designed by: Oluf Jensen
Price: $75-120

RC-CH1924
Title / English: Child Under Apple Branch
Title / Danish: Barn under æblegren
Designed by: Richard Bøcher
Price: $75-120

RC-CH1925
Title / English: Child with Apples
Title / Danish: Barn med æbler
Designed by: Richard Bøcher
Price: $75-120

RC-CH1926
Title / English: Boy with Toy Animal
Title / Danish: Dreng med legetøjsdyr
Designed by: Richard Bøcher
Price: $75-120

RC-CH1927
Title / English: Girl Under Umbrella
Title / Danish: Pige under paraply
Designed by: Richard Bøcher
Price: $75-120

RC-CH1928
Title / English: Boy with Dog
Title / Danish: Dreng med hund
Designed by: Richard Bøcher
Price: $75-120

RC-CH1929
Title / English: Boy in a Washtub with a Sail
Title / Danish: Dreng i balje med sejl
Designed by: Richard Bøcher
Price: $75-120

RC-CH1930
Title / English: Girl with Bucket
Title / Danish: Pige med spand
Designed by: Richard Bøcher
Price: $150-250

RC-CH1931
Title / English: Boy Sailing Ship
Title / Danish: Dreng sejler med skib
Designed by: Richard Bøcher
Price: $150-250

RC-CH1932
Title / English: Boy with Watering Can
Title / Danish: Dreng med vandkande
Designed by: Richard Bøcher
Price: $150-250

RC-CH1933
Title / English: Boy with Toy Horse
Title / Danish: Dreng med legetøjshest
Designed by: Richard Bøcher
Price: $150-250

RC-CH1934
Title / English: Boy Digging in the Sand
Title / Danish: Dreng graver i sandet
Designed by: Richard Bøcher
Price: $150-250

RC-CH1935
Title / English: Girl with Teddy Bear
Title / Danish: Pige med bamse
Designed by: Richard Bøcher
Price: $150-250

RC-CH1936
Title / English: Boy with Ball
Title / Danish: Dreng med bold
Designed by: Richard Bøcher
Price: $200-300

RC-CH1937
Title / English: Boy on Scooter
Title / Danish: Dreng på løbehjul
Designed by: Richard Bøcher
Price: $200-300

RC-CH1938
Title / English: Boy with Kite
Title / Danish: Dreng med drage
Designed by: Richard Bøcher
Price: $200-300

RC-CH1939
Title / English: Boy with Bucket and Broom
Title / Danish: Dreng med kost og spand
Designed by: Richard Bøcher
Price: $200-300

RC-CH1940
Title / English: Girl with Bouquet
Title / Danish: Pige med buket
Designed by: Richard Bøcher
Price: $200-300

Royal Copenhagen Portraits of Old Copenhagen Plates / RC-PC

Produced in 1977, all of the Portraits of Old Copenhagen plates are 10 3/4" in diameter. This is a series of twelve plates that picture buildings from the old days in Copenhagen. All the portraits were designed by the famous Danish illustrator, Mads Stage.

RC-PC1
Title: The Stock Exchange
Price: $50-100

RC-PC2
Title: The Thorvaldsen Museum
Price: $50-100

RC-PC3
Title: The Naval Church
Price: $50-100

RC-PC4
Title: The Gate to the King's Garden
Price: $50-100

RC-PC5
Title: The Gate to the Citadel ("The Zealand Gate")
Price: $50-100

RC-PC6
Title: The Museum of Arts and Crafts
Price: $50-100

RC-PC7
Title: The Entrance to the "Round Tower"
Price: $50-100

RC-PC8
Title: The Naval Hospital at Christianshavn
Price: $50-100

RC-PC9
Title: The Summer Palace of Christian IV
Price: $50-100

RC-PC10
Title: The Odd Fellow Lodge
Price: $50-100

RC-PC11
Title: Amalienborg Palace, Frederik VIII' House
Price: $50-100

RC-PC12
Title: Charlottenborg
Price: $50-100

Royal Copenhagen Commemorative Plates / RC-CM

The first Commemorative Plate was produced for the Scandinavian Fair held in Copenhagen in 1888. This plate [as illustrated number 1A, crown with three wavy lines with square ends] was exhibited on each corner of the fringe on the Royal Copenhagen Porcelain factory stand. Queen Louise of Denmark wished to receive a plate similar to those displayed on the corners of the exibition stand. She was presented with one that had a crown and three wavy lines with indented ends [as illustrated by number 1]. This became the first production plate and was in demand by the Danish aristocracy of the time.

Following the success of the first plate, the factory started producing plates to commemorate royal events, anniversaries, and special occasions in 1888. The plates produced were initiated by Royal Copenhagen Porcelain themselves, Danish royalty, and various companies, private organizations, and charities. Production has continued up to the present, with the most productive times being from 1897 to 1919 and 1970 to 1979.

This book covers the period up to 1970 and the numbers used are those in the book, *Royal Copenhagen Porcelain Manufactory Plates*, published in 1971. Also included are some of the plates produced up to the 1960s that were left out of the 1971 publication. NOTE: There were many commemerative plates produced after 1970, which are not included in this edition. Some of them can be seen on the following websites:

www.danishporcelain.com
www.danishglass.com

RC-CM1
Year: 1888
Description / English: The Scandinavian Exhibition in Copenhagen for Industry, Agriculture, and Art. Crown over three wavy lines.
Description / Danish: Den Nordiske Industri, Landbrugs-og Kunstundstilling i København
Designed by: Arnold Krog
Number of copies / size: 1,200 copies, 6 3/4", 17 1/2 cm
Price: $300-400

RC-CM1A
Year: 1888
Description / English: The Scandinavian Exhibition in Copenhagen for Industry, Agriculture, and Art. Crown over three wavy lines.
Description / Danish: Den Nordiske Industri, Landbrugs-og Kunstundstilling i København
Designed by: Arnold Krog
Number of copies / size: 6 3/4", 17 1/2 cm
Price: $1000-1500

RC-CM2
Year: 1892
Description / English: King Christian IX's and Queen Louise's Golden Wedding. Crowned face-to-face monogram C $_9$ L and the year 1892 over three wavy lines.
Description / Danish: Christian IX.s og droning Louise's guldbryllup. Kronet spejlmonogram C $_9$ L og årstal 1892 over bølgelinier.
Designed by: Arnold Krog
Number of copies / size: 1,200 copies, 6 3/4", 17 1/2 cm
Price: $100-150

RC-CM3
Year: 1894
Description / English: Crown Prince Frederik's and Crown Princess Louise's Silver Wedding. Crowned face-to-face monogram FL and years 1869-1894 over three wavy lines.
Description / Danish: Kronprins Frederiks og Kronprinsesse Louises sølvbryllup. Kronet spejlmonogram FL og 1869-1894.
Designed by: Arnold Krog
Number of copies / size: 1,200 copies, 7", 18 cm
Price: $100-150

RC-CM3A (LARGE)
Year: 1894
Description / English: Crown Prince Frederik's and Crown Princess Louise's Silver Wedding. Crowned face-to-face monogram FL and years 1869-1894 over three wavy lines.
Description / Danish: Kronprins Frederiks og Kronprinsesse Louises sølvbryllup. Kronet spejlmonogram FL og 1869-1894.
Designed by: Arnold Krog
Number of copies / size: 11 3/4" / 29.75cm
Price: $5000-6000
Same as RC-CM3

RC-CM4 (right)
Year: 1895
Description / English: Women's exhibition in Copenhagen "past and present"; three wavy lines, and flower motif
Inscription: KVINDERNES UDSTILLING 1895
Description / Danish: Kvindernes Udstilling fra Fortid og Nutid I København; t.v. tre bølgelinier, f.n. afblomstret løvetand
IndskriftÆ: KVINDERNES UDSTILLING 1895
Designed by: Arnold Krog
Number of copies / size: 1,200, 7", 18 cm
Price: $80-130

RC-CM5
Year: 1895
Description / English: Diploma of honor of the women's exhibition in Copenhagen. Stylized rising sun over three wavy lines.
Inscription: DIPLOM VED KVINDERNES HÆDERS-UDSTILLING 1895.
Description / Danish: Kvindernes Udstilling hædersdiplom. Stiliseret, opgående sol over tre bølgelinier. Indskrift:
Designed by: Suzette Holten (Skovgaard)
Number of copies / size: 13 copies, 8 3/4", 22 1/2 cm
Price: $5000-6000
No picture available

RC-CM6
Year: 1896
Description / English: The wedding of Princess Louise of Denmark to Prince Friederich of Schaumburg-Lippe. Crowned monogram LF and year MDCCCLXXXXVI (1896) over three wavy lines.
Description / Danish: Prinsesse Louises bryllup med prins Friederich af Schaumburg+Lippe. Kronet monogram LF og årstal MDCCCLXXXXVI (1896). F.n. tre bølgelinier.
Designed by: Arnold Krog
Number of copies / size: 1,200 copies.
6 3/4", 17 1/2 cm
Price: $80-130

RC-CM7
Year: 1896
Description / English: The wedding of Prince Carl of Denmark to Princess Maud of Great Britain and Ireland. Crowned monogram CM and year MDCCCLXXXXVI (1896) over three wavy lines.
Description / Danish: Prins Carls bryllup med Prinsesse Maud af Storbritannien og Irland. Kronet monogram CM og årstal MDCCCLXXXXVI (1896). F.n. tre bølgelinier.
Designed by: Arnold Krog
Number of copies / size: 1,200 copies,
6 3/4", 17 1/2 cm
Price: $80-130

RC-CM8
Year: 1897
Description / English: The wedding of Princess Ingeborg of Denmark to Prince Carl of Sweden. Crowned face-to-face monogram CI and the year 1897.
Description / Danish: Prinsesse Ingeborgs bryllup med prins Carl af Sverige. Kronet spejlmonogram CI og 1897.
Designed by: Arnold Krog
Number of copies / size: 1,200 copies.
6 3/4", 17 1/2 cm
Price: $80-130

RC-CM7A (WITH GOLD)
Year: 1896
Description / English: The wedding of Prince Carl of Denmark to Princess Maud of Great Britain and Ireland. Crowned monogram CM and year MDCCCLXXXXVI (1896) over three wavy lines.
Description / Danish: Prins Carls bryllup med Prinsesse Maud af Storbritannien og Irland. Kronet monogram CM og årstal MDCCCLXXXXVI (1896). F.n. tre bølgelinier.
Designed by: Arnold Krog
Number of copies / size: 6 3/4", 17 1/2 cm
Price: $300-400

RC-CM9
Year: 1897
Description / English: The women's building in Copenhagen. Letters KB and the year 1896-1900 between two towers on a background of sunrise.
Description / Danish: Kvindernes Bygning I København. Bogstaver KB og 1896-1900 mellem to tårne, derover solstråler.
Designed by: Marianne Høst, 1896
Number of copies / size: 1,200 copies,
6 1/2", 17 cm
Price: $80-130

RC-CM10
Year: 1897
Description / English: Art and Industry Exhibition in Stockholm. Dome of building over which are three crowns.
Inscription: STOCKHOLM 1897. On the left crowned vase with the letters K.P.F. (Kongelige Porcelains Fabrik) and the year 1897.
Description / Danish: Kunst—go Industriudstillingen i Stockholm, Kuppel, derover tre kroner, f.n. indskrift: STOCKHOLM 1897, t.v. kronet vase med bogstaver K.P.F. (Kongelige Porcelains Fabrik) 1779.
Designed by: Arnold Krog
Number of copies / size: 1,200 copies, 7 1/4", 18 1/2 cm
Price: $80-130

RC-CM11
Year: 1897
Description / English: The royal crown of Sweden. Made on occasion of the Art and Industry Exhibition in Stockholm.
Description / Danish: Svensk kongekrone. Udført til Kunst- og Industriudstillingen i Stockholm.
Designed by: Arnold Krog
Number of copies / size: 100 copies, 9", 23 cm
Price: $400-600

RC-CM12
Year: 1897
Description / English: Three wavy lines. Made on occasion of the Art and Industry Exhibition in Stockholm.
Description / Danish: Tre bøogelinier. Udført til Kunst- og Industriudstillingen i Stockholm.
Designed by: Arnold Krog
Number of copies / size: 100 copies, 9", 23 cm
Price: $400-600

RC-CM13
Year: 1897
Description / English: Bull in a landscape with barrow. Commissioned on occasion of the Jutland Farmer's association's exhibition in Aarhus.
Inscription: VNITIS VIRIBUS (by united efforts) and in a clover leaf the letters J.L.F. and years 1872-97.
Description / Danish: Jydske Landboforeningers udstilling i aarhus. Tyr i kløvermark med kæmpehøj. IndskriftÆ VNITIS VIRIBUS (Ved forenede kræfter), i kløverblad J.L.F. 1872-97.
Designed by: Arnold Krog
Number of copies / size: 1,200 copies,
7 1/4", 18 1/2 cm
Price: $80-130

RC-CM14
Year: 1897
Description / English: Dragon pierced by rapier with guard formed by three rings. The point forms the figure 1 in the year 1897. Commissioned by the Independent Order of Odd Fellows for its hospital on Iceland.
Inscription: SCTO GEORGIO IUVANTE (by the help of Saint George).
Description / Danish: Odd Fellow Ordenens hospital på Island. Drage genemstukket af kårde, hvis parerplade er danet af tre ringe og hvis spids danner I-tallet i 1897. Indskrift: SCTO GEORGIO IUVANTE (Ved Skt. Georgs hjælp).
Designed by: Arnold Krog
Number of copies / size: 1,500 copies, 7 1/4", 18 1/2 cm
Price: $100-150

RC-CM15
Year: 1897
Description / English: Saint George killing the dragon. On the left the city-arms of Copenhagen under which is found the three rings of the Independent Order of Odd Fellows. Commissioned by the order for its hospital on Iceland.
Inscription: AEGROTANTIUM MEDICUS (The healer of the suffering).
Description / Danish: Odd Fellow Ordenens hospital på Island. Skt. Georg og dragen. T.v. Københavns byvåben med ordenens tre ringe under bølgelinierne. Indskrift: AEGROTANTIUM MEDICUS)de lidendes læge).
Designed by: Arnold Krog
Number of copies / size: 100 copies, 11 3/4", 30 cm
Price: $1200-1400

RC-CM16
Year: 1897
Description / English: Queen Louise's 80th birthday. Oval platter with crowned, relieved circumference. Face to face monogram L composed of leaves under which the date 18-17-7 Septmb-1897.
Description / Danish: Dronning Louises 80-årsdag. Oval platte med kronet ramme i relief. Spejlmonogram L dannet af blade, derunder: 1817-7 Septmb.-1897.
Designed by: Arnold Krog
Number of copies / size: 1,200 copies, 9 1/4", 23 1/2 cm
Price: $200-300

RC-CM16A (WITH GOLD)
Year: 1897
Description / English: Queen Louise's 80th birthday. Oval platter with crowned, relieved circumference. Face to face monogram L composed of leaves under which the date 18-17-7 Septmb-1897.
Description / Danish: Dronning Louises 80-årsdag. Oval platte med kronet ramme i relief. Spejlmonogram L dannet af blade, derunder: 1817-7 Septmb.-1897.
Designed by: Arnold Krog
Number of copies / size: 9 1/4", 23 1/2 cm
Price: $300-400

RC-CM17
Year: 1898
Description / English: King Christian IX's 80th birthday. Matching number 16. Face to face monogram C9, under which the date and years 1818-8 April-1898.
Description / Danish: Christian IX.s 80-årsdag. Pendant til 16. Spejlmonogram C9, herunder: 1818-8 April-1898.
Designed by: Arnold Krog
Number of copies / size: 1,200 copies. 9 1/4", 23 1/2 cm
Price: $200-300

RC-CM17A (WITH GOLD)
Year: 1898
Description / English: King Christian IX's 80th birthday. Matching number 16. Face to face monogram C9, under which the date and years 1818-8 April-1898.
Description / Danish: Christian IX.s 8- årsdag. Pendant til 16. Spejlmonogram C9, herunder: 1818-8 April-1898.
Designed by: Arnold Krog
Number of copies / size: 9 1/4", 23 1/2 cm
Price: $300-400

RC-CM18
Year: 1898
Description / English: Prince Christian's (later King Christian X) wedding to Princess Alexandrine of Mecklenburg. The edge shaped in three curves. Crown and the year 1898 under which face to face monogram C.A.
Description / Danish: Prins Christians bryllup med hertuginde Alexandrine af Mecklenburg. Kant I tre buer, krone og årstal 1898, derunder spejlmonogram CA.
Designed by: Arnold Krog
Number of copies / size: 2,500 copies, 6 3/4", 17 1/2 cm
Price: $80-130

RC-CM18A (WITH GOLD)
Year: 1898
Description / English: Prince Christian's (later King Christian X) wedding to Princess Alexandrine of Mecklenburg. The edge shaped in three curves. Crown and the year 1898 under which face to face monogram C.A.
Description / Danish: Prins Christians bryllup med hertuginde Alexandrine af Mecklenburg. Kant I tre buer, krone og årstal 1898, derunder spejlmonogram CA.
Designed by: Arnold Krog
Number of copies / size: 6 3/4", 17 1/2 cm
Price: $300-400

RC-CM19
Year: 1898
Description / English: Crowned navigational buoy with the inscription DANMARK positioned outside Elsinore Castle with seagulls in the air. Commissioned by the Tourist Association of Denmark.
Inscription: 18 D.T.F. 98 (Tourist Association of Denmark).
Description / Danish: Turistforeningen. Svungen kant. Kronet klokkebøje betegnet DANMARK ud for Kronborg, derover måger. Indskrift: D.T.F. 1898 (Danmarks Turistforening).
Designed by: Arnold Krog
Number of copies / size: 800 copies, 7 1/4", 18 1/2 cm
Price: $100-150

RC-CM20
Year: 1898
Description / English: Flower motif with inscription I and L.U. NAKSKOV 1898 (Industrial and Agricultural Exhibition in Nakskov). Commissioned by the exhibition.
Description / Danish: Industri- og Landbrugsudstillingen i Nakskov. Kartebolleplante med tre blomster. Indskrift f.o.: I og L.U. NAKSKOV 1898.
Designed by: Arnold Krog
Number of copies / size: 500 copies, 7 3/4", 20 cm
Price: $150-200

RC-CM21
Year: 1898
Description / English: The monument commemorating the Danish soldier in the war with Slesvig-Holsten 1848-50 (sculp. H.V. Bissen). Commissioned by the committee for the celebration of the 50th anniversary of the war, celebrated in the Royal Gardens of Rosenborg (Copenhagen).
Inscription: FOR KONGE OG FOR LAND (For King and For Country) 1848-1898.
Description / Danish: Landsoldaten. Udført på bestilling fra komiteen for festen i Kongens Have i 50 året for krigen i 1848. H.V. Bissens monument i Fredericia og indskrift: FOR KONGE OG FOR LAND 1848-1898.
Designed by: Arnold Krog
Number of copies / size: 850 copies, 7 1/4", 18 1/2 cm
Price: $120-200

RC-CM22
Year: 1898
Description / English: Icelandic falcon on a dragon pierced by a rapier with guard formed by three rings, cf. no 14. Commissioned by the Independent Order of Odd Fellows for its hospital on Iceland.
Description / Danish: Odd Fellow Ordenens hospital på Island. Den islandske falk siddende på en drage, der er genemboret med kårde, hvis parerplade er danet af tre ringe (sml. 14).
Designed by: Arnold Krog
Number of copies / size: 2,500 copies, 8 1/2", 22 cm
Price: $100-150

RC-CM23
Year: 1898
Description / English: Coat of arms. In the shield an eagle's foot, on the helmet armed hand between two eagle-wings. Commissioned by the wine-merchants I.C.Teilmann on occasion of their 25th anniversary.
Inscription: 1873-1898.
Description / Danish: Teilman-platte. Fremstillet for vinhandlerfirmet I.C. Teilman til dets 25-års jubilæum. Våben med bjørneklo, på hjelmen væbnet arm mellem to vinger. 1873-1898.
Designed by:
Number of copies / size: 600 copies, 6 3/4", 17 1/2 cm
Price: $200-250

RC-CM24
Year: 1898
Description / English: The cenotaph on Skamlingsbanken (Hill in the southern part of Jutland). Three shields, inscription on the left F.D.S.S., in the middle of coat of arms of Slesvig and to the right SANDHED OG RET (Truth and Justice). Commissioned by Sønderjysk Centralforening.
Description / Danish: Sønderjysk Centralforening. Støtten på Skamlingsbanken og derunder tre skjolde hvori i midten Slesvigs løver, t.h. SANDHED OG RET, t.v. bogstaverne F.D.S.S.
Designed by: Arnold Krog
Number of copies / size: 1,200 copies, 8 3/4", 22 1/2 cm
Price: $80-130

RC-CM25
Year: 1898
Description / English: Thistle and two butterflies in ornamental border. Commissioned by Kunstforeningen af 18 November (Art Society of 18 November).
Description / Danish: Kunstforeningen af 18. november. Tidsel med to sommerfugle, ornamental bort.
Designed by: Gotfred Rode
Number of copies / size: 300 copies, 8 1/4", 21 cm
Price: $350-500

RC-CM26
Year: 1899
Description / English: Clouds, advancing soldiers and officer on horseback. Commemorative plate for the 50th anniversary of the battle of Fredericia.
Inscription: FREM GIK DE DANSKE DRENGE TIL SEJR OG TIL DØD. (The Danish soldiers marched on to victory and death); below the inscription 1849- 6 JULI-1899 FREDERICIA.
Description / Danish: 6. juli-platte. Fremstillet til 50 årsdagen for Fredericiaslaget d. 6. juli 1849. Fremrykkende soldater med officer til hest, derover i skyer indskrift: FREM GIK DE DANSKE DRENGE TIL SEJR OG TIL DØD. F.n. 1849- 6 JULI-1899 FREDERICIA.
Designed by: Arnold Krog
Number of copies / size: 200 copies, 12 1/2", 32 cm
Price: $800-1000

RC-CM27
Year: 1899
Description / English: Barrow and rising sun. Commemorative plate for the 50th anniversary of the battle of Fredericia 6th july 1849 and for the general Olaf Rye, who died in the battle.
Inscription: 1849-FREDERICIA-1899 6 JULI. On barrow OLAF RYE D. 6 JULI 1849.
Description / Danish: 6. Juli platte. Sol over dysse med indskrift: OLAF RYE D. 6. JULI 1849. Desuden indskrift: 1849 – FREDERICIA – 1899 6. JULI.
Designed by: Arnold Krog
Number of copies / size: 1,000 copies,
6 3/4", 17 1/2 cm
Price: $80-130

RC-CM28
Year: 1899
Description / English: Polar bear pierced by rapier with guard formed by three rings, cf. no 14. Commissioned by the Independent Order of Odd Fellows for its hospital on Iceland.
Inscription: CAPTIVORUM LIBERATOR (Liberator of the captives).
Description / Danish: Old Fellow Ordenens hospital på Island. Isbjørn gennemboret af kårde, hvis parerplade er danned af tre ringe.(samme som 14, 29, 30) Indskrift: CAPTIVORUM LIBERATOR (de fangnes befrier).
Designed by: Arnold Krog
Number of copies / size: 1,900 copies, 15", 38 cm
Price: $3000-4000

RC-CM29
Year: 1899
Description / English: A geyser on Iceland. In the foreground a dragon pierced by rapier with guard formed by three rings. Commissioned by the Independent Order of Odd Fellows for its hospital on Iceland.
Insciription: AEGROTANTIUM MEDICUS (The Healer of Suffering).
Description / Danish: Old Fellow Ordenens hospital på Island. Den hede springkilde Geysir, i forgrunden en drage gennemboret af en kårde (samme som 14, 28, 30). Indskrift: AEGROTANTIUM MEDICUS (same som 15).
Designed by: Arnold Krog
Number of copies / size: 200 copies, 11", 28 cm
Price: $550-650

RC-CM30
Year: 1899
Description / English: The Icelandic volcano Hekla in eruption. In the foreground a dragon pierced by rapier with guard formed by three rings. Commissioned by Independent Order of Odd Fellows for its hospital on Iceland.
Inscription: CAPTIVORUM LIBERATOR (Liberator of the captives).
Description / Danish: Old Fellow Ordenens på Island. Hekla i udbrud, i forgrunden en drage gennemboret af kårde, hvis parerplade er danned af tre ringe (samme som 14, 28, 29) Indskrift: CAPTIVORUM LIBERATOR (samme som 28)
Designed by: Arnold Krog
Number of copies / size: 200 copies, 11", 28 cm
Price: $550-650

RC-CM31
Year: 1899
Description / English: Skogafos waterfall, in the foreground half submerged in the water a dragon pierced by rapier with guard formed by three rings. Commissioned by the Independent Order of Odd Fellows for its hospital on Iceland.
Description / Danish: Old Fellow Ordenens hospital på Island. Skogafors, i forgrunden halvt skjult i vandet en drage gennemboret af kårde, hvis parerplade er danned af tre ringe (samme som 14, 28, 29, 30) Indskrift: PAVPERVM PROTECTOR (De fattiges beskytter)
Designed by: Arnold Krog
Number of copies / size: 200 copies, 11", 28 cm
Price: $550-650

RC-CM32
Year: 1899
Description / English: Armed mason on scaffolding. Commissioned by the Free Mason Lodge in Denmark.
Inscription: DEVS INCEPTIS NOSTRIS FAVEAT (May God favor our enterprises) and the year 1899 on the mason's tub.
Description / Danish: Frimurerplatte. Harnisklædt murer på stilads med balje hvorpå 1899. Indskrift: DEVS INCEPTIS NOSTRIS FAVEAT (Måtte Guds begundstige vore forehavender).
Designed by: N. Fristrup
Number of copies / size: 600 copies, 8 3/4", 22 cm
Price: $300-400

RC-CM33
Year: 1899
Description / English: Insignia and letters I.O.O.F. Commissioned by the Independent Order of Odd Fellows in Denmark.
Description / Danish: Odd Fellow platte. Ordenens symboler og bokstaver I.O.O.F. (Independet Order of Oddfellows).
Designed by: Arnold Krog
Number of copies / size: 500 copies, 7", 18 cm
Price: $200-250

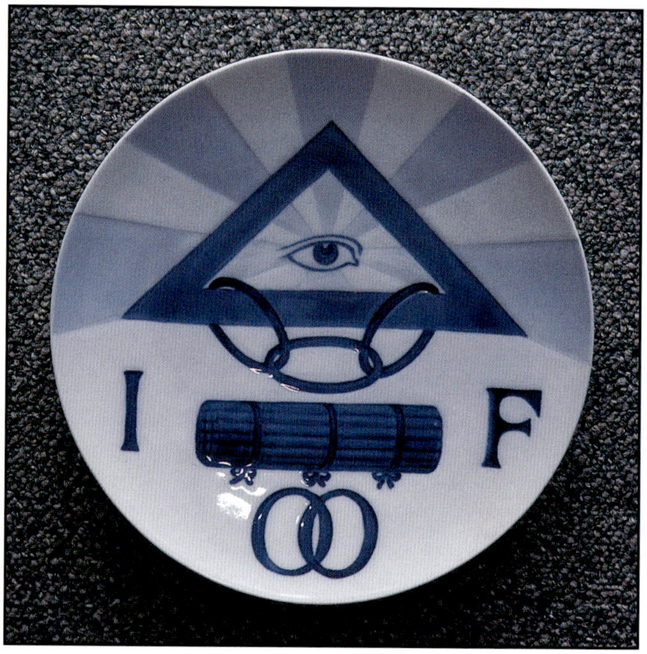

RC-CM34
Year: 1899
Description / English: Masonic insignia and year 1899. Commissioned by the Free Mason Lodge in Denmark.
Description: Danish: Frimurerplatte. Ordenens symboler og 1899
Designed by: N. Fristrup
Number of copies / size: 800 copies, 7"
Price: $140-170

RC-CM35
Year: 1899
Description / English: Eagle on branch. Below the towers of the city and three wavy lines and above the years 1874-1899. Commissioned by the students of 1874 on the occasion of their 25th anniversary.
Inscription: COELESTEM ADSPICIT LVCEM (It beholds the heavenly light) – the inscription over the entrance to the university of Copenhagen.
Description / Danish: 1874-studenternes 25 års jubilæum. Ørn på gren. Indskrift: COLESTEM ADSPICIT LVCEM (Den skuer det himmelske lys), indskrift over indgangen til Københavns Universitet, og 1874-1899. F.N. Københavns tårne over bølgelinier.
Designed by: Arnold Krog
Number of copies / size: 100 copies, 7", 18 cm
Price: $1000-1500

RC-CM36
Year: 1899
Description / English: The Royal Theatre in Copenhagen. Made on occasion of the 25th anniversary of the opening of the new building.
Inscription: MDCCCLXXIV (1874)– XV OCTOBER – MDCCCXCIX (1899) and beloved face-to-face monogram FV (King Frederik V).
Description / Danish: Det Kongelige Theater. Facaden i aftenlys. Indskrift: MDCCCLXXIV (1872)– XV OCTOBER – MDCCCXCIX (1899) and beloved face-to-face monogram FV (Frederik V). Udført i anledning af 25 året for bygningens indvielse.
Designed by: Oluf Jensen
Number of copies / size: 35 copies, 8 1/2", 22 cm
Price: $4000-4500

RC-CM37
Year: 1900
Description / English: Viking ship steering Southwest. In the sail the Danish arms over three wavy lines. Commemorating the Danish Participation in the World Exhibition in Paris that year.
Inscription: ANNO 1900
Description / Danish: Verdensudstillingen i Paris. Udført til minde om den danske deltagelse. Vikingeskib stævner mod sydvest, i sejlet dansk rigsvåben over tre bølgelinier. Indskrift: ANNO 1900
Designed by: Arnold Krog
Number of copies / size: 600 copies, 7 1/4", 18 1/2 cm
Price: $160-200

RC-CM38
Year: 1900
Description / English: Norwegian mountainside and fjord with Viking ship under sail.
Inscription: D.N.V. (Danish-Norwegian Friendship Association) and the year 1900.
Description / Danish: Nordlandsplatte. Klippevæg mod vand og vikingeskib med sejl i hvis ene hjørne bogstaverne D.N.V. (Dansk Norsk Venskabsforening) og 1900
Designed by: Arnold Krog
Number of copies / size: 50 copies, 11", 28 cm
Price: $3000-5000
No picture available

RC-CM39
Year: 1901
Description / English: Sphinx sitting on globe and holding snake in its claw. Sunrise and the years 1901 on top of plate. Below urn with the year 1900, commemorating the turn of the century.
Description / Danish: "Verdensplatte." På over del af jordkugle en sfinks der holder en slange fast med sin ene klo, derover i sollys årstallet 1901, f. n. urne med 1900. Udført i anledning af århundredeskiftet.
Designed by: Arnold Krog, 1899
Number of copies / size: 500 copies, 8 3/4", 22 1/2 cm
Price: $200-300

RC-CM40
Year: 1901
Description / English: Thistles
Inscription: GLASGOW 1901. Commissioned by the exhibition in Glasgow in 1901.
Description / Danish: Glasgow-platte. Fremstillet i anledning af udstilling i Glasgow. Tidsel og indskrift: GLASGOW 1901.
Designed by: Arnold Krog
Number of copies / size: 262 copies, 7 1/4", 18 1/2 cm
Price: $300-350

RC-CM41
Year: 1901
Description / English: The Goose tower in Vordingborg. In the foreground flowering chestnuts. Commissioned by the exhibition in Vordingborg.
Inscription: VORDINGBORG 1901
Description / Danish: Vordingborg-platte. Fremstillet i anledning af udstilling i Vordingborg. Gåsetårnet og i forgrunden blomstrende kastanie. Indskrift: VORDINGBORG 1901.
Designed by: Oluf Jensen
Number of copies / size: 455 copies, 7 3/4", 20 cm
Price: $200-300

RC-CM42
Year: 1902
Description / English: The coronation of King Edward VII of Great Britain and Ireland and Queen Alexandra. Crowned monogram EA, below the year MCMII (1902)and three wavy lines.
Inscription: REX ET IMP. REG.
Description / Danish: Engelsk kroningsplatte fremstillet i anledning af kong Edward VII.s og dronning Alexandras kroning. Kronet monogram EA. derunder MCMII (1902) og tre bølgelinier. F.n. indskrift: REX. ET IMP. REG.
Designed by: Arnold Krog
Number of copies / size: 1,000 copies,
6 3/4", 17 1/2 cm
Price: $100-140

RC-CM43
Year: 1903
Description / English: Hourglass and the years 1878-1903, above three rings, below the same symbol and the letters I.O.O.F. Commissioned by the Independent Order of Odd Fellows on occasion of their 25th anniversary.
Description / Danish: Odd Fellow Ordenens 25-års jubilæum. Timeglas mellem årstallene 1878 og 1903, de tre ringe og bogstaver I.O.O.F. (Independent Order of Odd Fellows).
Designed by:
Number of copies / size: 250 copies, 7 1/4", 18 1/2 cm
Price: $250-350

RC-CM44
Year: 1903
Description / English: Crowned monogram MA
Inscription: MAIFEST 1903 (May-day festival). Made on occasion of a festival under the protection of the princesses Marie and Alexandrine.
Description / Danish: Majfest-platte. Protektricer prinsesse Marie og prinsesse Alexandrine. Kronet monogram MA. Indskrift: MAIFEST 1903.
Designed by: Arnold Krog
Number of copies / size: 500 copies, 6", 15 cm
Price: $160-200

RC-CM45
Year: 1903
Description / English: The town hall of Gentofte. The plate in the form of a shield.
Inscription: GIENTOFTE KOMMUNES RAADHUS 1903 (Town hall of Gentofte urban district).
Description / Danish: Gentofte rådhus. Skjold med rådhusbygningen i Charlottenlund. Indskrift GIENTOFTE KOMMUNES RAADHUS 1903.
Designed by: A. Thejll
Number of copies / size: 225 copies, 8", 20 1/2 cm
Price: $400-500

RC-CM46 (closed border)
Year: 1903
Description / English: The 40th anniversary of King Christian IX. Crowned face to face monogram and the years 1863-1903.
Description / Danish: Christian IX.s 40års regerings-jubilæum. Kronet spejlmonogram og 1863–1903.
Designed by: Arnold Krog
Number of copies / size: 1,200 copies, 7 3/4", 20 cm
Price: $90-150

RC-CM47
Year: 1903
Description / English: Ornamental design with 4 crowns.
Inscription: ST. LOVIS EXHIBITION ANO MCMIV (1904).
Description / Danish: Udstilling i St. Louis. Gitterornament omsluttet af fire kroner. Indskrift St. LOVIS EXHIBITION ANNO MCMIV (1904).
Designed by: Arnold Krog
Number of copies / size: 500 copies, 7", 18 cm
Price: $170-250

RC-CM46A (Lace border)
Year: 1903
Description / English: The 40th anniversary of King Christian IX. Crowned face to face monogram and the years 1863-1903.
Description / Danish: Christian IX.s 40års regeringsjubilæum. Kronet spejlmonogram og 1863–1903.
Designed by: Arnold Krog
Number of copies / size: 40 copies, 7 3/4", 20 cm
Price: $2500-3500

RC-CM48
Year: 1904
Description / English: Star shining over font from which two snakes are drinking. Below initials D.A.F. (Danish Teetotaller's Association) and the years 1879-1904. Commissioned by the association for its 25th anniversary.
Description / Danish: Afholdsforeningens 25-års jubilæum. Stjerne der lyser over en skål hvoraf to giftslanger drikker. Derunder initialer D.A.F. (Danmarks Afholdsforening) og 1879 – 1904.
Designed by: Arnold Krog
Number of copies / size: 1,000 copies, 7", 18 cm
Price: $100-150

RC-CM49
Year: 1904
Description / English: Ribe Cathedral. In the foreground, three crowned lions. Made on the occasion of the completion of the restoration.
Description / Danish: Ribe Domkirke. Fremstillet til minde om restaureringens fuldførelse. I forgrunden f.n. tre kronede løver.
Designed by: H.C. Amberg
Number of copies / size: 200 copies, 11", 28 cm
Price: $400-600

RC-CM50
Year: 1904
Description / English: The coat of arms of the Bulow family and the years 1154-1904. Commissioned by the Bulow family to commemorate its 750th anniversary.
Description / Danish: Bulow-slægtens 750 års jubilæum. Våben og årstal 1154 – 1904.
Designed by:
Number of copies / size: 700 copies, 8 3/4", 22 1/2 cm
Price: $2000-3500
No picture available

RC-CM51
Year: 1904
Description / English: The coat of arms of the Holstein family. The shield vertically halved with one and a half rose to the right and unfolded wing to the left. On the helmet an oxen head with a wing between the horns.
Description / Danish: Slægten Holstein. Våben lodret delt skjold med en hel og en halv rose i højre, en udslået vinge i venstre felt. På hjelmen et oksehoved med en vinge mellem hornene.
Designed by:
Number of copies / size: 7 3/4", 20 cm
Price: $2000-3500
No picture available

RC-CM52
Year: 1905
Description / English: Lake with swans. Above a flowering chestnut. Commemorating Hans Christian Andersen's 100th anniversary.
Inscription: 1805-H.C. ANDERSEN-1905.
Description / Danish: H.C. Andersens 100 års fødselsdag. Sø med svaner, f.o. kastanie i blomst. Indskrift: 1805 – H.C. ANDERSEN – 1905.
Designed by: Oluf Jensen
Number of copies / size: 800 copies, 7 3/4", 20 cm
Price: $100-150

RC-CM53
Year: 1905
Description / English: Stallion standing in front of a tree.
Inscription: DEN JYDSKE INDUSTRI – OG LANDBRUGS – UDSTILLING HORSENS MCMV (Industrial and agricultural exhibition for Jutland in Horsens).
Description / Danish: Horsens-udstilling. Stående hingst foran et træ. Indskrift: DEN JYDSKE INDUSTRI – OG LANDBRUGS UDSTILLING HORSENS MCMV.
Designed by: Arnold Krog
Number of copies / size: 7 3/4", 20 cm
Price: $120-200

RC-CM54
Year: 1905
Description / English: The mythological heroine Gefion plowing with her four oxen. A shield with initials D.S.S.S.L. and below the years 1880 – 1905. Commissioned by the agricultural exhibition in Copenhagen 1905.
Description / Danish: Landbrugsudstilling i København. Gefion pløjer. F.o. skjold med initialer D.S.S.S.L., derunder 1880 – 1905.
Designed by: Knud Kyhn
Number of copies / size: 454 copies, 8 3/4", 22 1/2 cm
Price: $200-300

RC-CM55
Year: 1905
Description / English: Seal with a salmon in its mouth. In the background sailing boats. Below a fishing-net with a laurel wreath. Commissioned by the association.
Inscription: XX AARSMØDE 1905, monogram FF (Fishery Association) and crowned initials V and M (Prince Valdemar and Princess Marie, protectors of the fishery exhibition).
Description / Danish: Fiskeriudstilling. Farvand med sejlskibe og sæl med laks. F.n. net med krans og indskrift: XX AARSMØDE 1905, spejlmonogram FF (Fiskeriforeningen) samt kronede monogrammer V og M (Prins Valdemar og Prinsesse Marie, udstillingens protektorer).
Designed by: Arnold Krog
Number of copies / size: 666 copies, 7 3/4", 20 cm
Price: $150-200

RC-CM56
Year: 1905
Description / English: Frigate. In the background a West Indian coast. Below the monograms F5 and C9 (King Frederik 5 and King Christian 9). Commissioned by the Independent Order of Odd Fellows, which founded a hospital in St. Croix.
Inscription: PATRIA INTEGRA (A healthy country) 1755-1905.
Description / Danish: Odd Fellow Ordenens hospital på St. Croix, Dansk Vestindien. Sejlskib udfor kyst, derunder monogrammer F5 og C9 og 1755 – 1905. Indskrift: PATRIA INTEGRA (Et sundt fædreland) samt ordenens symbol.
Designed by: Oluf Jensen
Number of copies / size: 300 copies, 7 3/4", 20 cm
Price: $200-250

RC-CM56A (LARGE)
Year: 1905
Description / English: Frigate. In the background a West Indian coast. Below the monograms F5 and C9 (King Frederik 5 and King Christian 9). Commissioned by the Independent Order of Odd Fellows, which founded a hospital in St. Croix.
Inscription: PATRIA INTEGRA (A healthy country) 1755-1905.
Description / Danish: Odd Fellow Ordenens hospital på St. Croix, Dansk Vestindien. Sejlskib udfor kyst, derunder monogrammer F5 og C9 og 1755 – 1905. Indskrift: PATRIA INTEGRA (Et sundt fædreland) samt ordenens symbol.
Designed by: Oluf Jensen
Number of copies / size: 12 copies, 11 3/4", 30 cm
Price: $3000-4000
Same picture as RC-CM56

RC-CM57
Year: 1905
Description / English: Nursing sister. In the background the hospital in Copenhagen. Above crowned face to face monogram L (Queen Louise), below NOVEMBER 1905. Commemorating the 40th anniversary of the foundation of the nursing sister's motherhouse.
Description / Danish: Diakonissestiftelsen. Stående diakonisse, i baggrunden hospitalet på Peter Bangsvej i København. F.o. Kronet spejlmonogram L (Dronning Louise), f.n. NOVEMBER 1905. Udført i anledning af moderhusets 40 års indvielsesdag.
Designed by: Christian Thomsen
Number of copies / size: 7 3/4"
Price: $170-210

RC-CM57A (LARGE)
Year: 1905
Description / English: Nursing sister. In the background the hospital in Copenhagen. Above crowned face to face monogram L (Queen Louise), below NOVEMBER 1905. Commemorating the 40th anniversary of the foundation of the nursing sister's motherhouse.
Description / Danish: Diakonissestiftelsen. Stående diakonisse, i baggrunden hospitalet på Peter Bangsvej i København. F.o. Kronet spejlmonogram L (Dronning Louise), f.n. NOVEMBER 1905. Udført i anledning af moderhusets 40 års indvielsesdag.
Designed by: Christian Thomsen
Number of copies / size: 11 3/4"
Price: $3000-4000
Same picture as RC-CM57

RC-CM58
Year: 1906
Description / English: The coat of arms of the Flach family. Shield with asymmetric 5-pointed star. On helmet two drinking horns. Commissioned by tanner Flach in Aarhus on his 40th anniversary.
Description / Danish: Slægten Flach. Våben med asymmetrisk, femoddet stjerne. På hjelmen to vesselhorn. Udført til garver Flach i Aarhus, 40 års jubilæum.
Designed by:
Number of copies / size: 7 1/2", 19 cm
Price: $2500-3500

RC-CM59
Year: 1906
Description / English: Mercury staff with letters F.D.H. (Association of Danish Commercial Travelers) in a shield around which 5 motifs showing various means of transport. Below the years 1866-1906. Commissioned by F.D.H. on occasion of its 40th anniversary.
Description / Danish: Foreningen af danske handelsrejsende. Merkurstav med skjold hvori bogstaverne F.D.H. derom 5 medailloner med motiver fra forskellig befordring og f.n. årstallene 1866 – 1906. Fremstillet til foreningens 40 års jubilæum.
Designed by: Arnold Krog
Number of copies / size: 1,000 copies, 7 3/4", 20 cm
Price: $90-120

RC-CM60
Year: 1906
Description / English: The accession to the throne of King Frederik VIII. Crowned plate with face to face monogram F8L. (Queen Louise) and the year 1906.
Description / Danish: Tronbestigelsen. Ramme i relief med krone og perlestaf, spejlmonogram F8L (Frederik 8 og Louise) 1906.
Designed by: Arnold Krog
Number of copies / size: 1,500 copies, 8 3/4", 22 cm
Price: $100-150

RC-CM61
Year: 1906
Description / English: Coronation of King Haakon VII and Queen Maud of Norway. Crowned face to face monogram H7M and the year 1906.
Description / Danish: Norsk kroningsplatte. Kronet spejlmonogram H7 (Haakon 7) og M (Maud) 1906.
Designed by: Arnold Krog
Number of copies / size: 1,500 copies, 7 3/4", 20 cm
Price: $90-130

RC-CM62
Year: 1906
Description / English: The towers of Copenhagen with hill in the background. Wroght iron fence with the year 1904 and face-to-face monogram JF (Journalist's Association). Commissioned by this association to commemorate the foundation in 1904.
Description / Danish: Journalistforbundets stiftelse. I baggrunden et bjerg, i forgrunden svaler over Københavns tårne samt gitter med spejlmonogram JF 1904 (Da Forbundet blev stiftet).
Designed by: Arnold Krog
Number of copies / size: 300 copies, 8 3/4", 22cm
Price: $250-350

RC-CM63
Year: 1906
Description / English: The evangelist St. John and the eagle of a rock. Above a crowned ribbon. Commissioned by the Freemason lodge St. John in Aalborg on the occasion of its 50th anniversary.
Inscription: ET SPIRITUS EST QUI TESTATUR QUOD SPIRITUS VERITAS EST (And the spirit witnesses that the spirit is truth). Below 5856 – 11.15 Cimbria 5906.
Description / Danish: Cimbria. Frimurerlogen St. Johannes i Aalborg. 50 års jubilæum. Evangelisten Johannes på ørn over klippe med våben i oval. F.o. kronet bånd med indeskrift: ET SPIRITUS EST QUI TESTATUR QUOD SPIRITUS VERITAS EST (Og det er ånden der vidner at ånd er sandhed). F.n. 5856 – 11.15. 5906 Cimbria (1856 – 1906).
Designed by: Christian Thomsen
Number of copies / size: 800 copies, 8 3/4" , 22cm
Price: $150-200

RC-CM63A (LARGE)
Year: 1906
Description / English: The evangelist St. John and the eagle of a rock. Above a crowned ribbon. Commissioned by the Freemason lodge St. John in Aalborg on the occasion of its 50th anniversary.
Inscription: ET SPIRITUS EST QUI TESTATUR QUOD SPIRITUS VERITAS EST (And the spirit witnesses that the spirit is truth). Below 5856-11.15 Cimbria 5906.
Description / Danish: Cimbria. Frimurerlogen St. Johannes i Aalborg. 50 års jubilæum. Evangelisten Johannes på ørn over klippe med våben i oval. F.o. kronet bånd med indeskrift: ET SPIRITUS EST QUI TESTATUR QUOD SPIRITUS VERITAS EST (Og det er ånden der vidner at ånd er sandhed). F.n. 5856 – 11.15. 5906 Cimbria (1856 – 1906).
Designed by: Christian Thomsen
Number of copies / size: 11 copies, 13", 32.75 cm
Price: $3000-5000
Same picture as RC-CM63

RC-CM64
Year: 1906
Description / English: Commemorative plate for King Christian IX. Crowned laurel wreath and face to face monogram C9.
Description / Danish: Christian IX.s mindeplatte. Kronet krans med spejlmonogram C9.
Designed by: Arnold Krog
Number of copies / size: 1,500 copies,
5 1/2", 14 CM
Price: $80-150

RC-CM65
Year: 1906
Description / English: Red cross nursing sister in landscape. Above crowned monogram L (Queen Louise), below inscription NOVEMBER 1906, Commissioned for the Danish Virgin Island's nursing and children home under protection of Queen Louise.
Description / Danish: Vestindisk Syge – og Børnehjem. Røde Kors sygeplejerske i landskab. F.o. Dronning Louises kronede monogram, f.n. NOVEMBER 1906.
Designed by: Christian Thomsen
Number of copies / size: 300 copies, 7 3/4", 20 cm
Price: $250-350

RC-CM66
Year: 1906
Description / English: Landscape with a church-tower against starlit sky. In the foreground palms. Commissioned by the Danish Virgin Islands' church fund.
Inscription: SOLI DEO GLORIA (Glory only to God).
Description / Danish: Vestindisk Kirkesag. Landskab med kirketårn under stjernehimmel, i forgrunden palmer. Indskrift: SOLI DEO GLORIA (Gud alene æren).
Designed by: Christian Thomsen
Number of copies / size: 300 copies, 7 3/4", 20 cm
Price: $200-300

RC-CM67
Year: 1906
Description / English: The westfront of Viborg Cathedral in ornamental frame with the city arms of Viborg. Commemorating the completion of the frescoes by Joachim Skovgaard in the church.
Inscription: A. DOM. MCMVI (anno domini 1906)
Description / Danish: Viborg Domkirke. Vestfacaden i firpasramme med ornamentik og byvåben. Indskrift: A. DOM. MCMVI (anno domini 1906), i dette år fuldførtes Joachim Skovgaards vægfresker.
Designed by: Arnold Krog
Number of copies / size: 243 copies, 11", 28 cm
Price: $400-600

RC-CM68
Year: 1907
Description / English: The Good Samaritan. Made on the occasion of the Red Cross Society's 30th anniversary.
Inscription: INTER ARMA CARITAS (Charity in war) 1877-1907.
Description / Danish: Den barmhjertige samaritan. Indskrift: INTER ARMA CARITAS (Næstekærlighed i krig). Udført til Røde Kors 30 års jubilæum 1877 – 1907.
Designed by: Christian Thomsen
Number of copies / size: 300 copies, 7 3/4", 19.5 cm
Price: $200-300

RC-CM68A (LARGE)
Year: 1907
Description / English: The Good Samaritan. Made on the occasion of the Red Cross Society's 30th anniversary.
Inscription: INTER ARMA CARITAS (Charity in war) 1877-1907.
Description / Danish: Den barmhjertige samaritan. Indskrift: INTER ARMA CARITAS (Næstekærlighed i krig). Udført til Røde Kors 30 års jubilæum 1877 – 1907.
Designed by: Christian Thomsen
Number of copies / size: 15 copies, 11 3/4", 29.5 cm
Price: $3000-4000
Same picture as RC-CM68

RC-CM69
Year: 1907
Description / English: Mail coach surrounded by the Danish, Norwegian and Swedish arms. Above a crowned coach horn and the year 1907.
Inscription: DET NORDISKE POSTMØDE I KJØBENHAVN (The Scandinavian postal conference in Copenhagen)
Description / Danish: Nordisk Postmøde i København. Kuglepost omgivet af det danske, det norske og det svenske våben. F.o. kronet posthorn og 1907. Indskrift: DET NORDISKE POSTMØDE I KJØBENHAVN.
Designed by: Karl Hansen-Reistrup
Number of copies / size: 8 3/4", 22 cm
Price: $2500-4000
No picture available

RC-CM70
Year: 1907
Description / English: Mail coach on Copenhagen waterfront. In the background the skyline of the town. Above the three Scandinavian arms in coach horns. To the right a milestone with inscription: DET NORDISKE POSTMODE I KJOBENHAVN (The Scandinavian postal conference in Copenhagen)
Description / Danish: Nordisk Postmøde (jfr. 69), variant. Kuglepost på Strandvejen, i baggrunden byens silhouet. F.o. bladhang med de tre våben, t.h. milepæl med indskrift som 69.
Designed by: Karl Hansen-Reistrup
Number of copies / size: 11", 28 cm
Price: $4000-5000
No picture available

RC-CM71
Year: 1907
Description / English: Aarhus Cathedral. Two sitting figures (St. Clemens and St. Paul), two towers, the sun and the moon, below wavy lines – a free composition over the city arms of Aarhus. Commemorating the beginning of the restoration of the church
Inscription: AARHUS 1907
Description / Danish: Aarhus Domkirke. Bygningen mellem to siddende figurer, Skt. Clemens og Skt. Paul, f.n. bølger. Indfattet i ramme med to tårne, sol – og månetegn. Kompositionen bygget over Aarhus byvåben. Indskrift: Aarhus 1907. (Det år den store istandsættelse påbegyndtes under Hack Kampmanns ledelse.)
Designed by: Arnold Krog
Number of copies / size: 11", 27.7 cm
Price: $400-600

RC-CM73
Year: 1907
Description / English: The city arms of Aarhus and a Mercury staff. Commissioned by this association on its 10th anniversary.
Inscription: AARHUS HANDELSREJSENDE-FORENING 1897-25 April - 1907 (The Association in Aarhus of Commercial Travelers).
Description / Danish: Aarhus Handelsrejsendeforening. Byvåben og merkurstav. Indskrift: AARHUS HANDELSREJSENDEFORENING 1897 – 25. APRIL – 1907 (10 års jubilæum).
Designed by: Christian Thomsen
Number of copies / size: 300 copies, 8 1/2", 22 cm
Price: $200-350

RC-CM72
Year: 1907
Description / English: Scene from the island of Fanoe. The beach with a sailing boat and the full moon.
Inscription: FANO over three wavy lines.
Description / Danish: Fanø – platte. Strandmotiv med båd og fuldmåne. Indskrift: FANØ, derunder tre bølgelinier.
Designed by: Oluf Jensen
Number of copies / size: 7 3/4", 20 cm
Price: $300-500

RC-CM74
Year: 1907
Description / English: Landscape with cow.
Inscription: S.A.L.S 50 AARS JUBILAEUMS SKUE FAABORG 1907 (The Agricultural Society in Svendborg County, 50th anniversary show in Faaborg).
Description / Danish: Dyrskue i Faaborg. Landskab med græssende ko. Indskrift: S.A.L.S. (Svendborg Amts Landøkonomiske Selskab) 50 AARs JUBILÆUMS SKUE FAABORG 1907.
Designed by: Godfred Rode
Number of copies / size: 208 copies, 7 3/4", 20 cm
Price: $250-400

RC-CM75
Year: 1907
Description / English: Cross and in the background silhouette of an island. Commissioned in aid of the Virgin Island's Church fund.
Inscription: PAX IN TERRA (Peace on Earth).
Description / Danish: Vestindisk Kirkesag. Ornamentalt kors, i baggrunden profil af en ø. Indskrift: PAX IN TERRA (fred på jorden).
Designed by: Arnold Krog
Number of copies / size: 250 copies, 7 3/4", 20 cm
Price: $270-350

RC-CM76
Year: 1907
Description / English: Mother with child and cradle. Above crowned face to face monogram L (Queen Louise). Commissioned in aid of Queen Louise's day nursery in the Danish Virgin Islands.
Inscription: MANVS QV AE CVNAS MOVET MVNDVM REGIT (The hand that rocks the cradle governs the world)
Description / Danish: Dronning Louises vuggestue i dansk Vestindien. Mor med barn ved en vugge. F.o. kronet spejlmonogram L. Indskrift: MANVS QV Æ CVNAS MOVET MVNDVM REGIT (Den hånd der rører vuggen styrer verden).
Designed by: Christian Thomsen
Number of copies / size: 7 3/4", 20 cm
Price: $500-1000

RC-CM77
Year: 1907
Description / English: Crowned M and anchor (Monogram of Princess Marie) in sunrays, which penetrate a cloud. Commissioned by the Independent Order of Odd Fellows in aid of its hospital in the Danish Virgin Islands.
Inscription: BENEDIC. DEO ET MORERE. Below the year 1907 and three rings.
Description / Danish: Odd Fellow Ordenens hospital i Dansk Vestindien. F.o. kronet M (Prinsesse Marie) og anker i solstråler der bryder gennem en sky. Indskrift: BENEDIC. DEO ET MORERE; f.n. ringsymbol og 1907.
Designed by: Arnold Krog
Number of copies / size: 430 copies, 6", 15 cm
Price: $125-160

RC-CM77A (LARGE)
Year: 1907
Description / English: Crowned M and anchor (Monogram of Princess Marie) in sunrays, which penetrate a cloud. Commissioned by the Independent Order of Odd Fellows in aid of its hospital in the Danish Virgin Islands.
Inscription: BENEDIC. DEO ET MORERE. Below the year 1907 and three rings.
Description / Danish: Odd Fellow Ordenens hospital i Dansk Vestindien. F.o. kronet M (Prinsesse Marie) og anker i solstråler der bryder gennem en sky. Indskrift: BENEDIC. DEO ET MORERE; f.n. ringsymbol og 1907.
Designed by: Arnold Krog
Number of copies / size: 15 copies, 11 1/4", 30 cm
Price: $4000-5000
Same picture as RC-CM77

RC-CM78
Year: 1907
Description / English: The motif is a copy of a 4 ore stamp. Commissioned by the Philatelist Club.
Inscription: FRIMAERKEUDSTILLING MCMVII (Stamp exhibition 1907).
Description / Danish: Frimærkeudstilling. Kopi af 4 øres mærke. Indskrift: FRIMÆRKE UDSTILLING MCMVII (1907). Afholdt af Filatelistklubben.
Designed by: Arnold Krog
Number of copies / size: 457 copies, 7 1/4", 18 1/2 cm
Price: $300-400

RC-CM79
Year: 1907
Description / English: Koldinghus Castle ruin: In the foreground the lake. Commemorating the centenary of the fire that ruined the castle.
Inscription: 1808-30 MARTS-1908.
Description / Danish: Koldinghus. 100- årsdagan for slottets brand. Slotssøen med ruinen i baggrunden. Indskrift: 1808 – 30 MARTS – 1908.
Designed by: Oluf Jensen
Number of copies / size: 600 copies, 8 3/4", 22 cm
Price: $150-200

RC-CM80
Year: 1907
Description / English: Royal Life Guard on duty at Amalienborg castle, garlanded by two medallions in which the crowned monograms of F3 (King Frederik III) 1658 and F8 (King Frederik VIII) 1908. Commemorating the 250th anniversary of the Royal Life Guard Regiment.
Description / Danish: Livgardens 250 års jubilæum. Garder på vagt ved Amalienborg. Guirlande med kronede monogrammer F3 (Frederik III) 1658 and F8 (King Frederik 8) 1908.
Designed by: Arnold Krog
Number of copies / size: 825 copies, 9", 23 cm
Price: $200-300

RC-CM81
Year: 1907
Description / English: Two crossed colors with shield. Commemorating the 250th anniversary of the battalion.
Inscription: 30 Nov 1657-1907 and below 6. BATAILLON: round the edge, the major battles in which the battalion took part: NYBORG 1659 – WISMAR 1675 – RYGEN 1715 – TRELDESKANSEN 1849 – DYBBOL 1848 – 64.
Description / Danish: 6. Bataillons 250 års jubilæum. Pyramide af to faner og en standard med skjold og indskrift: 30 NOV. 1657 – 1907 og f.n. 6. BATAILLION. På kanten NYBORG 1659 – WISMAR 1675 – RYGEN 1715 – TRELDESKANSEN 1849 – DYBBØL 1848 – 64 (Slag i hvilke bataillonen har deltaget).
Designed by: Arnold Krog
Number of copies / size: 350 copies, 8 3/4", 22 1/2 cm
Price: $200-300

RC-CM81A (LARGE)
Year: 1907
Description / English: Two crossed colors with shield. Commemorating the 250th anniversary of the battalion.
Inscription: 30 Nov 1657-1907 and below 6. BATAILLON: round the edge, the major battles in which the battalion took part: NYBORG 1659 – WISMAR 1675 – RYGEN 1715 – TRELDESKANSEN 1849 – DYBBOL 1848 – 64.
Description / Danish: 6. Bataillons 250 års jubilæum. Pyramide af to faner og en standard med skjold og indskrift: 30 NOV. 1657 – 1907 og f.n. 6. BATAILLION. På kanten NYBORG 1659 – WISMAR 1675 – RYGEN 1715 – TRELDESKANSEN 1849 – DYBBØL 1848 – 64 (Slag i hvilke bataillonen har deltaget).
Designed by: Arnold Krog
Number of copies / size: 36 copies, 12 1/2", 32 cm
Price: $2500-3500
Same picture as RC-CM81

RC-CM82
Year: 1907
Description / English: The Cathedral of Saint Canut in Odense viewed from the southeast. Below, a leaf motif with the city arms
Inscription: ODENSE 1908.
Description / Danish: Odense – platte. Skt. Knuds kirke set fra sydøst. F.n. bladværk med byvåben og indskrift: ODENSE 1908.
Designed by: Arnold Krog
Number of copies / size: 212 copies, 11", 28 cm
Price: $350-450

RC-CM83
Year: 1907
Description / English: Monogram H.R.F. (Hoteliers' and Restaurateurs' Association) 1908 surrounded by stylized pheasants.
Description / Danish: Kogekunstudstilling. Monogram H.R.F. (Hotel – og Restauratør Foreningen) 1908 i ornamental ramme med fasaner.
Designed by: Christian Thomsen
Number of copies / size: 372 copies, 7 3/4", 20 cm
Price: $200-300

RC-CM84
Year: 1908
Description / English: Scene from the beach at Fanø with bathing wagon and a girl.
Inscription: FANO.
Description / Danish: Fanø – platte. Strandmotive med fanøpige og badevogne. Indskrift: FANØ.
Designed by: Arnold Krog
Number of copies / size: 215 copies, 7 3/4", 20 cm
Price: $300-400

RC-CM85
Year: 1908
Description / English: Crowned anchor with a triangle. Commissioned by the Freemason Lodge St. Johannes Ft. Clemens Orient in Aarhus founded 1871.
Inscription: ST. CLEMENS.
Description / Danish: Frimurerlogen Skt. Clemens i Aarhus. Anker med krone og trekant hvori Skt. Clemens. Udført til logen Skt. Johannes Skt. Clemens Orient, stiftet 1871.
Designed by: Arnold Krog
Number of copies / size: 331 copies, 7 3/4", 20 cm
Price: $200-300

RC-CM86
Year: 1908
Description / English: Oval crowned platter. Lamb lying on a rock. Danish flag and triangle. Commissioned by the freemason lodge St. Clemens in Aarhus.
Inscription: ST. CLEMENS and round the border: SUB CRUCE CLEMENTIA CRESCIT (under the cross clemency grows).
Description / Danish: Frimurerlogen Skt. Clemens i Aarhus. Kronet ovalt skjold med lam med korsfane på en klippe. Indskrift: ST. CLEMENS (I trekant) samt f.n. SUB CRUCE CLEMENTIA CRESCIT (Under korset vokser medfølelsen).
Designed by: Arnold Krog
Number of copies / size: 29 copies, 15", 38 cm
Price: $3000-5000

RC-CM87
Year: 1908
Description / English: See Royal Copenhagen Christmas Plate list (see RC-1908)
No picture available

RC-CM88
Year: 1908
Description / English: Ballet Dancer.
Inscription: TERPSICHORE J.F. 1908 (The Journalist's Association).
Description / Danish: Balletdanserinde. Indskrift: TERPSICHORE J.F. 1908 (Journalistforeningen).
Designed by: Christian Thomsen
Number of copies / size: 250 copies, 7 1/4", 18 1/2 cm
Price: $190-230

RC-CM89
Year: 1909
Description / English: Danish flag and coat of arms. In the background the cathedral of Aarhus and Marselisborg Castle in sunrise.
Inscription: LANDSUDSTILLINGEN I AARHUS 1909 (National exhibition in Aarhus).
Description / Danish: Udstilling i Aarhus. Dannebrog over rigsvåbenet. I baggrunden domkirken og Marselisborg. Indskrft: LANDSUDSTILLINGEN I AARHUS 1909.
Designed by: Arnold Krog
Number of copies / size: 1,460 copies, 7 3/4", 20 cm
Price: $85-130

RC-CM90
Year: 1909
Description / English: See Royal Copenhagen Christmas Plate list. (see RC-1909)
No picture available

RC-CM91
Year: 1909
Description / English: Viking ship with the Danish coat of arms and the word CARITAS in the sail. On the stone with an agave plant the inscription MESSINA 1908. The plate was issued for the benefit of the Danish relief mission to Messina after the earthquake on the 28th of December, 1908, where 60,000 people died.
Description / Danish: Messina – platte. Vikingeskib med dansk rigsvåben og CARITAS i sejlet, på sten med agave indskrift MESSINA 1908. Ved katastrofen den 28. december omkom 60.000 mennesker. Platten blev fremstillet til fordel for den danske hjælp.
Designed by: Arnold Krog
Number of copies / size: 1,107 copies, 7 1/4", 18 1/2 cm
Price: $95-140

RC-CM92
Year: 1909
Description / English: Elephant with young.
Inscription: 1859 ZOOLOGISK HAVE KOBENHAVN 1909 (The Zoological Garden)
Description / Danish: Zoologisk Haves 50 års jubilæum. Elefant med unge. Indskrift: 1859 – ZOOLOGISK HAVE KØBENHAVN 1909.
Designed by: V.Th. Fischer
Number of copies / size: 392 copies, 7 3/4", 20 cm
Price: $250-350

RC-CM93
Year: 1909
Description / English: Farmer plowing his fields.
Inscription: MARIBO AMTS OKONOMISKE SELSKAB 1809-1909 (Mutual aid society of Maribo county).
Description / Danish: Mand der pløjer. Indskrift: MARIBO AMTS ØKONOMISKE SELSKAB 1809 – 1909. Udført til selskabets 100 års jubilæum.
Designed by: Christian Thomsen
Number of copies / size: 238 copies, 7 3/4", 20 cm
Price: $230-260

RC-CM94
Year: 1909
Description / English: Rock with a cross and three portraits with the names HOEG-HAGEN-MYLIUS ERICHSEN-BRONLUND (names of 3 explorers who died in Greenland).
Inscription: DANMARK EKSPEDITIONEN TIL GRØNLANDS NORDOST KYST (Danish Expedition to Greenland's Northeastern Coast) 1906-1908.
Description / Danish: Danmark – Ekspeditionen. Klippe med kors og tre portrætter betegnet HØEG – HAGEN – MYLIUS ERICHSEN – BRØNLUND (de tre omkomne). Indskrift: DANMARK EKSPEDITIONEN TIL GRØNLANDS NORDOST KYST 1906 – 1908.
Designed by: Harald Moltke
Number of copies / size: 624 copies, 9", 23 cm
Price: $250-350

RC-CM95
Year: 1909
Description / English: Dog sleds.
Inscription: DANMARK EKSPEDITIONEN TIL GRØNLANDS NORDOST KYST (Danish Expedition to Greenland's Northeastern Coast) 1906-1908.
Description / Danish: Danmark – Ekspeditionen. Hundeslæder. Indskrift: DANMARK EKSPEDITIONEN TIL GRØNLANDS NORDOST KYST 1906 – 1908.
Designed by: Harald Moltke
Number of copies / size: 341 copies, 9", 23 cm
Price: $250-350

RC-CM96
Year: 1909
Description / English: Greenlandic hunter in kayak between icebergs.
Inscription: DENMARK EKSPEDITIONEN TIL GRØNLANDS NORDOST KYST (Danish Expedition to Greenland's Northeastern Coast) 1906-1908.
Description / Danish: Danmark – Ekspeditionen. Grønlandsk fanger i Kaiak mellem isfjelde.
Designed by: Harald Moltke
Number of copies / size: 315 copies, 9", 23 cm
Price: $250-350

RC-CM97
Year: 1909
Description / English: The wedding of Prince Harald of Denmark to Princess Helena of Slesvig – Holstein – Sønderborg – Glucksborg. Crowned monogram HH and ribbon.
Inscription: MAI MCMIX (1909)
Description / Danish: Prins Haralds bryllup med prinsesse Helena af Slesvig – Holstein – Sønderborg – Glucksborg. Kronet monogram HH og skriftbåand med MAI MCMIX (1909)
Designed by: Arnold Krog
Number of copies / size: 1,653 copies,
6 3/4", 17 1/2 cm
Price: $75-125

RC-CM98
Year: 1909
Description / English: The Frigate Jylland. Commissioned by the society for preservation of the ship.
Inscription: JYLLAND.
Description / Danish: Fregatten Jylland. Indskrift: JYLLAND. Fremstillet som hjælp til skibets bevarelse.
Designed by: Christian Blache
Number of copies / size: 496 copies, 7 3/4", 20 cm
Price: $225-275

RC-CM99
Year: 1909
Description / English: The Frigate Jylland. Commissioned by the society for preservation of the ship.
Inscription: JYLLAND surrounded by anchor-chain and crowned shield.
Description / Danish: Fregatten Jylland. Ankerkædebort og kronet skilt med JYLLAND. Jfr. 98.
Designed by: Christian Blache
Number of copies / size: 18 copies, 11 3/4", 30 cm
Price: $5000-6000

RC-CM100
Year: 1909
Description / English: Crowned shield with the cross of St. Andrew and four roses. Commissioned by the Freemason lodge of St. Andrew in Aarhus founded in 1908.
Inscription: DE FIRE ROSERCARITATE DEI Tthe four roses – by charity of God).
Description / Danish: Frimurerlogen "De Fire Roser" i Aahus. Kronet skjold med Andreaskors og fire roser. Indskrift: DE FIRE ROSER – CARITATE DEI (Ved Guds Kærlighed). Udført til logen Skt. Andreas, stiftet 1908.
Designed by: Arnold Krog
Number of copies / size: 127 copies, 7 3/4", 20 cm
Price: $400-600

RC-CM101
Year: 1909
Description / English: Oval plate shaped as a crowned shield. Motif, inscription and commission as no 100.
Description / Danish: Frimurerlogen De fire Roser i Aarhus. Ovalt, kronet skjold med motiv og indskrift som 100.
Designed by: Arnold Krog
Number of copies / size: 28 copies, Height 15", 38 cm
Price: $4000-5000

RC-CM102
Year: 1909
Description / English: Statue of Liberty and Elsinore Castle. Commissioned by the American Exhibition in Aarhus.
Inscription: AMERIKA – DANMARK 1909.
Description / Danish: Amerikansk udstilling i Aarhus. Frihedsgudinden og Kronborg, indskrift: AMERIKA – DANMARK 1909.
Designed by: Arnold Krog
Number of copies / size: 396 copies, 7 3/4", 20 cm
Price: $220-260

RC-CM103
Year: 1909
Description / English: Copenhagen city arms and the year 1909. Initials I.M.C. (International Congress for Raw Material Testing).
Description / Danish: International Materialprøve kongres. Københavns byvåben med 1909 og initialer I.M.C.
Designed by: Arnold Krog
Number of copies / size: 25 copies, 7 3/4", 20 cm
Price: $2500-4000

RC-CM104
Year: 1909
Description / English: Commemorative plate for Princess Marie. Crowned laurel wreath with anchor and letter M. Same model as number 64
Description / Danish: Prinsesse Maries mindeplatte. Kronet krans (samme model som 64) hvori bogstavet M og et anker.
Designed by: Arnold Krog
Number of copies / size: 2,756 copies, 5 1/2", 14 cm
Price: $100-150

RC-CM105
Year: 1910
Description / English: See Royal Copenhagen Christmas Plate list. (see RC-1910)
No picture available

RC-CM106
Year: 1910
Description / English: Two Greenlanders.
Inscription: DANMARK EKSPEDITIONEN 1906-1908. HENDRIK – TOBIAS.
Description / Danish: Danmark Ekspeditionen. To grønlændere. Indskrift: DANMARK EKSPEDITIONEN 1906 – 1908. HENDRIK – TOBIAS.
Designed by: Harold Moltke
Number of copies / size: 5 copies, 12 1/4", 31 cm
Price: $4000-5000
No picture available

RC-CM109
Year: 1910
Description / English: Woman with boy carrying a sword, surrounded by border with lions and hearts, the initials D.K.F. and the year 1910. Commissioned by Danish Women Association for the Defense of Denmark, founded in 1907.
Description / Danish: Forsvarsplatte. Ung dreng med sværd foran siddende kvinde. På kanten løver og hjerter samt initialer D.K.F. 1910. Udført til Danske Kvinders Forsvarsforening (stiftet 1907).
Designed by: Christian Thomsen.
Number of copies / size: 2,423 copies, 6", 15 cm
Price: $70-100

RC-CM110
Year: 1910
Description / English: Aircraft over sailing ship in Copenhagen roads. Commissioned by the Aeronautical Society to commemorate the flight from Copenhagen to Malmo.
Inscription: ROBERT SVENDSEN KJØBENHAVN 17 JULI 1910 MALMØ.
Description / Danish: Robert Svendsens sundflyvning. Fly over sejlskib. Indskrift: ROBERT KJØBENHAVN 17 JULI 1910 MALMØ. Bestilt af Aeronautisk Selskab.
Designed by: Christian Thomsen
Number of copies / size: 251 copies, 7 3/4", 20 cm
Price: $260-400

RC-CM111
Year: 1911
Description / English: Small Christmas Plate. Snow covered landscape with a lake, trees and church: starlit sky.
Inscription: Jul 1911.
Description / Danish: Lille juleplatte. Landskab med sø og snedækket træ, i baggrunden en kirke; stjernehimmel. Indskrift: JUL 1911.
Designed by: Stephan Ussing
Number of copies / size: approx. 120 copies, 6", 15 1/2 cm
Price: $10,000-15,000

RC-CM112
Year: 1911
Description / English: See Royal Copenhagen Christmas Plate list

RC-CM113
Year: 1911
Description / English: The building belonging to the Association of Commercial Travelers, in a border of flowers. Below a Mercury staff.
Inscription: HANDELSREJSENDEFORENINGEN AF 1886. 1911 PAASKE LØRDAG (Easter Eve), the latter date and year indicating the opening of the building.
Description / Danish: Foreningen af Handelsrejsende. Foreningens bygning i blomsterkrans, f.n. merkurstav. Indskrift: HANDELSREJSENDEFORENINGEN AF 1886. 1911 PAASKE LØRDAG.
Designed by: Bent Helweg-Møller
Number of copies / size: 812 copies, 7 3/4", 20 cm
Price: $130-150

RC-CM114
Year: 1911
Description / English: Commemorative plate for Bishop Thomas Skat Rørdam with portrait in profile. Round the border ornamental motif and four medallions with the years 1832, 1909, the monogram T.S.R. and a cross.
Description / Danish: Mindeplatte for biskop Thomas Skat Rørdam. På kanten fire ansatser til korsarme; portræt i profil derom krans med medailloner hvori et kors, årstallene 1832 og 1909 samt monogram T.S.R.
Designed by: Bent Helweg-Møller
Number of copies / size: 205 copies, 7 3/4", 20 cm
Price: $300-400

RC-CM107
Year: 1910
Description / English: Mother nursing her child. Commissioned by the Grandduches of Hessen in Germany.
Inscription: WOHLFARSTSTELLER 1910 SAUGLINGS UND MUTTERFURSORGE. (Welfare plate, baby and mother care).
Description / Danish: Tysk barneplejeplatte. Diende barn. Indskrift: WOHLFARTSTELLER 1910 SAUGLINGS UND MUTTERFURSORGE. Udført på foranledning af Storhertuginden af Hessen.
Designed by: Christian Thomsen
Number of copies / size: 480 copies, 6 3/4", 17 1/2 cm
Price: $150-250

RC-CM108
Year: 1910
Description / English: West Indian landscape with woman and child. Commissioned by the West Indian Church and kindergarden fund under protection of the Queen.
Inscription: ALIOS JUVANDO IPSI GAUDEMUS (By helping others we make ourselves happy) and the year MCMX (1910). Above face to face monogram L (Queen Louise).
Description / Danish: Vestindisk platte. Kvinde og negerbarn i landskab med palmer. Indskrift: ALIOS JUVANDO IPSI GAUDEMUS (Ved at hjælpe andre glæder vi os selv) MCMX (1910). F.o. kronet spejlmonogram L (Dronning Louise). Udført til fordel for Dronningens Kirke – og Børnehjemssag.
Designed by: Christian Thomsen
Number of copies / size: 251 copies, 8", 20 1/2 cm
Price: $250-350

RC-CM115
Year: 1911
Description / English: Racing boats in the Sound. In the background the Middelgrund Fortress. Commissioned by the racing boat club in Copenhagen.
Description / Danish: Kaproningsplatte. I baggrunden Middelgrundsfortet. Udført for Roklubforeningen.
Designed by: Bent Helweg-Møller
Number of copies / size: 174 copies, 7 3/4", 20 cm
Price: $350-400

RC-CM116
Year: 1911
Description / English: The coronation of King George V and Queen Mary of Great Britain and Ireland. Crowned monogram GM and the year MCMXI (1911).
Description / Danish: Engelsk kroningsplatte. Kronet monogram GM (George V og Mary) MCMXI (1911).
Designed by: Arnold Krog
Number of copies / size: 1,936 copies,
6 3/4", 17 1/2 cm
Price: $90-140

RC-CM117
Year: 1911
Description / English: Crowned coach horn. Made on the occasion of the 200th anniversary (faithful and vigilant) of the Danish Postal service as a crown institution.
Inscription: TRO OG AGTSOM – MDCCXI (1711) – MCMXI (1911).
Description / Danish: Postplatte. Krone over posthorn. Indskrift: TRO OG AGTSOM – MDCCXI (1711) – MCMXI (1911). Udført i anledning af Det danske Postvæsens 200 års jubilæum som statsinstitution.
Designed by: Oluf Jensen
Number of copies / size: 492 copies, 6", 15 cm
Price: $150-200

RC-CM118
Year: 1911
Description / English: The granary of Carlsberg. Wide border formed by ears of corn. Carlsberg plate. Commissioned by brewer Carl Jacobsen on the occasion of the centenary of his father J.C. Jacobsen's birth September 2, 1811. All used as presents from Carl Jacobsen.
Inscription: GL. CARLSBERG (Old Carlsberg).
Description / Danish: Kornmagasinet på Carlsberg. Bred kant af aks. Indskrift: GL. CARLSBERG. Carlsberg – platter. Bestilt af brygger Carl Jacobsen i anledning af 100 – året for faderen J.C. Jacobsens fødsel den 2. september 1811. Fordelt som gaver fra Carl Jacobsen.
Designed by: Bent Helweg-Møller
Number of copies / size: 135 copies, 9 3/4", 25 cm
Price: $500-600

RC-CM119
Year: 1911
Description / English: The peristyle at Carlsberg. Commissioned by brewer Carl Jacobsen on the occasion of the centenary of his father J.C. Jacobsen's birth September 2, 1811. All used as presents from Carl Jacobsen.
Inscription: J.C. JACOBSEN. SØJLEGAARD PAA GL. CARLSBERG. Carlsberg plate.
Description / Danish: Søjlegården på Gl. Carlsberg. Indskrift: J.C. JACOBSEN, SØJLEGAARD PAA GL. CARLSBERG. Carlsberg – platter. Bestilt af brygger Carl Jacobsen i anledning af 100 – året for faderen J.C. Jacobsens fødsel den 2. september 1811. Fordelt som gaver fra Carl Jacobsen.
Designed by: Bent Helweg-Møller
Number of copies / size: 161 copies, 9 3/4", 25 cm
Price: $500-600

RC-CM120
Year: 1911
Description / English: The Carlsberg research laboratories. Carlsberg plate. Commissioned by brewer Carl Jacobsen on the occasion of the centenary of his father J.C. Jacobsen's birth September 2, 1811. All used as presents from Carl Jacobsen.
Inscription: CARLSBERG LABORATORIUM J.C. JACOBSEN 2 SEPTEMBER 1811-1911.
Description / Danish: Carlsberg Laboratorium. Indskrift: CARLSBERG LABORATORIUM J.C. JACOBSEN 2 SEPTEMBER 1811 – 1911. Carlsberg – platter. Bestilt af brygger Carl Jacobsen i anledning af 100 – året for faderen J.C. Jacobsens fødsel den 2. september 1811. Fordelt som gaver fra Carl Jacobsen.
Designed by: Bent Helweg-Møller
Number of copies / size: 200 copies, 9 3/4", 25 cm
Price: $500-600

RC-CM121
Year: 1911
Description / English: The Neptune fountain outside Frederiksborg castle in Hillerød. Brewer J.C. Jacobsen donated the fountain. Carlsberg plate. Commissioned by brewer Carl Jacobsen on the occasion of the centenary of his father J.C. Jacobsen's birth September 2, 1811. All used as presents from Carl Jacobsen.
Description / Danish: Neptunbrønden på Frederiksborg. Springvandet bekostet af brygger Jacobsen. Carlsberg – platter. Bestilt af brygger Carl Jacobsen i anledning af 100 – året for faderen J.C. Jacobsens fødsel den 2. september 1811. Fordelt som gaver fra Carl Jacobsen.
Designed by: Bent Helweg-Møller
Number of copies / size: 158 copies, 9 3/4", 25 cm
Price: $500-600

RC-CM122
Year: 1911
Description / English: The Palmhouse in the Botanical Gardens in Copenhagen. The palmhouse was designed and donated by J.C. Jacobsne. Carlsberg plate. Commissioned by brewer Carl Jacobsen on the occasion of the centenary of his father J.C. Jacobsen's birth September 2, 1811. All used as presents from Carl Jacobsen.
Inscription: 2 SEPTEMB 1811-1911 and face-to-face monogram JCJ.
Description / Danish: Palmehuset i Botanisk Have i København. Tegnet og bekostet af J.C. Jacobsen. Indskrift: 2 SEPTEMB. 1811 – 1911 og spejlmonogram J.C.J. Carlsberg – platter. Bestilt af brygger Carl Jacobsen i anledning af 100 – året for faderen J.C. Jacobsens fødsel den 2. september 1811. Fordelt som gaver fra Carl Jacobsen.
Designed by: Bent Helweg-Møller
Number of copies / size: 137 copies, 9 3/4", 25 cm
Price: $500-600

RC-CM123
Year: 1911
Description / English: Frederiksborg Castle. J.C. Jacobsen financed the restoration of the castle after a fire in 1859 and conversion into a museum for Danish national history. Carlsberg plate. Commissioned by brewer Carl Jacobsen on the occasion of the centenary of his father J.C. Jacobsen's birth September 2, 1811. All used as presents from Carl Jacobsen.
Description / Danish: Frederiksborg Slot. Genopførelsen efter branden 1859 og indrettelsen af det nationalhistoriske museum bekostet af J.C. Jacobsen. Carlsberg – platter. Bestilt af brygger Carl Jacobsen i anledning af 100 – året for faderen J.C. Jacobsens fødsel den 2. september 1811. Fordelt som gaver fra Carl Jacobsen.
Designed by: Bent Helweg-Møller
Number of copies / size: 194 copies, 9 3/4", 25 cm
Price: $500-600

RC-CM124
Year: 1911
Description / English: The Royal Danish Society of Sciences and Letters, Copenhagen. The Carlsberg Foundation donated the building. Carlsberg plate. Commissioned by brewer Carl Jacobsen on the occasion of the centenary of his father J.C. Jacobsen's birth September 2, 1811. All used as presents from Carl Jacobsen.
Inscription: 1811-1911 and face-to-face monogram LCJ.
Description / Danish: Det Kongelige Danske Videnskabernes Selskab. Bygningen på Dantes Plads, bekostet af Carlsbergfondet. Indskrift: 1811 – 1911. Carlsberg – platter. Bestilt af brygger Carl Jacobsen i anledning af 100 – året for faderen J.C. Jacobsens fødsel den 2. september 1811. Fordelt som gaver fra Carl Jacobsen.
Designed by: Bent Helweg-Møller
Number of copies / size: 125 copies, 9 3/4", 25 cm
Price: $500-600

RC-CM125
Year: 1911
Description / English: The castle ruin Lindos on the island of Rhodos. Excavations by Christian Blinkenberg, the archeologist, 1902-05. Financed by the Carlsberg Foundation. Carlsberg plate. Commissioned by brewer Carl Jacobsen on the occasion of the centenary of his father J.C. Jacobsen's birth September 2, 1811. All used as presents from Carl Jacobsen.
Description / Danish: Borgen Lindos på Rhodos. Christian Blinkenbergs udgravninger 1902 – 05 bekostet af Carlsbergfondet. Carlsberg – platter. Bestilt af brygger Carl Jacobsen i anledning af 100 – året for faderen J.C. Jacobsens fødsel den 2. september 1811. Fordelt som gaver fra Carl Jacobsen.
Designed by: Bent Helweg-Møller
Number of copies / size: 143 copies, 9 3/4", 25 cm
Price: $500-600

RC-CM126
Year: 1911
Description / English: Face to face monogram L.C.J. Carlsberg plate. Commissioned by brewer Carl Jacobsen on the occasion of the centenary of his father J.C. Jacobsen's birth September 2, 1811. All used as presents from Carl Jacobsen.
Inscription: CARLSBERG 2DEN SEPTR. 1811-1911 in border of hop-leaves.
Description / Danish: Humlekrans i relief omkring spejlmonogram J.C.J. og indskrift: CARLSBERG 2DEN SEPTR. 1811 – 1911. Carlsberg – platter. Bestilt af brygger Carl Jacobsen i anledning af 100 – året for faderen J.C. Jacobsens fødsel den 2. september 1811. Fordelt som gaver fra Carl Jacobsen.
Designed by: Bent Helweg-Møller
Number of copies / size: 575 copies, 4", 10.5 cm
Price: $160-220

RC-CM126A (Large)
Year: 1911
Description / English: Face to face monogram L.C.J. Carlsberg plate. Commissioned by brewer Carl Jacobsen on the occasion of the centenary of his father J.C. Jacobsen's birth September 2, 1811. All used as presents from Carl Jacobsen.
Inscription: CARLSBERG 2DEN SEPTR. 1811-1911 in border of hop-leaves.
Description / Danish: Humlekrans i relief omkring spejlmonogram J.C.J. og indskrift: CARLSBERG 2DEN SEPTR. 1811 – 1911. Carlsberg – platter. Bestilt af brygger Carl Jacobsen i anledning af 100 – året for faderen J.C. Jacobsens fødsel den 2. september 1811. Fordelt som gaver fra Carl Jacobsen.
Designed by: Bent Helweg-Møller
Number of copies / size: 156 copies, 10 1/4", 26 cm
Price: $800-1000
See RC-CM126

RC-CM127
Year: 1911
Description / English: Danish Viking ship. Made to commemorate the 1000th anniversary for the Danish Viking Rollo's conquest of Normandy 911.
Inscription: DANMARK ROUEN MCMXI (1911).
Description / Danish: Rouen – platte. Dansk vikingeskib. Indskrift: DANMARK ROUEN MCMXI. Udført i 1000 året for Rollos togt til Normandiet 911.
Designed by: Arnold Krog
Number of copies / size: 131 copies, 6", 17 1/2 cm
Price: $350-500

RC-CM128
Year: 1912
Description / English: Viking sounding a lure. Commissioned by the Copenhagen Rifle Corps
Inscription: VÆR ØVET TIL DAAD NAAR LUREN KALDER (be prepared to fight when the lure is sounded) 1862-1912 and K.S. (The Copenhagen Rifle Corps).
Description / Danish: Skytteplatte. Lurblæser og indskrift: VÆR ØVER TIL DAAD NAAR LUREN KALDER 1862 – 1912 K.S. Udført til Københavns Skytteforening.
Designed by: Bent Helweg-Møller
Number of copies / size: 375 copies, 7 3/4", 20 cm
Price: $200-300

RC-CM129
Year: 1912
Description / English: See Royal Copenhagen Christmas Plate list

RC-CM130
Year: 1912
Description / English: Old couple sitting in a garden. Commissioned on occasion of the 50th anniversary of the old people's home "Alderstrøst," belonging to the Artisan's Association.
Inscription: HAANDVÆRKERFORENINGENS STIFTELSE ALDERSTRØST 1862-1912.
Description / Danish: Alderstrøst. Ældre par på havebænk. Indskrift: HAANDVÆRKERFORENINGENS STIFTELSE ALDERSTRØST 1862 – 1912. Udført til stiftelsens 50 års jubilæum.
Designed by: Christian Thomsen
Number of copies / size: 399 copies, 7 3/4", 20 cm
Price: $200-300

RC-CM131
Year: 1912
Description / English: Saint Canute's Cathedral in Odense. In the foreground three swans on a lake. Below, crowned monogram L (Queen Louise). Commissioned by the Odense-branch of the Queen Louise Association.
Description / Danish: Skt. Knuds kirke i Odense. Tre svaner på sø i forgrunden, bagved kirken set fra øst. F.n. i skjold et kronet spejlmonogram L (Louise). Bestilt af Louise foreningens Odense filian.
Designed by: Christian Thomsen
Number of copies / size: 490 copies, 6 3/4", 17 1/2 cm
Price: $150-200

RC-CM132
Year: 1912
Description / English: The Castle of Kalmar (Sweden).
Description / Danish: Kalmar – platte. Kalmar Slot.
Designed by: Oluf Jensen
Number of copies / size: 125 copies, 7 3/4", 20 cm
Price: $350-450

RC-CM133
Year: 1912
Description / English: Scene from the beach at The Skaw. In the foreground a rowing boat.
Inscription: SKAGEN (the Skaw).
Description / Danish: Skagen – platte. Motiv fra stranden med båd betegnet SKAGEN
Designed by: Arnold Krog
Number of copies / size: 139 copies, 7 3/4", 20 cm
Price: $350-450

RC-CM134
Year: 1912
Description / English: Viking ship with three-fork masthead, three wavy lines, and fish and shields with the Danish, Norwegian, and Swedish arms.
Inscription: FISKERI OG MOTORUDSTILLING (Exhibition for Fishery and Ship's Engines) KØBENHAVN 1912.
Description / Danish: Fiskeriudstilling i København. Vikingeskib med treforket mast over stiliserede bølger og tre skjolde med det danske, norske og svenske våben. Indskrift: FISKERI OG MOTORUDSTILLING KØBENHAVN 1912.
Designed by: Bent Helweg-Møller
Number of copies / size: 291 copies, 6", 15 cm
Price: $200-300

RC-CM136
Year: 1912
Description / English: Young Viking receiving sword from a woman.
Inscription: D.K.F. 1912 (Danish Women's Association for the Defence of Denmark). Cf. no. 109.
Description / Danish: Forsvarsplatte. Ung viking modtager et sværd af en kvinde. Indskrift: D.K.F. 1912. Bestilt af Danske Kvinders Forsvarsforening, jfr. kat. 109.
Designed by: Christian Thomsen
Number of copies / size: 1,677 copies, 6", 15 cm
Price: $70-100

RC-CM135
Year: 1912
Description / English: Royal Danish hussar in landscape. Round the edge a garland with two cartridepouches carrying crowned monograms F5 and F VIII (King Frederik V and King Frederik VIII). Commissioned by the Royal Hussar Regiment on occasion of its 150th anniversary.
Inscription: GARDEHUSARREGIMENTET 1762-1912.
Description / Danish: Gardehusar – platte. Udført til regimentets 150 års jubilæum. Patrontasker med F5 og FVIII (Frederik 5. og Frederik 8). Indskrift: GARDEHUSAR REGIMENTET 1762 – 1912.
Designed by: Arnold Krog
Number of copies / size: 359 copies, 9 1/2", 24 cm
Price: $300-400

RC-CM137
Year: 1912
Description / English: Crowned coronation plate made on occasion of the ascension to the throne of King Christian X and Queen Alexandrine. Face to face monogram CXA and the year 1912.
Description / Danish: Tronbestigelsen. Platte med krone og perlestaf samt spejlmonogram CXA (Christian X og Alexandrine) 1912.
Designed by: Arnold Krog
Number of copies / size: 2,179 copies, 9", 23 cm
Price: $80-150

RC-CM138
Year: 1912
Description / English: Crowned commemorative plate for King Frederik VIII. Laurel wreath in the center face to face monogram F8 and the year MCMXII (1912).
Description / Danish: Frederk VIII.s mindeplatte. Kronet krans med spejlmonogram F8 MCMXII (1912).
Designed by: Arnold Krog
Number of copies / size: 1,975 copies,
5 1/2", 14 cm
Price: $80-100

RC-CM139
Year: 1912
Description / English: Native with cart walking on a road lined with palm trees. Commissioned by charities in the Danish Virgin Islands.
Description / Danish: Vestingdisk platte. Slave med kærre i palmealle.
Designed by: Christian Thomsen
Number of copies / size: 424 copies, 6", 15 cm
Price: $175-250

RC-CM140
Year: 1912
Description / English: Peasant in his cart drawn by team of oxen on a Jutland moor. Below the town hall of Herning. Commissioned by the town council in Herning on occasion of the granting of municipal charter in 1912.
Inscription: HERNING 1882-1912.
Description / Danish: Herning – platte. Studevogn på hedevej. F.n. Herning rådhus i krans samt indskrift: HERNING 1882 – 1912. Fremstillet i anledning af byens købstadsrettigheder, som den fik i 1912.
Designed by: Oluf Jensen.
Number of copies / size: 285 copies, 7 3/4", 20 cm
Price: $200-250

RC-CM141
Year: 1913
Description / English: See Royal Copenhagen Christmas Plate list
No picture available

RC-CM142
Year: 1913
Description / English: Landscape with trees and a Danish Fjord. Commissioned by the Danish Tourist Association on occasion of its 25th anniversary.
Inscription: 1888 DTF (Danish Tourist association) 1913 and DER ER ET YNDIGT LAND (There is a Lovely Country), the first line of one of the Danish national songs.
Description / Danish: Danmarks Turistforening. Landskab med træer og vand. På en sten indhugget 1888 D.T.F. 1913. F.n. indskrift: DER ER ET YNDIGT LAND. Fremstillet i anledning af foreningens 25 års jubilæum.
Designed by: Oluf Jensen
Number of copies / size: 573 copies, 6 3/4", 17 1/2 cm
Price: $150-200

RC-CM143
Year: 1913
Description / English: The west front of the cathedral (The Church of Our Lady) in Copenhagen. Commissioned by the Danish Tourist Association.
Description / Danish: Vor Frue kirke i København. Vestfacaden. Bestilt af Turistforeningen.
Designed by: Bent Helweg-Møller
Number of copies / size: 163 copies, 11", 28 cm
Price: $360-500

RC-CM144
Year: 1913
Description / English: Landscape with farm. Commissioned By the Danish committee of the exhibition in San Francisco, cf. no. 155 and 157.
Inscription: TIL DANMARKS RÆ SAN FRANCISCO CAL. 1915 (To the Honor of Denmark).
Description / Danish: San Francisco – platte. Landskab med gård. I forgrunden en græssende ko. Indskrift: TIL DANMARKS RÆ SAN FRANCISCO CAL. 1915 (jfr. kat. 155 og 157).
Designed by: Arnold Krog
Number of copies / size: 1,197 copies, 6 3/4", 17 1/2 cm
Price: $125-150

RC-CM145
Year: 1913
Description / English: Imagined scene on "Tivoli" - the founder Georg Carstensen and the goddess Fortuna driving on the big dipper. Commissioned on occasion of the garden's 70th anniversary.
Inscription: TIVOLIS STIFTER GEORG CARSTENSEN 1843-1913.
Description / Danish: Tivoliplatte. Georg Carstensen og Fortuna i rutschebanen. Indskrift: TIVOLIS STIFTER GEORG CARSTENSEN 1843 – 1913. Udført i anledning af Tivolis 70 års jubilæum.
Designed by: Christian Thomsen
Number of copies / size: 626 copies, 6 3/4", 17 1/2 cm
Price: $120-200

RC-CM146
Year: 1913
Description / English: Exhibition hall in Landskrona (Sweden). Round the border 3 crowns and 2 horns of plenty. Made on occasion of the exhibition to commemorate Landskrona's 500th anniversary.
Inscription: LANDSKRONA 1413-1913.
Description / Danish: Landskrona – platte. Udstillingsbygning, på kanten tre kroner og fyldhorn. Indskrift: LANDSKRONA 1413 – 1913 samt tre bølgelinier. Udført til udstillingen i anledning af byens 500 års jubilæum.
Designed by: Bent Helweg-Møller
Number of copies / size: 120 copies, 7 3/4", 20 cm
Price: $400-600

RC-CM147
Year: 1914
Description / English: See Royal Copenhagen Christmas Plate list
No picture available

RC-CM148
Year: 1914
Description / English: The mill of Dybbøl with a laurel wreath border. Made on occasion of the 50th anniversary of the battle at Dybbøl.
Inscription: 1864-1914 C IX and C X (the Kings Christian IX and Christian X).
Description / Danish: Veteranplatte. Dybbøl Mølle. Bladkrans i relief. Indskrift: 1864 – 1914 C IX og C X med krone. Fremstillet i anledning af 50 året for Dybbølslaget.
Designed by: Arnold Krog
Number of copies / size: 2,814 copies, 7 3/4", 19.5 cm
Price: $75-125

RC-CM149
Year: 1914
Description / English: Exhibition halls in Malmo (Sweden) and the city arms of the town.
Inscription: DEN BALTISKE UDSTILLING (The Baltic Exhibition) 1914.
Description / Danish: Baltisk Udstilling i Malmø. Perspektiv med udstillingsbygninger. F.n. Malmø byvåben. Indskrift: DEN BALTISKE UDSTILLING 1914.
Designed by: Bent Helweg-Møller
Number of copies / size: 265 copies, 7 1/2", 18 1/2 cm
Price: $250-400

RC-CM150
Year: 1914
Description / English: The naval battle of Helgoland (Denmark v. Germany). Commissioned by the Navy Clubs on occasion of the 50th anniversary of the victory at Helgoland.
Inscription: 1864 HELGOLAND 1914 9. Maj.
Description / Danish: Helgoland – platte. Linieskib i kamp. Indskrift: HELGOLAND 1864 MAJ 1914. Bestilt af Marineforeningen i anledning af 50 årsdagen for Soslaget.
Designed by: Christian Benjamin-Olsen
Number of copies / size: 1,761 copies, 7 3/4", 19.5 cm
Price: $100-140

RC-CM151
Year: 1914
Description / English: Scene from Frankfurt am Main (Germany). Bridge over the river Main. Commissioned by the firm Nic. Franz's Nachfolger in F.a.M.
Description / Danish: Frankfurt a.M. Motiv med bro over floden. Udført for firmaet Nic. Franzs Nachfolger i F.a.M.
Designed by: Oluf Jensen
Number of copies / size: 1,017 copies, 6 3/4", 17 1/2 cm
Price: $500-700

RC-CM154
Year: 1914
Description / English: Silhouette of Queen Alexandra of Great Britain and Ireland. Made on occasion of the Queen's 70th birthday. Silhouette by Else Hasselriis.
Inscription: 1844 ALEXANDRA 1914.
Description / Danish: Dronning Alexandra. Silhouet og indskrift: 1844 ALEXANDRA 1914. Udført i anledning af dronningens 70-års fødselsdag. Silhouet af Else Hasselriis.
Designed by: Arnold Krog
Number of copies / size: 929 copies, 7 3/4", 20 cm
Price: $150-200

RC-CM152
Year: 1915
Description / English: See Royal Copenhagen Christmas Plate list
No picture available

RC-CM153
Year: 1914
Description / English: Crowned face-to-face monogram A (Queen Alexandrine). Commissioned by the charity "Dronningens Juleindsamling" (The Queen's Christmas fund).
Inscription: HVER ER SIN GAVE LIG VÆRE SIG FATTIG ELLER RIG (A gift is appreciated equally whether it comes from rich or poor).
Description / Danish: Alexandrine – platte. Kronet spejlmonogram A (Alexandrine). Insdkrift: HVER ER SIN GAVE LIG VÆRE SIG FATTIG ELLER RIG. Udført til Centralforeningen Dronningens Juleindsamling.
Designed by: Arnold Krog
Number of copies / size: 599 copies, 7 1/2", 19 cm
Price: $150-250

RC-CM155
Year: 1914
Description / English: Crowned mark of the Royal Copenhagen Porcelain Factory, the year 1915 and inscription SAN FRANCISCO. Made on occasion of the factory's participation in the world exhibition.
Description / Danish: San Francisco. Den kgl. Porcelainsfabriks deltagelse i verdensudstillingen. Indskrift: SAN FRANCISCO 1915.
Designed by: Arnold Krog
Number of copies / size: 557 copies, 7", 18 cm
Price: $200-300

RC-CM156
Year: 1914
Description / English: The building in Copenhagen belonging to the insurance company Haand i Haand. Commissioned for the company's 25th anniversary.
Inscription: HAAND I HAAND 1890-1915.
Description / Danish: Forsikringsselskabet Haand i Haands bygning i København. Indskrift: HAAND I HAAND 1890 – 1915. Bestilt til selskabets 25-års jubilæum.
Designed by: Oluf Jensen
Number of copies / size: 421 copies, 7", 18 cm
Price: $175-225

RC-CM157
Year: 1915
Description / English: The arms of California. Made on occasion of the world exhibition.
Description / Danish: Verdensudstillingen i San Francisco.
Inscription: STATE OF CALIFORNIA – SAN FRANCISCO 1915.
Staten Californias segl med indskrift: STATE OF CALIFORNIA – SAN FRANCISCO 1915.
Designed by: Gotfred Rode.
Number of copies / size: 179 copies, 9 3/4", 25 cm
Price: $900-1400

RC-CM158
Year: 1915
Description / English: Triangular plate with the silhouettes of the Kings of Denmark, Norway and Sweden and the arms of each country. Made on occasion of the meeting of the three Scandinavian Kings in Malmo (Sweden). Silhouettes by Else Hasselriis.
Inscription: MALMO DEC. MCMXIV (1914) REGIS AD EXEMPLAR (example for a king).
Description / Danish: Kongemødet i Malmø. Trekantet platte med silhouetter af Gustaf V, Haakon VII og Chistian X, det danske, norske og svenske våben samt indskrift: MALMØ DEC. MCMXIV (1914) REGIS AD EXEMPLAR (En konge till monster). Silhouetter af Else Hasselriis.
Designed by: Arnold Krog
Number of copies / size: 3,610 copies, 7 3/4", 20 cm
Price: $100-150

RC-CM159
Year: 1915
Description / English: Saint George and the dragon. Inscription: BELLUM (war). Made for charity during the way.
Description / Danish: Krigsplatte. Skt. Georg og dragen. Indskrift: BELLUM (krig).
Designed by: Louis Moe
Number of copies / size: 2,123 copies, 8 1/2", 22cm
Price: $125-150

RC-CM160
Year: 1915
Description / English: Child garlanding a lamb with flowers. Made for charity during the war.
Inscription: PAX (Peace).
Description / Danish: Fredsplatte. Barn bekranser et lam. Indskrift: PAX (fred).
Designed by: Louis Moe
Number of copies / size: 8 1/2", 22 cm
Price: $150-250

RC-CM161
Year: 1916
Description / English: See Royal Copenhagen Christmas Plate list
No picture available

RC-CM162
Year: 1916
Description / English: The entrance to Frederiksberg Castle. Danish arms and oak leaves. Commissioned by the academy on occasion of its 100th anniversary.
Inscription: 1816 ELEVSKOLEN 1916 (The Army Cadet Academy).
Description / Danish: Hærens elevskoles platte. Indgangen til Frederiksberg slot. Indskrift: 1816 ELEVSKOLEN 1916. F.n. rigsvåben med egeløv. Fremstillet til skolens 100-års jubilæum.
Designed by: Oluf Jensen
Number of copies / size: 683 copies, 6 3/4", 17 cm
Price: $120-200

RC-CM163
Year: 1916
Description / English: The hydro at Wiesbaden (Germany). Commissioned by the firm W. Weitz Wiesbaden.
Inscription: AQUIS MATTIACIS (The Roman name for the hydro (Plinius)).
Description / Danish: Wiesbadenplatte. Kurhuset med indskrift over søjlefronten AQUIS MATTIACIS. Udført på bestilling for firmaet W. Weitz i Wiesbaden.
Designed by: Oluf Jensen
Number of copies / size: 6 3/4", 17 cm
Price: $1500-2500
No picture available

RC-CM164
Year: 1916
Description / English: Danish landscape with flag and corn sheaf. Round the border lions and hearts (From the Danish Coat of Arms). Commissioned by the Danmark-Samfundet (The Denmark Association).
Inscription: DANMARK OG DANMARKS ÆRE (Denmark and the honor of Denmark).
Description / Danish: Danmarksamfundet. Landskab med splitflag i neg og indskrift: DANMARK OG DANMARKS ÆRE. F.n. løver og hjerter. Udført på bestilling af Danmark – Samfundet, hvem overskuddet tilfaldt.
Designed by: Arnold Krog
Number of copies / size: 1,044 copies, 8", 20 1/2 cm
Price: $120-180

RC-CM165
Year: 1916
Description / English: The Good Samaritan. The symbol of the Odd Fellows. Commissioned by the Independent Order of Odd Fellows.
Inscription: I DECEMBER 1881-1916
Description / Danish: Odd Fellow – platte. Den barmhjertige Samaritan. Indskrift: I DECEMBER 1881 – 1916 samt ringsymbolet.
Designed by: Christian Thomsen
Number of copies / size: 890 copies, 7 3/4", 20 cm
Price: $135-200

RC-CM166
Year: 1917
Description / English: See Royal Copenhagen Christmas Plate list
No picture available

RC-CM167
Year: 1917
Description / English: Nurse with a tray. Commissioned by the Red Cross Society in Denmark.
Inscription: INTER ARMA SILENT MUSAE LOQUITUR CARITAS (In the war, the Muses are silent but charity speaks).
Description / Danish: Røde Kors. Stående sygeplejerske med bakke. Indskrift: INTER ARMA SILENT MUSAE LOQUITUR CARITAS (I krig tier muserne, barmhjertigheden taler).
Designed by: Christian Thomsen
Number of copies / size: 360 copies, 7 1/2", 19 cm
Price: $350-450

RC-CM168
Year: 1917
Description / English: Two men greeting each other. Commissioned by the Independent Order of Odd Fellows.
Inscription: 16 April 1887-1917.
Description / Danish: Odd Fellow – platte. To mænd mødes. Indskrift: 26 APRIL 1887 – 1917. Symboler med tre ringe.
Designed by: Christian Thomsen
Number of copies / size: 587 copies, 8", 20 1/2 cm
Price: $140-200

RC-CM169
Year: 1917
Description / English: Landscape with a road. Commissioned by the association.
Inscription: FORENINGEN AF HANDELSREJSENDE FOR ØS.L.D. (The Association of Commercial Travelers on Zealand) 1907 27 MARTS 1917.
Description / Danish: Handelsrejsende – platte. Landskab med vej. Indskrift: FORENINGEN AF HANDELSREJSENDE FOR ØS.L.D. 1907 27 MARTS 1917.
Designed by: Oluf Jensen
Number of copies / size: 174 copies, 6 3/4", 17 1/2 cm
Price: $250-300

RC-CM170
Year: 1917
Description / English: The actor Olaf Poulsen. Commissioned by the Association of Actors.
Inscription: 1867 OLAF POULSEN 1917.
Description / Danish: Olaf Pouseln – platte. Skuespilleren Olaf Poulsen i kostume. Indskrift: 1867 OLAF POULSEN 1917. Udført tl fordel for Skuespillerforeningen.
Designed by: Christian Thomsen
Number of copies / size: 765 copies, 9", 23 cm
Price: $150-200

RC-CM171
Year: 1917
Description / English: The fortress Trekroner. Commissioned by the Coast – Artillery Association.
Inscription: I. ARTBATL. KYSTARTRGMT. (1st Artillery Battalion of the Coast Defense Regiment) 1867-1917.
Description / Danish: Kystartilleri – platte. Fortet Trekroner. Indskrift: I. ARTBATL. KYSTARTRGMT (1ste Artilleribataillon, Kystartilleriregimentet) 1867 – 1917. Bestilt af K.A.F. (Kystartilleriforeningen).
Designed by: Christian Benjamin-Olsen
Number of copies / size: 511 copies, 8", 20 1/2 cm
Price: $175-225

RC-CM172
Year: 1917
Description / English: The 70th birthday of the dowager empress Dagmar of Russia. Crowned plate with roses. Silhouette by Else Hasselriis
Inscription: 1847 - DAGMAR - 1917.
Description / Danish: Kejserinde Dagmar 70-år. Ramme med krone og rose samt indskrift: 1847 – DAGMAR – 1917. Silhouette af Else Hasselriis.
Designed by: Christian Thomsen
Number of copies / size: 2,359 copies, 5 1/2", 14 cm
Price: $90-130

RC-CM173
Year: 1918
Description / English: Scene from Esbjerg harbor. Commissioned on occasion of the 50th anniversary of the city.
Inscription: ESBJERG 1868-1918.
Description / Danish: Esbjerg – platte. Motiv fra Esbjerg havn. Indskrift: ESBJERG 1868 – 1918. F.n. byvåben.
Designed by: Oluf Jensen
Number of copies / size: 417 copies, 8", 20 1/2 cm
Price: $175-225

RC-CM174
Year: 1918
Description / English: See Royal Copenhagen Christmas Plate list
No picture available

RC-CM175
Year: 1918
Description / English: Woman with two children. Commissioned on occasion of the 40th anniversary of the first lodge in Denmark of the Independent Order of Odd Fellows.
Inscription: DANMARK 1878-30 JUNI-1918
Description / Danish: Odd Fellow – platte. Kvinde med to børn. Indskrift: DANMARK 1878 – 30 JUNI – 1918. Fremstillet i anledning af 40-årsdagen for oprettelsen af den første loge i Danmark.
Designed by: Christian Thomsen
Number of copies / size: 1,570 copies, 8", 20 1/2 cm
Price: $75-125

RC-CM176
Year: 1918
Description / English: Elsinore Castle with man-of-war in the foreground. Commissioned by the museum, which was founded in 1914 and opened in 1915.
Inscription: HANDELS OG SØFARTS MUSEET PAA KRONBORG (The Mercantile Navy Museum of Kronborg). Commissioned by the museum, which was founded in 1914 and opened in 1915.
Description / Danish: Orlogsskib ved Kronborg. Indskrift: HANDELS OG SFARTS MUSEET PAA KRONGBORG. (Museet stiftet 1914 og indviet 1915).
Designed by: Christian Benjamin-Olsen
Number of copies / size: 1,435 copies, 8 1/4", 21 cm
Price: $125-160

RC-CM177
Year: 1918
Description / English: The powder magazine in Frederikshavn. Commissioned on occasion of the 100th anniversary of the granting of municipal charter of the town.
Inscription: 1818-FREDERIKSHAVN-1918.
Description / Danish: Frederikshavn – platte. Krudttårnet. Indskrift: 1818 – FREDERIKSHAVN – 1918. Fremstillet til byens 100-års jubilæum som købstad.
Designed by: Oluf Jensen
Number of copies / size: 7 3/4", 20 cm
Price: $150-200

RC-CM178
Year: 1918
Description / English: Large christmas plate. Motif: Shepherds in the Field.
Description / Danish: Hyrder på mark julenat. To stående rygfigurer.
Designed by: Gotfred Rode
Number of copies / size: 49 copies, 11 3/4", 30 cm
Price: $5000-7000

RC-CM179
Year: 1918
Description / English: Memorial plate for 100th Anniversary of the birth of King Christian IX. Crowned plate with leaf border monogram C IX
Inscription: MED GUD FOR ÆRE OG RET (With God for Honor and Right) 8DE APRIL 1818-1918
Description / Danish: Mindeplatte i hundredåret for Christian IX.s fødsel. Krans med krone og bladværk. Indskrift: MED GUD FOR ÆRE OG RET C IX 8DE APRIL 1818 – 1918.
Designed by: Christian Thomsen
Number of copies / size: 3,063 copies, 6 3/4", 17 1/2 cm
Price: $75-125

RC-CM180
Year: 1918
Description / English: Beer jug.
Inscription: KORPORATIONEN AF BEVÆRTERE I KØBENHAVN OG OMEGN 1818-1918 (The Corporation of Publicans in Copenhagen and surroundings).
Description / Danish: Beværter – platte. Fajancekande og indskrift: KORPORATIONEN AF BEV ÆRTERE 1818 – 1918 I KØBENHAVN OG OMEGN.
Designed by: Ellinor Selchau
Number of copies / size: 600 copies, 10", 25 1/2 cm
Price: $150-200

RC-CM181
Year: 1918
Description / English: Old building on the Frederiksholms Kanal in Copenhagen housing the Army Supply Corps. Commissioned by The Supply Officers' Association.
Inscription: FORPLEJNINGSKORPSET I OCTOBER 1868 - 1918 (The Army Supply Corps)
Description / Danish: Forplejningskorpsets bygning ved Frederiksholms Kanal. Indskrift: FORPLEJNINGSKORPSET I OKTOBER 1868 – 1918. Bestilt af Intendanturforeningen.
Designed by: Oluf Jensen
Number of copies / size: 603 copies, 6 3/4", 17 1/2 cm
Price: $150-200

RC-CM182
Year: 1918
Description / English: Moses being rescued from the Nile by Pharaoh's daughter. Commissioned by the Independent Order of Odd Fellows for the charitable institution the Rebecca-sisters' Home for Foundlings.
Inscription: DOMINO NON NOSTRIS VIRIBUS FRETI (Let us trust in God not in our own strength)
Description / Danish: Odd Fellow – platte. Moses bjerges på Nilen. Indskrift: DOMINO NON NOSTRIS VIRIBUS FRETI (Stolende på Herren, ikke på vore kræfter). F.n. ringsymbolet. Udført til fordel for Rebekkasføstrenes hittebørnshjem.
Designed by: Christian Thomsen
Number of copies / size: 1,325 copies, 9", 23 cm
Price: $100-150

RC-CM183
Year: 1918
Description / English: The Danish Flag falling from heaven at the battle of Reval in 1219. 700th Anniversary of the flag.
Description / Danish: Valdemars – platte. Dannebrog falder ned fra himlen under slaget ved Reval. Indskrift: 1219 – 15 JUNI – 1919. Fremstillet i anledning af 700-årsdagen for flagets modtagelse.
Designed by: Christian Thomsen
Number of copies / size: 32823 copies,
7 1/4", 19 cm
Price: $100-150

RC-CM184
Year: 1918
Description / English: The cathedral in Roskilde with fountain in the foreground.
Inscription: KONG HROAR 1893-19 NOVEMBER-1918. Commissioned by the Independent Order of Odd Fellows for the Roskilde lodge King Hroar on occasion of its 25th anniversary.
Description / Danish: Odd Fellow – platte. Logen Kong Hroar i Roskildes 25-års jubilæum. Indskrift: KONG HROAR 1893 – 19 NOVEMBER – 1918.
Designed by: Christian Thomsen
Number of copies / size: 352 copies, 7 3/4", 20 cm
Price: $150-200

RC-CM185
Year: 1919
Description / English: Thyra Danebod, Queen of Denmark, in the 10th century. Made on occasion of the reunification with the northern part of Slesvig.
Inscription: LEDET ER I LAVE (The fence is resotred) 1919 – meaning the border to Germany.
Description / Danish: Sønderjyllandsplatte. Thyra Danebod. Indskrift: LEDET ER I LAVE 1919. Fremstillet i anledning af genforeningen.
Designed by: Christian Thomsen
Number of copies / size: 4,411 copies, 9 3/4", 25 cm
Price: $100-150

RC-CM186
Year: 1919
Description / English: Mother and child looking at sunrise. So called peace-plate.
Inscription: FOR ANDEN GANG JORD AF HAVET GRØN OG HERLIG SER OPSTIGE - VØLVENS SPAADOM (For the second time the earth emerges from the sea green and wonderful - the Voluspa) from the Elder Edda.
Description / Danish: Fredsplтte. Mor og søn ser mod opgående sol. Indskrift: FOR ANDEN GANG JORD AF HAVET GRØN OG HERLIG SER OPSTIGE – VØLVENS SPAADOM (Fra en ældre Edda).
Designed by: Gotfred Rode
Number of copies / size: 3,488 copies, 8 3/4", 22 1/2 cm
Price: $100-120

RC-CM187
Year: 1919
Description / English: See Royal Copenhagen Christmas Plate list

RC-CM188
Year: 1919
Description / English: Landscape with Danish flag. Made on occasion of the reunification with Northern Slesvig
Inscription: GIV TID OG HVAD DU DRØMTE SKØNT DU SKAL I SANDHED SKUE 1919 (Have patience and you will see your dreams come true).
Description / Danish: Søndenå – platte. Landskab med Dannebrog vajende. Indskrift: GIV TID OG HVAD DU DRØMTE SKØNT DU SKAL I SANDHED SKUE 1919. Fremstillet i anledning af genforeningen.
Designed by: Oluf Jensen
Number of copies / size: 5,054 copies, 6", 15 cm
Price: $60-100

RC-CM189
Year: 1919
Description / English: Blacksmith forging the three rings of the Odd Fellows. Commissioned by the Independent Order of Odd Fellows.
Inscription: SEMPER ARDENS (Always burning) V.K.S. 1819 - 1919.
Description / Danish: Odd Fellow – platte. Smed der sammensmeder de tre ringe. Indskrift: SEMPER ARDENS (altid brændende) V.K.S. 1819 – 1919.
Designed by: Christian Thomsen
Number of copies / size: 1,500 copies, 9", 23 cm
Price: $100-150

RC-CM190
Year: 1919
Description / English: Same motif as no. 48. Commissioned on the 40th anniversary of the Danish Teetotaller's Association.
Inscription: 1879 DAF 1919.
Description / Danish: Afholdsplatte. Samme motiv som kat. 48. Indskrift: 1879 DAF 1919. Danmarks Afholdsforenings 40 års jubilæum.
Designed by: Arnold Krog
Number of copies / size: 157 copies, 7 1/2", 19 cm
Price: $350-450

RC-CM191
Year: 1920
Description / English: See Royal Copenhagen Christmas Plate list

RC-CM192
Year: 1920
Description / English: The memorial for the volunteers from Norway, Sweden and Finland who died in the wars against Germany, situated near Østerport in Copenhagen.
Inscription: FALDNE FOR DANMARK (They died for Denmark) 1848 - 1849 - 1850 - 1864.
Description / Danish: Mindeplatte for faldne frivillige. Mindesmærket i bastionen ved Østerport i København. Indskrift: FALDNE FOR DANMARK 1848 – 1849 – 1850 – 1864. Nordmænd, svenskere og finner symboliseret ved de tre rigsvåben.
Designed by: Arthur Boesen
Number of copies / size: 802 copies, 7 3/4", 19 1/2 cm
Price: $120-200

RC-CM193
Year: 1920
Description / English: The city arms of Aarhus. Commissioned on occasion of the 35th anniversary.
Inscription: AARHUS BRANDKORPSFORENING (Aarhus Fire Brigade Association) 1885-1920.
Description / Danish: Aarhus Brandkorps – platte. Aarhus byvåben og indskrift: AARHUS BRANDKORPSFORENING 1885 – 1920.
Designed by: Ellinor Selchau
Number of copies / size: 367 copies, 9", 23 cm
Price: $300-500

RC-CM194
Year: 1920
Description / English: Saint Ansgar preaching. Commissioned by the Independent Order of Odd Fellows for the 25th anniversary of the lodge 27 Ansgar in Aalborg.
Inscription: ANSGAR 1895-11 OKTOBER-1920.
Description / Danish: Odd Fellow – platte. Ansgar prædiker. Indskrift: ANSGAR 1895 – 11 OKTOBER – 1920. Udført til loge 27 Ansgar i Aalborg i anledning af 25 års jubilæet.
Designed by: Christian Thomsen
Number of copies / size: 592 copies, 8 1/2", 22 1/2 cm
Price: $150-200

RC-CM195
Year: 1920
Description / English: The 50th birthday of King Christian X. Crowned monogram C X
Inscription: MIN GUD MIT LAND MIN AERE (My God, My Country, My Honor) 1870-1920 26 September.
Description / Danish: Christian X.s 50 års fødselsdag. Kronet C X og indskrift: MIN GUD MIT LAND MIN ÆRE 1870 – 1920 26 SEPTEMBER.
Designed by: Hans Henrik Hansen
Number of copies / size: 2,601 copies, 8 1/4", 21 cm
Price: $75-100

RC-CM196
Year: 1920
Description / English: The Norway gate into the Citadel of Copenhagen. Commissioned by the Association of Old Soldiers
Inscription: I REGIMENTS SOLDATERFORENING I. 15. 21 BATL. (The association of old soldiers from the first regiment's 1st, 15th and 21st battalion).
Description / Danish: Norgesporten I Kastellet. Indskrift: 1. REGIMENTS SOLDATER FORENING 1. 15. 21. BATL.
Designed by: Oluf Jensen
Number of copies / size: 7", 18 cm
Price: $75-100

RC-CM197
Year: 1920
Description / English: The old and the new building of the Copenhagen Student's Association. Commissioned by the association on its 100th anniversary.
Inscription: STUDENTERFORENINGEN 1820 16 JULI 1920.
Description / Danish: Studenterforeningen. Den gamle og den nye bygning. Indskrift: STUDENTERFORENINGEN 1820 16 JULI 1920. Udført til 100-års jubilæet.
Designed by:
Number of copies / size: 1,229 copies, 7", 18 cm
Price: $60-100

RC-CM198
Year: 1921
Description / English: See Royal Copenhagen Christmas Plate list

RC-CM199
Year: 1921
Description / English: The silver wedding of King Haakon VII and Queen Maud of Norway. Crowned initials H7M and the years 1896 22 JULI 1921.
Description / Danish: Kong Haakon VIIs og Dronning Mauds sølvbryllup. Kronede initialer H 7 M og indskrift: 1896 22 JULI 1921.
Designed by: Oluf Jensen
Number of copies / size: 606 copies, 7", 18 cm
Price: $150-250

RC-CM200
Year: 1921
Description / English: The wedding of Princess Margrethe of Denmark to Prince Rene of Bourbon Parma. Crowned initials MR and the year MCMXXI (1921). Round the border, fleur-de-lis.
Description / Danish: Prinsesse Margrethes bryllup med prins Rene af Bourbon Parma. Kronede initialer MR MCMXXI (1921), i borten franske liljer.
Designed by: Oluf Jensen
Number of copies / size: 1,124 copies,
6 3/4", 17 1/2 cm
Price: $75-100

RC-CM201
Year: 1921
Description / English: Danish Man-of-War in Artic Sea. Commissioned on occasion of the 200th anniversary for Hans Egede's expedition to Greenland.
Inscription: HANS EGEDE GRØNLAND 1721-1921. Below crowned Danish arms and flag.
Description / Danish: Hans Egede – platte. Dansk orlogsskib i isfyldt farvand. Indskrift: HANS EGEDE GRØNLAND 1721 – 1921. F.n. kronet rigsvåben og flag. Udført i 200 året for Hans Egedes rejse til Grønland.
Designed by: Christian Benjamin-Olsen
Number of copies / size: 9", 23 cm
Price: $200-250

RC-CM202
Year: 1921
Description / English: The 70th birthday of the dowager Queen Louise of Denmark. Crowned face to face monogram L
Inscription: 1851 31 OKTOBER 1921.
Description / Danish: Enkedronning Louises 70-års fødselsdag. Kronet spejlmonogram L og indskrift: 1851 31 OKTOBER 1921.
Designed by: Unknown
Number of copies / size: 6", 15 1/2 cm
Price: $150-200

RC-CM203
Year: 1922
Description / English: The entrance to Frederiksberg Gardens.
Inscription: FREDERIKSBERG BORGERFORENING 1882-1922 (The Civic Association of Frederiksberg) and the arms of F. (suburb of Copenhagen).
Description / Danish: Frederiksberg borgerforening. Indgangen til Frederiksberg Have. Indskrift: FREDERIKSBERG BORGERFORENING 1882 – 1922. F.n. Frederiksberg våben.
Designed by: Oluf Jensen
Number of copies / size: 634 copies, 7 3/4", 20 cm
Price: $150-250

RC-CM204
Year: 1922
Description / English: See Royal Copenhagen Christmas Plate list

RC-CM205
Year: 1922
Description / English: Woman with two children. Made for charity for the Bethlehem orphanage.
Inscription: BØRNEHJEMMET BETHLEHEM 1922 (Bethlehem, The Children's Home)
Description / Danish: Kvinde med to børn. Indskrift: BØRNEHJEMMET BETHLEHEM 1922.
Designed by: Christian Thomsen
Number of copies / size: 866 copies, 6", 15 cm
Price: $120-200

RC-CM206
Year: 1922
Description / English: Star over landscape. The organization L. financing two convalecent homes through the surplus made by the sale of L-matches. Commissioned on occasion of the 5th anniversary of the organization.
Inscription: LYSGLIMT.
Description / Danish: Lysglimt. Stjerne over landskab. Indskrift: LYSGLIMT. Institutionen L. driver to rekonvalescenshjem gennem overskuddet ved salg af tændstikker. Udført til 5 års jubilæet.
Designed by: Oluf Jensen
Number of copies / size: 7 1/2", 19 cm
Price: $100-150

RC-CM207
Year: 1922
Description / English: Harbor entrance with ship under sail, an iceberg in the background. Commissioned by the Freemason lodge St. John in Iceland.
Inscription: IN CORDE ET ANIMO UNUM (Unity in heart and mind). Above a star with the date 1-6 5919 (1919) ST. JOH. EDDA.
Description / Danish: Frimurerplatte. Havneløb med to fyr, i baggrunden et isfjeld. Indskrift: IN CORDE ET ANIMO UNUM (En i hjertet og i sindet). F.o. stjerne med dato 1 – 6 5919 (1919) ST. JOH. EDDA.
Designed by: Unknown
Number of copies / size: 300 copies, 7", 18 cm
Price: $350-450

RC-CM208
Year: 1922
Description / English: Viking ship in front of the Arctic coast. Commissioned by the Independent Order of Odd Fellows.
Inscription: 1897 I.O.O.F. ISLAND 1922 CONCORDIA PARVAE RES CRESCUNT (unity makes small things grow).
Description / Danish: Odd Fellow – platte. Vikingeskib og isfjelde. Indskrift: 1897 I.O.O.F. ISLAND 1922 CONCORDIA PARVÆ RES CRESCUNT (Gennem sammenhold vokser små ting).
Designed by: Oluf Jensen
Number of copies / size: 9", 23 cm
Price: $125-175

RC-CM209
Year: 1922
Description / English: The author and poet Ludvig Holberg standing in a square of Old Copenhagen. Made on occasion of the 200th anniversary of the foundation of the Danish theatre.
Inscription: LUDVIG HOLBERG 1722 - 26 SEPTEMBER - 1922.
Description / Danish: Holberg – platte. Indskrift: LUDVIG HOLBERG 1722 26 SEPTEMBER 1922. Udført i anledning af 200 året for oprettelsen af den danske skueplads.
Designed by: Richard Bøcher
Number of copies / size: 577 copies, 9", 23 cm
Price: $180-300

RC-CM210
Year: 1922
Description / English: King Christian X and Queen Alexandrine's Silver Wedding. Crowned face to face monogram CX A .
Inscription: 1898-26 APRIL-1923.
Description / Danish: Christian X.s og droning Alexandrines sølvbryllup. Kronet spejlmonogram CX A. Indskrift: 1898 – 26 APRIL – 1923.
Designed by: Oluf Jensen
Number of copies / size: 8 1/2", 22 cm
Price: $85-125

RC-CM211
Year: 1923
Description / English: St. Andrew church, west front. Commissioned for the 50th anniversary of the church.
Inscription: SANKT ANDREAS KIRKE ORDRUP 1873-1923.
Description / Danish: Skt. Andreaskirken set fra vest. Indskrift: SANKT ANDREAS KIRKE ORDRUP 1873 – 1923.
Designed by: Richard Bøcher
Number of copies / size: 9", 23 cm
Price: $200-250

RC-CM212
Year: 1923
Description / English: The apostle St. Andrew with cross.
Inscription: cf. no. 211.
Description / Danish: Skt. Andreas – platte. Apostlen med kors. Indskrift som kat. 211.
Designed by: Richard Bøcher
Number of copies / size: 6", 15 1/2 cm
Price: $125-175

RC-CM213
Year: 1923
Description / English: See Royal Copenhagen Christmas Plate list

RC-CM214
Year: 1923
Description / English: Brick wall and tools. Commissioned by the guild on occasion of its 300th anniversary.
Inscription: KØBENHAVNS MURER OG STENHUGGERLAUG WER GOTT VERTRAUT HAT WOHL GEBAUT (The Copenhagen Bricklayer and Stonemason's Guild. He who trusts God, builds well) 1623-7 MARTS-1923.
Description / Danish: Murerlavets platte. Murværk, derover værktøj. Indskrift: KØBENHAVNS MURER OG STENHUGGERLAUG WER GOTT VERTRAUT HAT WOHL GEBAUT 1623 – 7 MARTS – 1923. Laugets 300-års jubilæum
Designed by: Oluf Jensen
Number of copies / size: 7", 18 cm
Price: $150-250

RC-CM215
Year: 1923
Description / English: Child in swaddling clothes. Made for charity for this home.
Inscription: PRINSESSE HELENAS BØRNEHJEM DANMARK (Princess Helena's Home for Children).
Description / Danish: Svøbelsesbarn. Indskrift: PRINSESSE HELENAS BØRNEHJEM DANMARK.
Designed by: Richard Bøcher
Number of copies / size: 7", 18 cm
Price: $125-175

RC-CM216
Year: 1923
Description / English: King Christian X and Queen Alexandrine's silver wedding. Crowned cartouche with the silhouettes of Their Majesties.
Inscription: 1898-26 APRIL-1923.
Description / Danish: Christian X.s og dronning Alexandrines sølvbryllup. Kronet kartouche med kongeparrets silhouetter. Indskrift: 1898 – 26 APRIL – 1923.
Designed by: Oluf Jensen
Number of copies / size: 9 3/4", 25 cm
Price: $80-125

RC-CM217
Year: 1923
Description / English: The ship Dana at sea. Commissioned to commemorate the Danish deep sea expedition to the Sargasso Sea.
Inscription: DANA EXPEDITIONEN 30 AUGUST 1921-11 JULI-1922.
Description / Danish: Dana – expeditionen, Skibet Dana til havs, i borten tang og fisk. Indskrift: DANA EXPEDITIONEN 30 AUGUEST 1921 – 11 JULI 1922.
Designed by: Christian Benjamin-Olsen
Number of copies / size: 7 3/4", 20 cm
Price: $2000-3000

RC-CM218
Year: 1923
Description / English: Polar Bear on an iceflow. Commissioned for the cement work's 25th anniversary.
Inscription: PORTLAND CEMENT FABRIKEN NORDEN 1898 AALBORG 1923.
Description / Danish: Portland Cement. Isbjørn og isbjerge. Indskrift: PORTLAND CEMENT FABRIKEN NORDEN 1898 AALBORG 1923. Virksomhedens 25-års jubilæum.
Designed by: Oluf Jensen
Number of copies / size: 368 copies, 8 1/2", 22 cm
Price: $200-300

RC-CM219
Year: 1923
Description / English: The Public School Sorø Academy
Inscription: SORØ AKADEMI.
Description / Danish: Sorø Akademi. Façade imod søen. Indskrift: SORØ AKADEMI.
Designed by: Oluf Jensen
Number of copies / size: 6", 10 1/2 cm
Price: $250-400

RC-CM220
Year: 1923
Description / English: Children on a bench. Commissioned on occasion of the 40th anniversary of the children's home "Bethlehem"
Inscription: 1883 – Bethlehem – 1923.
Description / Danish: Bethlehem. To børn på en bænk. Indskrift: 1883 – BETHLEHEM – 1923. Fremstillet i anlednig af børnehjemmet B.s 40-års jubilæum.
Designed by: Richard Bøcher
Number of copies / size: 397 copies, 6", 15 cm
Price: $150-200

RC-CM221
Year: 1923
Description / English: Landscape with cock in the foreground.
Inscription: EXPOSITION ALIMENTAIRE FRANCO DANOISE COPENHAGUE 1923 (Franco-Danish Food Exhibition).
Description / Danish: Fransk fødevareudstilling. Landskab med hane i forgrunden. Indskrift: EPOSITION ALIMENTAIRE FRANCO DANOISE COPENHAGUE 1923.
Designed by: Richard Bøcher
Number of copies / size: 6", 15 cm
Price: $250-350

RC-CM222
Year: 1924
Description / English: See Royal Copenhagen Christmas Plate list

RC-CM223
Year: 1924
Description / English: Two soldiers carrying a fallen comrade. Made on occasion of the 75th anniversary of the Battle of Fredericia.
Inscription: 1849 - 6 Juli-1924.
Description / Danish: 6. juli – platte. To soldater bærer falden kammerat. Indskrift: 1849 – 6 JULI – 1924. Fremstillet i anledning af 75 års dagen for Fredericiaslaget.
Designed by: Oluf Jensen
Number of copies / size: 7", 18 cm
Price: $100-150

RC-CM223A (LARGE)
Year: 1924
Description / English: Two soldiers carrying a fallen comrade. Made on occasion of the 75th anniversary of the Battle of Fredericia.
Inscription: 1849 - 6 Juli 1924.
Description / Danish: 6. juli – platte. To soldater bærer falden kammerat. Indskrift: 1849 – 6 JULI – 1924. Fremstillet i anledning af 75-års dagen for Fredericiaslaget.
Designed by: Oluf Jensen
Number of copies / size: 11 1/2", 29 cm
Price: $2500-4000
Same picture as RC-CM223

RC-CM224
Year: 1924
Description / English: Lighthouse. Commissioned by the Independent Order of Odd Fellow's Lodge "Vendsyssel" in Jutland on occasion of its 25th anniversary.
Inscription: VENDSYSSEL 1899 – 6 JUNI – 1924.
Description / Danish: Odd Fellow – platte. Fyrtaarn. Indskrift: VENDSYSSEL 1899 – 6 JUNI – 1924. Fremstillet til logen Vendsyssels 25-års jubilæum.
Designed by: Oluf Jensen
Number of copies / size: 337 copies, 9", 23 cm
Price: $200-300

RC-CM225
Year: 1924
Description / English: Sæby church. Made on occasion of the 400th anniversary of the town of Sæby (Jutland).
Inscription: 1524 – SÆBY – 1924.
Description / Danish: Sæby – platte. Landskab med Sæby Kirke. Indskrift: 1524 – SÆBY – 1924. Fremstillet til byens 400-års jubilæum.
Designed by: Oluf Jensen
Number of copies / size: 7", 18 cm
Price: $100-150

RC-CM226
Year: 1924
Description / English: Girl in the national costume of Fanø, sitting on a boat and knitting.
Inscription: Fanø 1924.
Description / Danish: Fanø – platte. Fanøpige, der strikker, siddende på en båd. Indskrift: FANØ 1924.
Designed by: Richard Bøcher
Number of copies / size: 7 3/4", 20 cm
Price: $300-400

RC-CM227
Year: 1924
Description / English: Veiled woman (Justitia) with chains. Made for the Dansk Arbejdsloge (Danish worker's lodge).
Inscription: VED FÆLLES KRAFT TIL FÆLLES GAVN HER SKABES VÆRN MOD NØD OG SAVN D.A.I. (By united strength and for the good community a fence is built against poverty and want).
Description / Danish: Dansk Arbejdsloge. Stående tilhyllet kvinde (Justitia) med lænker. Indskrift: VED FÆLLES KRAFT TIL FÆLLES GAVN HER SKABES VÆRN MOD NØD OG SAVN D.A.I. og fem medailloner med bostaverne A – O – L – P – J.
Designed by: Richard Bøcher
Number of copies / size: 8", 20 1/2 cm
Price: $125-175

RC-CM228
Year: 1924
Description / English: Viking ship.
Inscription: CRAYONS VIKING COPENHAGUE (The Viking Pencil factory in Copenhagen).
Description / Danish: Viking blyant. Vikingeskib. Indskrift: CRAYONS VIKING COPENHAGUE.
Designed by: Christian Benjamin-Olsen
Number of copies / size: 9", 23 cm
Price: $300-400

RC-CM229
Year: 1924
Description / English: Archer. Commissioned by the Independent Order of Odd Fellows.
Inscription: VENSKAB (Friendship) 1884 19 November – 1924.
Description / Danish: Odd Fellow – platte. Bueskytte. Indskrift: VENSKAB 1884 19 NOVEMBER – 1924.
Designed by: Richard Bøcher
Number of copies / size: 9", 23 cm
Price: $135-165

RC-CM230
Year: 1924
Description / English: Post rider and crown. Made on occasion of the 300th anniversary of the Royal Mail.
Inscription: TRO OG AGTSOM (Faithful and Diligent) 1624 – 1924 and the monograms C4 – CX (King Christian IV and King Christian X).
Description / Danish: Postplatte. Krone over postrytter i krans. Indskrift: TRO OG AGTSOM 1624 – 1924 C4 OG CX (Christian 4 og Christian X). Fremstillet i anledning af postvæsenets 300 års jubilæum.
Designed by: Richard Bøcher
Number of copies / size: 6", 15 1/2 cm
Price: $75-125

RC-CM231
Year: 1925
Description / English: See Royal Copenhagen Christmas Plate list

RC-CM232
Year: 1925
Description / English: Champs Elysees and the Triumphal Arch. Made on occasion of the world exhibition.
Inscription: PARIS 1925.
Description / Danish: Verdensudstillingen i Paris. Champs Elysees set mod Triumfbuen. Indskrift: PARIS 1925.
Designed by: Oluf Jensen
Number of copies / size: 7", 18 cm
Price: $300-400

RC-CM233
Year: 1925
Description / English: Sønderborg Castle. Commissioned by the Independent Order of Odd Fellow's lodge "Hertha" in Sønderbrg (Jutland).
Inscription: HERTHA SØNDERBORG.
Description / Danish: Odd Fellow – platte. Sønderborg slot. Indskrift: HERTHA SØNDERBORG.
Designed by: Oluf Jensen
Number of copies / size: 9", 23 cm
Price: $300-450

RC-CM234
Year: 1925
Description / English: Elsinore Castle. Commissioned by the Independent Order of Odd Fellows on the occasion of the 25th anniversary of its Elsinore lodge Hamlet.
Inscription: HAMLET 1900 – 25 NOVEMBER – 1925.
Description / Danish: Odd Fellow – platte. Kronborg. Indskrift: HAMLET 1900 25 NOVEMBE – 1925.
Designed by: Oluf Jensen
Number of copies / size: 9", 23 cm
Price: $125-175

RC-CM236
Year: 1925
Description / English: Korsør Citadel. Made on occasion of the 500th anniversary of Korsør's municipal charter.
Inscription: KORSOR 1425 – 1925.
Description / Danish: Korsør – platte. Fæstningen. Indskrift: KORSØR 1425 – 1925. Fremstillet i anledning af byens 500-års jubilæum.
Designed by: Oluf Jensen
Number of copies / size: 7 3/4", 20 cm
Price: $275-325

RC-CM235
Year: 1925
Description / English: Schooner with the town of Marstal in the background. Commissioned on occasion of the 100th anniversary of th harbor.
Inscription: MARSTAL HAVN 1825 – 1925 (Marstal Harbor).
Description / Danish: Marstal. Skonnert med byen i baggrunden. Indskrift: MARSTAL HAVN 1825 – 1925. Fremstillet til havnens 100-års jubilæum.
Designed by: Christian Benjamin-Olsen
Number of copies / size: 8", 20 1/2 cm
Price: $2000-3000

RC-CM237
Year: 1926
Description / English: Heraldic figure from the city arms of Hjørring. Commissioned on occasion of the 50th anniversary of the guild.
Inscription: HJØRRING HAANDVÆRKERFORENING 1876 23 JANUAR 1926 (The Artisan's Guild in Hjørring).
Description / Danish: Figur fra Hjørring byvåben og i baggrunden en bygning. Indskrift: HJØRRING HAANDVÆRKERFORENING 1876 23 JANUAR 1926.
Designed by: Richard Bøcher
Number of copies / size: 443 copies, 7 1/2", 19 cm
Price: $150-250

RC-CM238
Year: 1926
Description / English: See Royal Copenhagen Christmas Plate list

RC-CM239
Year: 1926
Description / English: Motorist and his car in Danish landscape. Made on occasion of the 25th anniversary of the Royal Danish Automobile Club
Inscription: KGL. DANSK AUTOMOBIL KLUB 1901 – 1926 (Royal Danish Automobile Club).
Description / Danish: Kongelig Dansk Automobilklub. Landskab med bilist siddende ved sin vogn. Indskrift: KGL. DANSK AUTOMOBIL KLUB 1901 – 1926.
Designed by: Richard Bøcher
Number of copies / size: 9", 23 cm
Price: $125-200

RC-CM240
Year: 1926
Description / English: Guardsman with halberd on the ramparts of Elsinore Castle. Made on occasion of the 500th anniversary of Elsinore's municipal charter.
Inscription: HELSINGOR 1426 - 1926. On the wall a crowned E (The Danish King Erik of Pommeren).
Description / Danish: Helsingør – platte. Vagtpost med hellebard på Kronbord; på muren plade med kronet E (Erik af Pommeren). Indskrift: HELSINGØR 1426 – 1926. Fremstillet i anledning af byens 500-års jubilæum.
Designed by: Christian Benjamin-Olsen
Number of copies / size: 8", 20 1/2 cm
Price: $150-200

RC-CM241
Year: 1926
Description / English: The Danish mythical hero Holger Danske sitting at a table with an hourglass. Commissioned by the Independent Order of Odd Fellows' lodge "Holger Danske" in Elsinore.
Inscription: HOLGER DANSKE 1886 – 15 JUNI – 1926.
Description / Danish: Odd Fellow – platte. Holger Danske ved bord med timeglas. Indskrift: HOLGER DANSKE 1886 15 JUNI 1926.
Designed by: Richard Bøcher
Number of copies / size: 9", 23 cm
Price: $150-200

RC-CM242
Year: 1926
Description / English: Løgum Monastery Church.
Inscription: LØGUMKLOSTER 1926.
Description / Danish: Løgum Kloster Kirken. Indskrift: LØGUMKLOSTER 1926.
Designed by: Oluf Jensen
Number of copies / size: 8", 20 1/2 cm
Price: $100-150

RC-CM243
Year: 1926
Description / English: Monk with a cross standing on a beach. Made to commemorate the 1100th anniversary for the conversion to Christianity of the Danes by St. Ansgar.
Inscription: 826 – ANSGAR – 1926.
Description / Danish: Ansgar – platte. Missionæren med kors på strandbred. Indskrift: 826 – ANSGAR – 1926. Fremstillet i 1100 året for kristendommens indførelse i Danmark.
Designed by: Richard Bøcher
Number of copies / size: 7", 18 cm
Price: $200-300

RC-CM244
Year: 1926
Description / English: View of the town Skive (Jutland) with the city-arms. Commissioned on occasion of the 600th anniversary of Skive's municipal charter.
Inscription: 1326 - SKIVE - 1926.
Description / Danish: Skive – platte. Bymotive, våben og indskrift: 1326 – SKIVE – 1926. Fremstillet til byens 600-års jubilæum.
Designed by: Oluf Jensen
Number of copies / size: 617 copies, 8", 20 1/2 cm
Price: $200-275

RC-CM245
Year: 1926
Description / English: The frigate Jylland saluting at sea outside Elsinore Castle.
Inscription: FOLKETS GAMLE MINDER FOLKET SAMMEN BINDER (The history of a nation binds its people together).
Description / Danish: Fregatten Jylland. Orlogsskibet saluterende ud for Kronborg. Indskrift: FOLKETS GAMLE MINDER FOLKET SAMMEN BINDER. F.n. rigsvåben.
Designed by: Christian Benjamin-Olsen
Number of copies / size: 1,903 copies, 8", 20 1/2 cm
Price: $125-175

RC-CM246
Year: 1926
Description / English: Airplane over Fujiyama. Made on occasion of the first flight between the two cities.
Inscription: KØBENHAVN – TOKIO 1926.
Description / Danish: Tokio – platte. Fly over Fuji. Indskrift: KØBENHAVN – TOKIO 1926. Fremstillet i anledning af flyvningen mellem de to byer.
Designed by: Arthur Boesen
Number of copies / size: 212 copies, 7 3/4", 20 cm
Price: $250-350

RC-CM249
Year: 1927
Description / English: View over Jutland landscape with the town of Nibe in the background. Below the city arms. Commissioned on occasion of the 200th anniversary of Nibe's municipal charter.
Inscription: 1727 – NIBE – 1927.
Description / Danish: Nibe – platte. Udsigt ned over byen, byvåben og indskrift: 1727 – NIBE – 1927. Fremstillet til byens 200-års købstadsjubilæum.
Designed by: Oluf Jensen
Number of copies / size: 114 copies, 8", 20 1/2 cm
Price: $500-700

RC-CM247
Year: 1927
Description / English: See Royal Copenhagen Christmas Plate list

RC-CM248
Year: 1927
Description / English: Landscape with farmhouse and flag. Commissioned by the Danish Home Guard movement.
Inscription: FRI MAND PAA FRI MANDS JORD - LANDEVÆRNET 1927 (Free man on his own land – Home Guard).
Description / Danish: Landeværnsplatte. Landskab med gård og dannebrog. Indskrift: FRI MAND PAA FRI MANDS JORD – LANDVEVÆRNET 1927.
Designed by: Oluf Jensen
Number of copies / size: 7 3/4", 20 cm
Price: $175-225

RC-CM250
Year: 1928
Description / English: Christiansborg Castle in Copenhagen seen from the inner court.
Inscription: CHRISTIANSBORG.
Description / Danish: Christiansborg – platte. Slottet set fra ridebanen. Indskrift: CHRISTIANSBORG.
Designed by: Oluf Jensen
Number of copies / size: 121 copies, 8", 20 1/2 cm
Price: $500-750

RC-CM251
Year: 1928
Description / English: See Royal Copenhagen Christmas Plate list

RC-CM252
Year: 1928
Description / English: The main building at J.P. Schmidt's tobacco factory in Fredericia (Jutland). Below a shield with the two lines of Slesvig. Commissioned on occasion of the firm's 150th anniversary.
Inscription: 1778 – J.P. SCHMIDTS JUN. – 1928.
Description / Danish: Tobaksfabrikken J.P. Schmidt jun. i Fredericia. F.n. skjold med de slesvigske løver og ved siderne tobaksplante. Indskrift: 1778 – J.P. SCHMIDT JUN. – 1928. Fremstillet i anledning af virksomhedens 150-års jubilæum.
Designed by: Oluf Jensen
Number of copies / size: 7", 18 cm
Price: $75-125

RC-CM253
Year: 1928
Description / English: Crowned anchor with initials V and M (Prince Valdemar and Princess Marie). Commissioned by Prince Valdemar and Princess Marie's benevolent fund.
Inscription: IKKE INTERESSE MEN KRÆLIGHED (Not out of interest but out of love).
Description / Danish: Prins Valdemars og Prinsesse Maries Fond. Kronet anker og bogstaver V og M. Indskrift: IKKE INTERESSE MEN KRÆLIGHED.
Designed by: Oluf Jensen
Number of copies / size: 232 copies, 8", 20 1/2 cm
Price: $300-500

RC-CM254
Year: 1928
Description / English: The Y.M.C.A. in Copenhagen seen from the Botanical Gardens. Commissioned on occasion of the association's 50th anniversary.
Inscription: 1878 – K.F.U.M. – 1928 16 SEPTEMBER.
Description / Danish: K.F.U.M. 50-års jubilæum. Foreningens bygning set fra Botanisk Have. Indskrift: K.F.U.M. 1878 – 16 SEPTEMBER – 1928.
Designed by: Oluf Jensen
Number of copies / size: 1,214 copies, 6", 11 1/2 cm
Price: $75-125

RC-CM255
Year: 1928
Description / English: Ship under construction at a shipyard.
Inscription: A/S BURMEISTER & WAINS MASKIN & SKIBSBYGGERI KØBENHAVN (The B&W Shipbuilding Co. in Copenhagen).
Description / Danish: Burmeister & Wain – platte. Skib under bygning. Indskrift: A/S BURMEISTER & WAINS MASKIN & SKIBSBYGGERI KØBENHAVN.
Designed by: Oluf Jensen
Number of copies / size: 6 1/4", 16 cm
Price: $500-750

RC-CM256
Year: 1929
Description / English: 150th anniversary plate for the Royal Copenhagen Porcelain Factory. Crown and three wavy lines. Incorporated already in 1775 the factory was taken over by the King in 1779.
Inscription: 29 JUNI 1779 – 1929.
Description / Danish: Den Kongelige Porcelainsfabriks 150-års jubilæumsplatte. Krone over tre bølgelinier. Indskrift: 29 JUNI 1779 – 1929.
Designed by: Oluf Jensen
Number of copies / size: 216 copies, 8", 20 1/2 cm
Price: $275-325

RC-CM257
Year: 1929
Description / English: See Royal Copenhagen Christmas Plate list

RC-CM258
Year: 1929
Description / English: Group from the Voluntary Rifle Corps. Commissioned on occasion of the 20th anniversary of the corps.
Inscription: KOBENHAVNS AMTS SKYTTEKORPS 1909 – 1929 (Copenhagen County Voluntary Rifle Corps).
Description / Danish: Amtsskyttekorpset. Gruppe af skytter med rekylgevær. Indskrift: KØBENHAVENS AMTS SKYTTEKORPS 1909 – 1929.
Designed by: Richard Bøcher
Number of copies / size: 169 copies, 7", 18 1/5 cm
Price: $400-600

RC-CM259
Year: 1929
Description / English: 150th anniversary plate for the Royal Copenhagen Porcelain Factory. Elsinore Castle, crown over three wavy lines
Description / Danish: Jubilæumsplakette. Kronborg og indskrift: 1779 – 1929 og krone over bølgelinier.
Designed by: Oluf Jensen
Number of copies / size: 1,815 copies, 6", 11 1/2 cm
Price: $75-130

RC-CM260
Year: 1927
Description / English: Main entrance. Commissioned by the Freemason's lodge in Copenhagen.
Inscription: GRATIA MEMORIA (Pleasant Memory) 1868 – 1927.
Description / Danish: Frimurerlogen i Klerkegade i København. Portal og indskrift: GRATIA MEMORIA (En kær erindring) 1868 – 1927.
Designed by: Richard Bøcher
Number of copies / size: 250 copies, 7", 18 cm
Price: $250-350

RC-CM261
Year: 1927
Description / English: Main entrance. Made for the Freemason's Lodge (The new building) in Copenhagen.
Inscription: FRED ENIGHED FREMGANG (Peace, Unity, Progress) 1927.
Description / Danish: Frimurerlogen på Blegdamsvej i København. Indskrift: FRED ENIGHED FREMGANG 1927.
Designed by: Richard Bøcher
Number of copies / size: 324 copies, 7", 18 cm
Price: $200-300

RC-CM262
Year: 1930
Description / English: See Royal Copenhagen Christmas Plate list

RC-CM263
Year: 1930
Description / English: King Christian X crossing the old border between Northern Slesvig and Denmark. Made on occasion of the 10th anniversary of the reunion of Northern Slesvig with Denmark.
Inscription: 1920 10 JULI 1930.
Description / Danish: Genforeningsplatte. Christian X rider over grænsen. Indskrift: 1920 10 JULI 1930. Fremstillet til 10-års dagen for Genforeningen.
Designed by: Richard Bøcher
Number of copies / size: 1,175 copies, 9 1/2", 24 cm
Price: $150-200

RC-CM264
Year: 1930
Description / English: A star lit sky and a globe with initials I.O.G.T. (Independent Order of Good Templar) 1880 13 MARTS 1930. Commissioned on occasion of the organization's 50th anniversary.
Description / Danish: Good Templar – platte. Stjernehimmel med jordglobe og initialer I.O.G.T. (Indepedent Order of Good Templar) 1880 13 MARTS 1930.
Designed by: Richard Bøcher
Number of copies / size: 304 copies, 7 1/2", 19 cm
Price: $200-300

RC-CM265
Year: 1931
Description / English: See Royal Copenhagen Christmas Plate list

RC-CM266
Year: 1931
Description / English: Greenland boy in winter clothes.
Inscription: HJÆLP GRØNLANDS BØRN TIL SUNDHED (Help Greenlands children to health).
Description / Danish: Grønlandsplatte. Grønlænderdreng i vinterdragt. Indskrift: HJÆLP GRØNLANDS BØRN TIL SUNDHED.
Designed by: Richard Bøcher
Number of copies / size: 7", 18 cm
Price: $300-500

RC-CM268
Year: 1932
Description / English: See Royal Copenhagen Christmas Plate list

RC-CM269
Year: 1932
Description / English: Elsinore Castle. The members meet once a year at Elsinore castle.
Inscription: DANSK SAMVIRKE (Danish Association of Danes living outside Denmark).
Description / Danish: Dansk Samvirke. Kronborgmotive og indskrift: DANSK SAMVIRKE.
Designed by: Oluf Jensen
Number of copies / size: 6", 12 1/2 cm
Price: $95-125

RC-CM267
Year: 1932
Description / English: Icelandic landscape. Commissioned by the Freemason's lodge on Iceland.
Inscription: UT OMNES UNUM SINT (Would all be united). Above a star with the year 5931 (1931) and ST. JOH. RUN ISLAND (St. John's Lodge, Iceland).
Description / Danish: Frimurerplatte. Islandsk landskab og indskrift: UT OMNES UNUM SINT (måttre alle være eet). F.o. stjerne med årstal 5931 (1931) ST. JOH. RUN ISLAND.
Designed by: Oluf Jensen
Number of copies / size: 7", 18 cm
Price: $500-1000

RC-CM270
Year: 1932
Description / English: The Eros statue at Piccadilly Circus. Commissioned on occasion of the exhibition in Copenhagen that year.
Inscription: THE ANGLO DANISH SOCIETY 1932. THE BRITISH EXHIBITION.
Description / Danish: Engelsk udstilling i København. Erosstatuen på Piccadilly Circus i London. Indeskrift: THE ANGLO DANISH SOCIETY 1932 THE BRITISH EXHIBITION.
Designed by: Richard Bøcher
Number of copies / size: 7 1/4", 18 1/2 cm
Price: $300-400

RC-CM271
Year: 1932
Description / English: St. Catharina Church in Ribe (Jutland).
Inscription: ST. CATHARINA RIPÆ 1932.
Description / Danish: Skt. Catharina Kirke i Ribe. Indskrift: ST. CATHARINA RIPÆ 1932.
Designed by: Richard Bøcher
Number of copies / size: 8", 20 1/2 cm
Price: $300-350

RC-CM272
Year: 1932
Description / English: Frederiksgaard on Fanø.
Inscription: FREDERIKSGAARD FANØ.
Description / Danish: Fanø – platte. Indskrift: FREDERIKSGAARD FANØ.
Designed by: Richard Bøcher
Number of copies / size: 7 1/4", 18 1/2 cm
Price: $400-500

RC-CM273
Year: 1933
Description / English: See Royal Copenhagen Christmas Plate list

RC-CM274
Year: 1933
Description / English: The Freemason's Lodge in Aarhus (Jutland). Commissioned on occasion of the 25th anniversary of the St. Andrew's lodge "The Four Roses".
Inscription: CARITATE DEI (By the grace of God) 1908 – 1933.
Description / Danish: Frimurer – platte. Logebygning i Aarhus. Indskrift: CARITATE DEI (Ved Guds kærlighed) 1908 – 1933. Fremstillet til Skt. Andreas logen De fire Roser O.R. Tegnet af Richard Bøcher.
Designed by: Richard Bøcher
Number of copies / size: 7", 18 cm
Price: $200-300

RC-CM275
Year: 1934
Description / English: See Royal Copenhagen Christmas Plate list

RC-CM276
Year: 1935
Description / English: See Royal Copenhagen Christmas Plate list

RC-CM277
Year: 1936
Description / English: See Royal Copenhagen Christmas Plate list

RC-CM278
Year: 1936
Description / English: The Danish Cooperative Cement Industries. Commissioned on occasion of the 25th anniversary.
Inscription: DANSK ANDELS CEMENTFABRIK 1911 10 NOVBR 1936.
Description / Danish: Dansk Andels Cementfabrik. Fabriksbygningerne og indskrift: DANSK ANDELS CEMENTFABRIK 1911 10 NOVBR 1936. Fremstillet til 25-års jubilæet.
Designed by: Richard Bøcher
Number of copies / size: 7", 18 cm
Price: $100-150

RC-CM279
Year: 1937
Description / English: See Royal Copenhagen Christmas Plate list

RC-CM280
Year: 1937
Description / English: King Christian X's silver jubilee. Crowned face to face monogram CX.
Inscription: MIN GUD MIT LAND MIN ÆRE (My God, My Country, My Honor) 1912 15 MAJ 1937.
Description / Danish: Christian X.s regeringsjubilæum. Kronet spejlmonogram CX og indskrift: MIN GUD MIT LAND MIN ÆRE 1912 15 MAJ 1937.
Designed by: Richard Bøcher
Number of copies / size: 7 1/2", 19 cm
Price: $150-180

RC-CM281
Year: 1937
Description / English: Landscape with dairy. Round the border leaves and below the letters D.D. (Danish Dairies).
Description / Danish: Mejeri – platte. Landskab med mejeri. I borten lurmærke og f.n. initialer D.D. (Danish Dairies).
Designed by: Richard Bøcher
Number of copies / size: 9 1/2", 24 1/2 cm
Price: $1000-2000

RC-CM282
Year: 1938
Description / English: See Royal Copenhagen Christmas Plate list see RC-38

RC-CM283
Year: 1938
Description / English: Detail from the liberty memorial in Copenhagen. Made on occasion of the 150th anniversary of the abolition.
Inscription: KONGEN BØD STAVNSBAANDET SKAL OPHØRE (the king decreed that adscription be abolished) 1788 – 1938.
Description / Danish: Frihedsstøtten. Udsnit af monumentet med de fire figurer. Indskrift: KONGEN BØD STAVNSBAANDET SKAL OPHØRE 1788 – 1938. Fremstillet i anledning af 150-året for stavnsbåndets ophævelse.
Designed by: Richard Bøcher
Number of copies / size: 7 1/4", 18 1/2 cm
Price: $100-150

RC-CM286
Year: 1939
Description / English: The Holy Teresia in a nun's garb. Commissioned by the Carmel convent in Lisieux, France.
Inscription: S. TERESIA A IESU INFANTE.
Description / Danish: Terese – platte. Den hellige Terese i nonnedragt. Indskrift: S. TERESIA A IESU INFANTE. Udført til klosteret Carmel i Lisieux.
Designed by: Richard Bøcher
Number of copies / size: 7 1/4", 18 1/2 cm
Price: $1500-2000

RC-CM287
Year: 1940
Description / English: See Royal Copenhagen Christmas Plate List

RC-CM288
Year: 1941
Description / English: See Royal Copenhagen Christmas Plate list

RC-CM289
Year: 1942
Description / English: See Royal Copenhagen Christmas Plate List

RC-CM290
Year: 1943
Description / English: See Royal Copenhagen Christmas Plate List

RC-CM291
Year: 1944
Description / English: See Royal Copenhagen Christmas Plate List

RC-CM292
Year: 1945
Description / English: See Royal Copenhagen Christmas Plate List

RC-CM293
Year: 1946
Description / English: See Royal Copenhagen Christmas Plate List

RC-CM294
Year: 1947
Description / English: See Royal Copenhagen Christmas Plate List

RC-CM295
Year: 1948
Description / English: See Royal Copenhagen Christmas Plate List

RC-CM296
Year: 1949
Description / English: See Royal Copenhagen Christmas Plate List

RC-CM297
Year: 1950
Description / English: See Royal Copenhagen Christmas Plate List

RC-CM298
Year: 1951
Description / English: See Royal Copenhagen Christmas Plate List

RC-CM299
Year: 1952
Description / English: See Royal Copenhagen Christmas Plate List

RC-CM300
Year: 1953
Description / English: See Royal Copenhagen Christmas Plate List

RC-CM301
Year: 1954
Description / English: See Royal Copenhagen Christmas Plate List

RC-CM302
Year: 1955
Description / English: See Royal Copenhagen Christmas Plate List

RC-CM303
Year: 1956
Description / English: See Royal Copenhagen Christmas Plate List

RC-CM304
Year: 1957
Description / English: See Royal Copenhagen Christmas Plate List

RC-CM305
Year: 1958
Description / Danish: See Royal Copenhagen Christmas Plate List

RC-CM306
Year: 1959
Description / English: See Royal Copenhagen Christmas Plate List

RC-CM307
Year: 1960
Description / English: See Royal Copenhagen Christmas Plate List

RC-CM308
Year: 1961
Description / English: King Frederik IX's and Queen Ingrid's silver wedding anniversary. Crowned face-to-face monogram F I.
Inscription: 1935. 24 MAJ 1960.
Description / Danish: Kong Frederik IX.s og dronning Ingrids sølvbryllup. Kronet spejlmonogram F I og indskrift: 1935. 24 MAJ 1960.
Designed by: Unknown
Number of copies / size: 8 1/4", 21 1/2 cm
Price: $60-100

RC-CM309
Year: 1961
Description / English: See Royal Copenhagen Christmas Plate List

RC-CM310
Year: 1962
Description / English: See Royal Copenhagen Christmas Plate List

RC-CM311
Year: 1962
Description / English: Two hussars of the Royal Hussar Regiment in uniforms from 1762 and 1962. Commissioned on occasion of the regiment's 200th anniversary.
Description / Danish: Gardehusarregimentets jubilæumsplatte. To husarer til hest i uniformer fra 1762 og 1962. Fremstillet til jubilæet. Indskrift: GARDEHUSARREGIMENTET 1762 – 1962.
Designed by: Kai Lange
Number of copies / size: 9 1/2", 24 1/2 cm
Price: $300-500

RC-CM312
Year: 1963
Description / English: See Royal Copenhagen Christmas Plate List

RC-CM313
Year: 1963
Description / English: The building belonging to the Danish Blacksmith's and Engine Worker's Union in Copenhagen. Commissioned on occasion of the union's 75th anniversary.
Inscription: Initials: D.S.M.F. 1888 – 1963.
Description / Danish: Dansk Smede – og Maskinarbejder Forbunds 75-års jubilæum. Forbundets bygning på Gammel Kongevej i København. F.n. initialer D.S.M.F. 1888 – 1963.
Designed by: Kai Lange
Number of copies / size: 14 1/4", 36 cm
Price: $3000-4000

RC-CM314
Year: 1964
Description / English: See Royal Copenhagen Christmas Plate list

RC-CM315
Year: 1965
Description / English: See Royal Copenhagen Christmas Plate list

RC-CM316
Year: 1966
Description / English: See Royal Copenhagen Christmas Plate list

RC-CM317
Year: 1967
Description / English: See Royal Copenhagen Christmas Plate list.

RC-CM318
Year: 1967
Description / English: Sugar mill on one of the Virgin Islands. Made to commemorate the 50th anniversary of the transfer to U.S.A. of the Danish Virgin Islands.
Inscription: THE UNITED STATES OF AMERICA 1917 – 1967 – SAINT CROIX SAINT THOMAS SAINT JOHN – 1966 DENMARK – 1917.
Description / Danish: Dansk Vestindien – platte. Fremstillet til minde om overdragelsen af de dansk vestindiske øer til U.S.A. i 1917. Gammel sukkermølle og indskrift: THE UNITED STATES OF AMERICA 1917 – 1967 – SAINT CROIX SAINT THOMAS SAINT JOHN – 1666 DENMARK – 1917.
Designed by: Kai Lange
Number of copies / size: 7", 18 cm
Price: $20-30

RC-CM319
Year: 1968
Description / English: See Royal Copenhagen Christmas Plate list

RC-CM320
Year: 1968
Description / English: Old houses in Frankfurt am Main (Germany).
Description / Danish: Frankfurt – platte. Gavlhuse i Frankfurt am Main.
Designed by: Kai Lange
Number of copies / size: 7", 18 cm
Price: $100-200
No picture available

RC-CM321
Year: 1968
Description / English: The church in Frederikshavn (Jutland). Made on occasion of the town's 150th anniversary.
Inscription: 1818 – 1968.
Description / Danish: Kirken i Frederikshavn. Indskrift: 1818 – 1968. Fremstillet i anledning af byens 150-års jubilæum.
Designed by: Kai Lange
Number of copies / size: 7", 18 cm
Price: $50-60

RC-CM322
Year: 1969
Description / English: See Royal Copenhagen Christmas Plate list

RC-CM323
Year: 1969
Description / English: The Dannebrog – the Danish flag – falling from heaven at the battle of Reval in 1219. Made on occasion of the 750th anniversary of the flag.
Inscription: 1219 – 15 JUNI – 1969.
Description / Danish: Valdemar – platte. Dannebrog falder fra himlen under slaget ved Reval. Indskrift: 1219 – 15 JUNI – 1969. Fremstillet i anledning af 750-års dagen for flagets modtagelse.
Designed by: Kai Lange
Number of copies / size: 7", 18 cm
Price: $30-40

RC-CM324
Year: 1969
Description / English: Moon plate. Moon landscape with footprints and the American flag. Made to commemorate the U.S.A. astronaut's first landing.
Inscription: VICTORIA SPATII (Conquest of Space) 1969.
Description / Danish: Måneplatte. Månelandskab med fodspor og amerikansk flag. Indskrift: VICTORIA SPATII 1969 (besejring af rummet). Fremstillet i anledning af amerikanske astronauters første landgang på månen.
Designed by: Sven Vestergard
Number of copies / size: 7", 18 cm
Price: $30-40

RC-CM325
Year: 1970
Description / English: The Mill of Dybbøll. Below the two lions of Slesvig and the years 1920 – 1970. Made on occasion of the 50th anniversary of the reunification of Northern Slesvig
Inscription: NORDSLESVIGS GENFORENING (The reunification of Northern Slesvig).
Description / Danish: Genforeningsplatte. Dybbøl mølle, f.n. Slesvigs løver og årstal 1920 – 1970. Indskrift: NORDSLESVIGS GENFORENING. Fremstillet i anledning af 50-året for genforeningen.
Designed by: Kai Lange
Number of copies / size: 7 3/4", 20 cm
Price: $30-40

RC-CM326
Year: 1970
Description / English: See Royal Copenhagen Christmas Plate list

Royal Copenhagen Commemorative Plates, Not in book Royal Copenhagen Porcelain Manafactory Plates, *published in 1971, the Grey Book / spec (Special)*

Here are a few of the plates not listed in the book, *Royal Copenhagen Porcelain Manafactory Plates*, published in 1971, known as "the grey book."

RC-CM387
Year: 1910
Description / English: Brussels 1910 World Fair
Designed by: Unknown
Number of copies / size: 3 3/4"

RC-CM388
Year: 1926
Description / English: 150th jubilee of the signing of the US constitution
Number of copies / size: 3 13/16"

RC-CM389
Year: 1923-1934
Description / English: The Royal Copenhagen factory
Description / Danish: Den Kongelige Porcelainsfabrik
Number of copies / size: 3 3/4"

RC-CM390
Year: pre 1923
Description / English: Danish Flag and Hamlets Kronborg in the background
Number of copies / size: 3 5/8"

RC-CM392
Year: 1938
Description / English: The 200 year jubilee for the abolishion of adscription
Description / Danish: 200-aars jubilaeum for Stavsbaandet ophaevelse
Number of copies / size: 5 1/8"

RC-CM391
Year: 1929
Description / English: Workers congress in Copenhagen 1929
Number of copies / size: 4 1/8"

RC-spec1 (special 1)
Year: 1912
Description / English: Chemnitz
Description / Danish: Chemnitz
Number of copies / size: 3 3/4", 9.5cm

RC-spec2
Year: 1923-1934
Description / English: Compliments of C. Caber Lumber Corporation, New York City
Number of copies / size: 3 3/4", 9.5cm

RC-spec16
Year: 1929
Description / English: Association of Danish Commercial Travellers
Number of copies / size: 3 3/4", 9.5cm

RC-spec3
Year: 1904
Description / English: Variation of RC-CM51
Number of copies / size: 8", 20cm

RC-spec5
Year: 1926
Description / English: Monogram in gold
Designed by: Unknown
Number of copies / size: 6 3/4", 17cm

RC-spec19
Year: pre 1923
Description / English: Danish royal and state seal in gold and overglaze
Number of copies / size: 8 3/4", 22cm

RC-spec4
Year: 1929
Description / English: Odd Fellow
Number of copies / size: 4 1/8", 10.5cm

RC-spec11
Year: 1909
Description / English: Overglaze and gold paintings of ships
Number of copies / size: 11 9/10, 30cm

RC-spec21
Year: 1926
Description / English: Lysglimt (flash), Also matchbox holder
Number of copies / size: 8 1/3", 21cm

RC-spec22
Year: 1923-1934
Description / English: Vejle and Aarhus
Number of copies / size: 6 1/3" x 4 1/8", 16cm x 10.5cm

RC-spec23
Year: pre 1923
Description / English: Copenhagen
Number of copies / size: 4 1/3" x 2.50, 11cm x 6.5cm

RC-spec24
Year: 1931
Description / English: 1881-1931
Number of copies / size: 6 1/3" x 4 1/3", 16cm x 11cm

RC-spec25
Year: pre 1923
Description / English: Copenhagen Scaninavian American Line
Number of copies / size: 6 1/3" x 4 1/3", 16cm x 11cm

RC-spec26
Year: 1888
Description / English: Unique plates from the 1888 exhxibition in Copenhagen for industry, agriculture and art. These were a part of Royal Copenhagen Exhibitions. "Kgl. Porcelain Fabrik" was spelled with a plate for each letter and were displayed as a border. We are interested in hearing if anybody should have some of these.
Designed by: Arnold Krog
Number of copies / size: 6 3/4", 17cm

Royal Copenhagen Shadow and Silhouette Plates / RC-S

The first of 15 different Royal Copenhagen Flora Danica Silhouette Portrait plates was produced in 1906 with Arnold Krog as the main designer. The plates were produced in varying quantities and prices ranging from $250 to $4000. Each plate measures 4.5" x 3.5" and features a picture of a Danish royal family member. They also feature a gilded crown and border with a flag and ribbons in the nationality of the family member. The first two plates of this series were made in five different variations found in the border and inscription. Though it is impossible to know exactly how many were produced, we are sure that some of the other plates were alsso made in variations. A few specilally designed plates were done in plain white; unfortunately, we do not know why they were made or what they were used for.

RC-S1
Title / English: King Christian IX of Denmark (1818-1906) reigned 1863-1906.
Title / Danish: Konge Christian IX
Designed by: Arnold Krog
Year: 1906

RC-S2
Title / English: Queen Louise (1817-1898), wife of King Christian IX.
Title / Danish: Dronning Louise
Designed by: Arnold Krog
Year: 1906

RC-S3
Title / English: Princess Marie (1865-1909), wife of Prince Valdemar third son of King Christian IX.
Title / Danish: Prinsesse Marie
Designed by: Arnold Krog
Year: 1909

RC-S4
Title / English: King Frederick VIII of Denmark (1843-1912) reigned 1906-1912.
Title / Danish: Konge Frederick VIII
Designed by: Arnold Krog
Year: 1912

RC-S5
Title / English: King George I of the Hellenes (Greece) (1843-1913) reigned 1863-1913. Second son of King Christian IX of Denmark.
Title / Danish: Konge George I
Designed by: Arnold Krog
Year: 1913

RC-S6
Title / English: Prince Ernst August, Duke of Cumberland and Duke of Brunswick (1845-1923). Husband of Princess Thyra of Denmark.
Title / Danish: Prins Ernst August
Designed by: Arnold Krog
Year: 1923

RC-S7
Title / English: Queen Alexandra of Great Britain (1844-1924) wife of King Edward VII and daughter of King Christian IX.
Title / Danish: Dronning Alexandra
Designed by: Arnold Krog
Year: 1924
No picture available

RC-S8
Title / English: Queen Alexandra of Great Britain (1844-1925) upon her death (similar to RC-S7).
Title / Danish: Dronning Alexandra
Designed by: Arnold Krog
Year: 1925
No picture available

RC-S9
Title / English: Queen Olga of Greece (1851-1926) reigned as consort of King George I of the Hellenes (see RC-S5).
Title / Danish: Dronning Olga
Designed by: Arnold Krog
Year: 1926
No picture available

RC-S10
Title / English: Queen Louise of Denmark (1851-1926) consort of King Frederick VIII (see RC-S4).
Title / Danish: Dronning Louise
Designed by: Arnold Krog
Year: 1926

RC-S11
Title / English: Empress (Tzarina) Dagmar of Russia (1847-1927). Daughter of King Christian IX.
Title / Danish: Tzarina Dagmar
Designed by: Arnold Krog
Year: 1927

RC-S12
Title / English: Princess Thyra of Denmark, Duchess of Cumberland and Duchess of Brunswick (1853-1933). Wife of Prince Ernst August (see RC-S6), and daughter of King Christian IX.
Title / Danish: Prinsesse Thyra
Designed by: Arnold Krog
Year: 1933
No picture available

RC-S13
Title / English: Prince Valdemar of Denmark (1858-1939) third son of King Christian IX and husband of Princess Marie (see RC-S3).
Title / Danish: Prins Valdemar
Designed by: Arnold Krog
Year: 1939
No picture available

RC-S14
Title / English: King Christian X of Denmark (1870-1947). Reigned 1912-1947. Eldest son of King Frederick VIII.
Title / Danish: Konge Christian X
Designed by: Arnold Krog
Year: 1947

RC-S15
Title / English: Queen Alexandrine of Denmark (1879-1952) wife of King Christian X.
Title / Danish: Dronning Alexandrine
Designed by: Arnold Krog
Year: 1952

Following are examples of the variations that were done to some of the plates, plus special issue plates.

Right:
RC-SS1
Title / English: King Christian IX of Denmark (1818-1906) reigned 1863-1906.
Title / Danish: Konge Christian IX
Designed by: Arnold Krog
Year: 1906

Left:
RC-SS2
Title / English: Queen Louise (1817-1898) wife of King Christian IX.
Title / Danish: Dronning Louise
Designed by: Arnold Krog
Year: 1906

Below:
RC-SS3
Title / English: King George I of the Helleness (Greece) (1843-1913) reigned 1863-1913. Second son of King Christian IX of Denmark.
Title / Danish: Konge George I
Designed by: Arnold Krog
Year: 1913

RC-SS4
Title / English: 1873-1923 23th of May
Year: 1923, occasion unknown

Royal Copenhagen Compass Series / Danske Kompasser / RC-DK

The Compass Series is very limited in number and features compasses from Denmark. All the plates are individually numbered and are priced at $30-60.

RC-DK1970
Title / Danish: Sladrekompas ca. 1785
Inscription: "Iver Jensen Borger i Kiobenhavn"
Quantity: 1000

RC-DK1971
Title / Danish: Sladrekompas ca. 1750
Inscription: "Jeg haaber med troen og kierlighed prætig at fortunen kommer fra gud almægtig Kiobenhavn O.P.S."
Quantity: 1250

RC-DK1972
Title / Danish: Sladrekompas 18. Aarh.
Inscription: "LWC"
Quantity: 1250

RC-DK1973
Title / Danish: Sladrekompas 1772
Inscription: "Koch i Kiobenhavn 1772"
Quantity: 1300

RC-DK1974
Title / Danish:
Inscription:
Quantity: 1500
No picture available

RC-DK1975
Title / Danish: Sladrekompas ca. 1825
Inscription: "Christian Lystrup Kiobenhavn"
Quantity: 2000

RC-DK1976
Title / Danish: Sladrekompas 1787
Inscription: "Fecit Gluckstadt 1787 F. Meyer"
Quantity: 1800

RC-DK1977
Title / Danish: Sladrekompas ca. 1800
Inscription: "JOHAN PHILIP WEILBACH KIØBENHAVN"
Quantity: 1600

RC-DK1979
Title / Danish: Sladrekompas ca. 1750-65
Inscription: "Peder Nielsen Brenoe Kiøbenhavn"
Quantity: 1500

RC-DK1978
Title / Danish: Sladrekompas ca. 1760
Inscription: "IVAR IENSSEN BORGER I KIØBENHAVN"
Quantity: 1500

RC-DK1980
Title / Danish: Sladrekompas ca. 1760
Inscription: "Christian IV.s skibskompas 1595 efter original i De Danske Kongers kronologiske Samling på Rosenborg Slot"
Quantity: 1500

Royal Copenhagen Christmas in Denmark or Dear Family Series / RC-DF

The Christmas in Denmark series, also known as the Dear Family series, was the only Royal Copenhagen full color series produced. They are all 8" in diameter.

RC-DF1991
Title / English: Bringing Home the Tree
Title / Danish: Træet vælges
Designed by: Hans Henrik Hansen
Price: $40-60

RC-DF1992
Title / English: Christmas Shopping
Title / Danish: Jule indkøb
Designed by: Hans Henrik Hansen
Price: $40-60

RC-DF1993
Title / English: The Skating party
Title / Danish: Skøjtefest
Designed by: Hans Henrik Hansen
Price: $40-60
No picture available

RC-DF1994
Title / English: The Sleigh Ride
Title / Danish: Kanetur
Designed by: Hans Henrik Hansen
Price: $40-60

RC-DF1995
Title / English: Christmas Tales
Title / Danish: Jule historier
Designed by: Hans Henrik Hansen
Price: $40-60

RC-DF1996
Title / English: Christmas Eve
Title / Danish: Jule aften
Designed by: Hans Henrik Hansen
Price: $40-60
No picture available

Royal Copenhagen Young Adventurer's Series / RC-YA

The Young Adventurer's series plates were designed by Sven Vestergaard in 1998. They are all 5 1/4" in diameter. This series was inspired by the impulsiveness and curiosity of children. The motif is executed in relief and hand-decorated in the classic cobalt blue underglaze design. Bing and Grøndahl also did a plate in 1990 with the same series name. It is not included in this book but could be considered part of the series. That particular plate is slighty larger in size.

RC-YA1998
Title / English: Parachuting

RC-YA1999
Title / English: Catch of the Day

RC-YA2000
Title / English: Airborne"

RC-YA2001
Title / English: Slip Sliding Away

RC-YA2002
Title / English: The First Leap

RC-YA2003
Title / English: Balloon Ride
No picture available

Royal Copenhagen Millennium Series / RC-M

Sven Vestergaard created the Millennium series in 2000. The series is supposed to project great hope for the future, as each design is natural and friendly to the environment. Each of the plates features Emma and Frederik on different adventures around the world. These plates measure 7 1/4".

RC-M2000

RC-M2001

RC-M2002
No picture available

RC-M2003
No picture available

RC-M2004
No picture available

Royal Copenhagen 2010 Plaquette Series / RC2010

Although Kai Lange designed most of the 2010 Plaquette series, Svend Vestergaard designed the Antique Car set. Each plaquette measures 3 1/4" in diameter and most feature a back stamp. Some of the back stamps include: the normal Aluminia "A " with three waves, the Royal Copenhagen crown with three waves, or either of the previous two with the series number "2010" and the piece number or the piece number only. It is the individual collector's decision whether to collect plaquettes with the same back stamp or whether to collect plaquettes with different back stamps.

RC2010-1
Title / English: Rosenberg Castle
Title / Danish: Rosenberg Slot
Designed by: Kai Lange 1950
Price: $10-15

RC2010-2
Title / English: Little Mermaid
Title / Danish: Langelinie
Designed by: Kai Lange 1950
Price: $10-15

RC2010-3
Title / English: Winter Landscape
Title / Danish: Vinter Landskab
Designed by: Kai Lange 1951
Price: $10-15

RC2010-4
Title / English: Barrows
Title / Danish: Kæmpehøj
Designed by: Kai Lange 1950
Price: $10-15

RC2010-5
Title / English: Kronborg Castle
Title / Danish: Kronborg Slot
Designed by: Kai Lange 1951
Price: $10-15

RC2010-7
Title / English: Østerlars Church
Title / Danish: Østerlars Kirke
Designed by: Kai Lange 1951
Price: $10-15

RC2010-9
Title / English: Maribo Cathedral
Title / Danish: Maribo Domkirke
Designed by: Kai Lange 1951
Price: $10-15

RC2010-6
Title / English: Frederiksborg Castle
Title / Danish: Frederiksborg Slot
Designed by: Kai Lange 1950
Price: $10-15

RC2010-8
Title / English: The Round Tower
Title / Danish: Rundetårn
Designed by: Kai Lange 1950
Price: $10-15

RC2010-10
Title / English: Our Savior's Church
Title / Danish: Vor Frelsers Kirke
Designed by: Kai Lange 1950
Price: $10-15

RC2010-11
Title / English: Church Tower at Hvidovre
Title / Danish: Hvidovre Kirketårn
Designed by: Kai Lange 1951
Price: $10-15

RC2010-12
Title / English: Dybbøl Mill
Title / Danish: Dybbøl Mølle
Designed by: Kai Lange 1950
Price: $10-15

RC2010-14
Title / English: Copenhagen Stock Exchange
Title / Danish: København Børsen
Designed by: Kai Lange 1950
Price: $10-15

RC2010-16
Title / English: H.C. Andersen's House, Odense
Title / Danish: H.C. Andersens Hus, Odense
Designed by: Kai Lange 1950
Price: $10-15

RC2010-13
Title / English: Amalienborg Palace
Title / Danish: Amalienborg Slot
Designed by: Kai Lange 1950
Price: $10-15

RC2010-15
Title / English: Copenhagen Town Hall
Title / Danish: KINSERT [RC-spec19] WITH PREVIOUS København Rådhus
Designed by: Kai Lange 1950
Price: $10-15

RC2010-17
Title / English: Frederiksberg Church
Title / Danish: Frederiksberg Kirke
Designed by: Kai Lange 1950
Price: $10-15

RC2010-18
Title / English: Rebild Park
Title / Danish: Rebild Bakker
Designed by: Kai Lange 1950
Price: $10-15

RC2010-19
Title / English: Viborg Cathedral
Title / Danish: Viborg Domkirke
Designed by: Kai Lange 1950
Price: $10-15

RC2010-21
Title / English: Færevejle Church
Title / Danish: Færevejle Kirke
Designed by: Kai Lange 1951
Price: $10-15

RC2010-23
Title / English: Old Town by Aarhus
Title / Danish: Den Gamle by Århus
Designed by: Kai Lange 1951
Price: $10-15

RC2010-20
Title / English: Little Belt Bridge
Title / Danish: Lillebæltsbroen
Designed by: Kai Lange 1951
Price: $10-15

RC2010-22
Title / English: Roskilde Cathedral
Title / Danish: Roskilde Domkirke
Designed by: Kai Lange 1951
Price: $10-15

RC2010-24
Title / English: Jens Bang's Stone House, Aalborg
Title / Danish: Jens Bangs Sten Hus, Ålborg
Designed by: Kai Lange
Price: $10-15

RC2010-25
Title / English: Hermitage Castle
Title / Danish: Eremitage Slot
Designed by: Kai Lange 1951
Price: $10-15

RC2010-26
Title / English: Goose Tower
Title / Danish: Gåsetårnet, Vordingborg
Designed by: Kai Lange 1951
Price: $10-15

RC2010-28
Title / English: Watchman Square in Aabenraa
Title / Danish: Vægterpladsen, Abenrå
Designed by: Kai Lange 1952
Price: $10-15

RC2010-30
Title / English: Fredensborg Castle
Title / Danish: Fredensborg Slot
Designed by: Kai Lange 1952
Price: $10-15

RC2010-27
Title / English: Randers Town Hall, Nils Ebbesens Statue
Title / Danish: Randers Rådhus, Nils Ebbesens Statue
Designed by: Kai Lange 1951
Price: $10-15

RC2010-29
Title / English: Ribe Cathedral
Title / Danish: Ribe Domkirke
Designed by: Kai Lange 1952
Price: $10-15

RC2010-31
Title / English: Fanø Island
Title / Danish: Fanø
Designed by: Kai Lange 1952
Price: $10-15

RC2010-32
Title / English: Tivoli Gate
Title / Danish: Tivoli
Designed by: Kai Lange 1952
Price: $10-15

RC2010-33
Title / English: Grundtvig's Church
Title / Danish: Grundtvigiskirken
Designed by: Kai Lange 1952
Price: $10-15

RC2010-35
Title / English: 6 Amager Square, Copenhagen
Title / Danish: Amager Torv 6, København
Designed by: Kai Lange 1952
Price: $10-15

RC2010-37
Title / English: Summer Spire Cliff of Møen
Title / Danish: Sommer Spiret, Møns Klint
Designed by: Kai Lange 1951
Price: $10-15

RC2010-34
Title / English: Marble Church
Title / Danish: Marmorkirken
Designed by: Kai Lange 1952
Price: $10-15

RC2010-36
Title / English: Gefion Fountain
Title / Danish: Gefion Springvandet
Designed by: Kai Lange 1952
Price: $10-15

RC2010-38
Title / English: Koldinghus Castle
Title / Danish: Koldinghus Slot
Designed by: Kai Lange 1952
Price: $10-15

RC2010-39
Title / English: Svendborg Harbor
Title / Danish: Svendborg Havn
Designed by: Kai Lange 1953
Price: $10-15

RC2010-40
Title / English: Haderslev Cathedral
Title / Danish: Haderslev Domkirke
Designed by: Kai Lange 1952
Price: $10-15

RC2010-42
Title / English: Frederiksborg Castle
Title / Danish: Frederiksborg Slot
Designed by: Kai Lange 1952
Price: $10-15

RC2010-44
Title / English: Dogsled in Greenland
Title / Danish: Hundeslæde, Grønland
Designed by: Kai Lange 1953
Price: $10-15

RC2010-41
Title / English: The Peasant Soldier of Fredericia
Title / Danish: Landsoldaten, Fredericia
Designed by: Kai Lange 1952
Price: $10-15

RC2010-43
Title / English: On the Lookout for Father in Greenland
Title / Danish: På udkig efter Får Grønland
Designed by: Kai Lange 1953
Price: $10-15

RC2010-45
Title / English: Fish Market on the Old Beach in Copenhagen
Title / Danish: Fisketorvet på Gammel Strand, København
Designed by: Kai Lange 1953
Price: $10-15

RC2010-46
Title / English: King's Lifeguards
Title / Danish: Kongens Libgard
Designed by: Kai Lange 1953
Price: $10-15

RC2010-47
Title / English: Flower Sellers
Title / Danish: Blomstertorvet Højbroplads
Designed by: Kai Lange 1952
Price: $10-15

RC2010-49
Title / English: Storks Nesting
Title / Danish: Storkerede
Designed by: Kai Lange 1954
Price: $10-15

RC2010-51
Title / English: Christian X Equestrian Statue by Sculptor Kvederis
Title / Danish: Nakskov, Chr. Xs Rytterstatue, Sklp. Kvederis
Designed by: Kai Lange 1954
Price: $10-15

RC2010-48
Title / English: Hans Christian Andersen in Kings Gardens
Title / Danish: Hans Christian Andersen i Kongens Havn
Designed by: Kai Lange 1952
Price: $10-15

RC2010-50
Title / English: Kalundborg Church
Title / Danish: Kalundborg Kirke
Designed by: Kai Lange 1954
Price: $10-15

RC2010-52
Title / English: Graasten Castle
Title / Danish: Gråsten Slot
Designed by: Kai Lange 1954
Price: $10-15

RC2010-53
Title / English: The Kings Yacht in Copenhagen Harbor
Title / Danish: Kongeskibet i, Københavns Havn
Designed by: Kai Lange 1954
Price: $10-15

RC2010-54
Title / English: The Water Tower, Esbjerg
Title / Danish: Vantårnet, Esbjerg
Designed by: Kai Lange 1954
Price: $10-15

RC2010-56
Title / English: Nyborg Castle
Title / Danish: Nyborg Slot
Designed by: Kai Lange 1954
Price: $10-15gf

RC2010-58
Title / English: Sorø Academy
Title / Danish: Sorø Akademi
Designed by: Kai Lange 1954
Price: $10-15

RC2010-55
Title / English: Commemorative Anchor, New Harbor
Title / Danish: Mindesmaerket, Nyhavn
Designed by: Kai Lange 1954
Price: $10-15

RC2010-57
Title / English: Gudhjem, Bornholm
Title / Danish: Gudhjem, Bornholm
Designed by: Kai Lange 1954
Price: $10-15

RC2010-59
Title / English: House of Czar in Nykøbing, Falster
Title / Danish: Czarens Hus, Nykøbing, Falster
Designed by: Kai Lange 1954
Price: $10-15

RC2010-60
Title / English: Aarhus Town Hall
Title / Danish: Århus Rådhus
Designed by: Kai Lange 1954
Price: $10-15

RC2010-61
Title / English: The Kings New Square
Title / Danish: Kongens Nytorv
Designed by: Kai Lange 1956
Price: $10-15

RC2010-63
Title / English: Dragør, Amager
Title / Danish: Dragør, Amager
Designed by: Kai Lange 1956
Price: $10-15

RC2010-65
Title / English: Sønderborg Castle
Title / Danish: Sønderborg Slot
Designed by: Kai Lange 1957
Price: $10-15

RC2010-62
Title / English: Danish Ferryboat
Title / Danish: Dansk Færge
Designed by: Kai Lange 1954
Price: $10-15

RC2010-64
Title / English: Danish Landscape
Title / Danish: Dansk Landskab
Designed by: Kai Lange 1957
Price: $10-15

RC2010-66
Title / English: Tønder Church
Title / Danish: Tønder Kirke
Designed by: Kai Lange 1957
Price: $10-15

RC2010-67
Title / English: Saint Buddolfi Church in Aalborg
Title / Danish: Buddolfi Kirke, Ålborg
Designed by: Kai Lange 1957
Price: $10-15

RC2010-68
Title / English: Køge Church
Title / Danish: Køge Kirke
Designed by: Kai Lange 1957
Price: $10-15

RC2010-70
Title / English: Christiansborg Palace
Title / Danish: Christiansborg Slot
Designed by: Kai Lange 1957
Price: $10-15

RC2010-72
Title / English: Open Air Museum at Sorgenfri Station
Title / Danish: Frilandsmuseet, Sorgenfri
Designed by: Kai Lange 1957
Price: $10-15

RC2010-69
Title / English: Changing of the Guard
Title / Danish: Vagtparaden
Designed by: Kai Lange 1957
Price: $10-15

RC2010-71
Title / English: Herlufsholm Boarding School
Title / Danish: Herlufsholm
Designed by: Kai Lange 1957
Price: $10-15

RC2010-73
Title / English: Windmill at Vejle
Title / Danish: Vejle Mølle
Designed by: Kai Lange 1958
Price: $10-15

RC2010-74
Title / English: Powder Magazine in Frederikshavn
Title / Danish: Krudtårnet, Frederikshavn
Designed by: Kai Lange 1958
Price: $10-15

RC2010-75
Title / English: Ebeltoft Town Hall
Title / Danish: Ebeltoft Radhus
Designed by: Kai Lange 1959
Price: $10-15

RC2010-77
Title / English: Fishermen
Title / Danish: Fiskere
Designed by: Kai Lange 1959
Price: $10-15

RC2010-79
Title / English: Willemoes Farm in Assens
Title / Danish: Willemoesgården, Assens
Designed by: Kai Lange 1960
Price: $10-15

RC2010-76
Title / English: The Farmer
Title / Danish: Landmanden
Designed by: Kai Lange 1959
Price: $10-15

RC2010-78
Title / English: Sky Mountain
Title / Danish: Himmelbjerget
Designed by: Kai Lange 1959
Price: $10-15

RC2010-80
Title / English: The Stockingmaker at Herning
Title / Danish: Hosenbinder, Herning
Designed by: Kai Lange 1960
Price: $10-15

RC2010-81
Title / English: Church Buried in Sand at Skagen
Title / Danish: Den Tilsandede Kirke, Skagen
Designed by: Kai Lange 1962
Price: $10-15

RC2010-82
Title / English: Kaleko Mill near Faaborg
Title / Danish: Kaleko Mølle ved Fåborg
Designed by: Kai Lange 1962
Price: $10-15

RC2010-84
Title / English: Training Ship "Denmark"
Title / Danish: Skolskibet Danmark
Designed by: Kai Lange 1954
Price: $10-15

RC2010-86
Title / English: Munkholm Bridge
Title / Danish: Munkholm Bro
Designed by: Kai Lange
Price: $25-30

RC2010-83
Title / English: The Girl with the Golden Horn at Horsens, by Sculptor Holger Christensen
Title / Danish: Pigen med guldhornet, Horsens, Skulptur Holger Christensen
Designed by: Kai Lange 1962
Price: $10-15

RC2010-85
Title / English: Rømø Church
Title / Danish: Rømø Kirke
Designed by: Kai Lange 1968
Price: $10-15

RC2010-87
Title / English: Skamlingsbanken
Title / Danish: Skamlingsbanken
Designed by: Kai Lange
Price: $25-30

RC2010-88
Title / English: The New Little Belt Bridge
Title / Danish: Den Nye Lillebeltsbro
Designed by: Kai Lange
Price: $25-30

RC2010-89
Title / English: Viking Ship
Title / Danish: Vikinge Skib
Designed by: Kai Lange
Price: $25-30

RC2010-90
Title / English: Rune Stone
Title / Danish: Rune Sten
Designed by: Kai Lange
Price: $25-30

RC2010-91
Title / English: Marselisborg Palace
Title / Danish: Marselisborg Slot
Designed by: Kai Lange
Price: $25-30

RC2010-92
Title / English: Kiobinghus 1645
Title / Danish: Kiobinghus 1645
Designed by:
Price: $25-30
No picture available

RC2010-93
Title / English: Tranekaer Langeland
Title / Danish: Tranekær Langeland
Designed by: Kai Lange
Price: $25-30picture not available

RC2010-94
Title / English: Aarhus Cathedral
Title / Danish: Åarhus Domkirke
Designed by:
Price: $25-30

RC2010-95
Title / English: The Lock Chamber, Hvide Sande
Title / Danish: Kammerslusen, Hvide Sande
Designed by:
Price: $50-100
No picture available

RC2010-96
Title / English: Sømaerket, Løkken
Title / Danish: Sømaerket Løkken
Designed by:
Price: $50-100

RC2010-97
Title / English: Egeskov Castle
Title / Danish: Egeskov Slot
Designed by:
Price: $50-100

Pictures not available from RC-2010-98 through RC-2010-150

RC2010-98
Title / English: Vørgård
Title / Danish: Vørgård
Designed by:
Price: $50-100

RC2010-99
Title / English: Lyngvig Light house
Title / Danish: Lyngvig Fyr
Designed by:

RC2010-101
Title / English: Chillion Castle near Geneva
Title / Danish: Chillion Slot nær Geneva
Designed by: Kai Lange
Price: $50-100

RC2010-101A
Title / English: Ringsted Church
Title / Danish: Ringsted Kirke
Designed by: Kai Lange
Price: $50-100

RC2010-102
Title / English: The Zurich Cathedral
Title / Danish: Domkirken i Zurich
Designed by: Kai Lange
Price: $50-100

RC2010-102A
Title / English: Musichouse in Aarhus
Title / Danish: Musikhuset i Aarhus
Designed by: Kai Lange
Price: $50-100

RC2010-103
Title / English: The Lion by Thorvaldsen Luzern
Title / Danish: Thorvaldsen's Løve i Luzern
Designed by: Kai Lange
Price: $50-100

RC2010-103A
Title / English: Odense Concert Hall
Title / Danish: Odense Koncerthus
Designed by: Kai Lange
Price: $50-100

RC2010-104
Title / English: Castagnola Church, Lugano
Title / Danish: Castagnola Kirken i Lugano
Designed by: Kai Lange
Price: $50-100

RC2010-105
Title / English: Spalentor Basel
Title / Danish: Spalentor Basel
Designed by: Kai Lange
Price: $50-100

RC2010-106
Title / English: Bundespalast in Bern
Title / Danish: Forbundespaldset i Bern
Designed by: Kai Lange
Price: $50-100

RC2010-120
Title / English: Ørebro Castle, Sweden
Title / Danish: Ørebro Slot
Designed by: Kai Lange
Price: $50-100

RC2010-121
Title / English: Kalmar Castle, Sweden
Title / Danish: Kalmar Slot
Designed by: Kai Lange
Price: $50-100

RC2010-122
Title / English: Vaderkvarn Øland, Sweden
Title / Danish Vaderkvarn Øland
Designed by: Kai Lange
Price: $50-100

RC2010-123
Title / English: Nørrelandsmotiv Moose, Sweden
Title / Danish: Nørrelandsmotiv Elg
Designed by: Kai Lange
Price: $50-100

RC2010-124
Title / English: Visby Ringmur Gotland, Sweden
Title / Danish: Visby Ringmur Gotland
Designed by: Kai Lange
Price: $50-100

RC2010-126
Title / English: Frøsø Kurkland, Jamtland, Sweden
Title / Danish: Frøsø Kurkland, Jamtland
Designed by: Kai Lange
Price: $50-100

RC2010-128
Title / English: Vatstene Castle Øestergotland, Sweden
Title / Danish: Vatstene Slot Øestergotland
Designed by: Kai Lange
Price: $50-100

RC2010-151
Title / English: Dion Bouton 1910
Title / Danish: Dion Bouton 1910
Designed by: Sven Vestergaard 1967
Theme: Auto
Price: $50-100

RC2010-152
Title / English: Renault 1902
Title / Danish: Renault 1902
Designed by: Sven Vestergaard 1967
Theme: Auto
Price: $50-100

RC2010-153
Title / English: Ford A 1903
Title / Danish: Ford A 1903
Designed by: Sven Vestergaard 1967
Theme: Auto
Price: $50-100

RC2010-154
Title / English: Delahaye 1907
Title / Danish: Delahaye 1907
Designed by: Sven Vestergaard 1967
Theme: Auto
Price: $50-100

RC2010-155
Title / English: Delaunay Belleville 1910
Title / Danish: Delaunay Belleville 1910
Designed by: Sven Vestergaard 1967
Theme: Auto
Price: $50-100

RC2010-156
Title / English: Rolls Royce 1911
Title / Danish: Rolls Royce 1911
Designed by: Sven Vestergaard 1967
Theme: Auto
Price: $50-100

RC2010-163
Title / English: Fishing Boat by St. Peter, Germany
Title / German: Fischkutter Bei St. Peter
Price: $50-100

RC2010-164
Title / English: Luneberg Heide, Germany
Title / German: Luneburger Heide
Price: $50-100

RC2010-165
Title / English: The Towers of Regensburg Cathedral, Germany
Title / German: Die Turme Des Domes Regensburg
Price: $50-100

RC2010-170
Title / English: Friesland, Germany
Title / German: Friesland
Price: $50-100

RC2010-175
Title / English: George Washington 1732-1799
Title / Danish: George Washington
Designed by: Kai Lange 1964
Theme: US President
Price: $50-100

RC2010-176
Title / English: Thomas Jefferson 1743-1826
Title / Danish: Thomas Jefferson 1743-1826
Designed by: Kai Lange 1964
Theme: US President
Price: $50-100

RC2010-177
Title / English: Abraham Lincoln 1809-1865
Title / Danish: Abraham Lincoln 1809-1865
Designed by: Kai Lange 1964
Theme: US President
Price: $50-100

RC2010-178
Title / English: Theodore Roosevelt 1858-1919
Title / Danish: Theodore Roosevelt 1858-1919
Designed by: Kai Lange 1964
Theme: US President
Price: $50-100

RC2010-179
Title / English: Franklin Roosevelt 1882-1945
Title / Danish: Franklin Roosevelt 1882-1945
Designed by: Kai Lange 1964
Theme: US President
Price: $50-100

RC2010-180
Title / English: John F. Kennedy 1917-1963
Title / Danish: John F. Kennedy 1917-1963
Designed by: Kai Lange 1964
Theme: US President
Price: $50-100

RC2010-181
Title / English: Lyndon B. Johnson
Title / Danish: Lyndon B. Johnson
Designed by: Kai Lange
heme: US President
Price: $50-100

RC2010-201
Title / English: Tiger
Title / Danish: Felis Tigris
Designed by: Kai Lange 1960
Theme: Zoo
Price: $50-100

RC2010-202
Title / English: Hamadras Baboon
Title / Danish: Papio Hamadryas
Designed by: Kai Lange 1960
Theme: Zoo
Price: $50-100

RC2010-203
Title / English: Penguins
Title / Danish: Spheniscidæ
Designed by: Kai Lange 1960
Theme: Zoo
Price: $50-100

RC2010-204
Title / English: Hamadras Baboons
Title / Danish: Papio Hamadryas
Designed by: Kai Lange 1960
Theme: Zoo
Price: $50-100

RC2010-205
Title / English: Burchells' Zebra
Title / Danish: Equus Burchelli
Designed by: Kai Lange 1960
Theme: Zoo
Price: $50-100

RC2010-206
Title / English: North American Bison
Title / Danish: Bison
Designed by: Kai Lange 1960
Theme: Zoo
Price: $50-100

RC2010-211
Title / English: Oslo Town Hall, Norway
Title / Danish: Oslo Raadhus
Designed by:
Price: $50-100

RC2010-212
Title / English: Winter in the Mountains
Title / Danish: Vinter paa Fjellet
Designed by:
Theme:
Price: $50-100

RC2010-215
Title / English: Waterfall
Title / Danish: Fosselfal
Designed by:
Price: $50-100

RC2010-216
Title / English: The Ship of Øseberg
Title / Danish: Øsebergskipet
Designed by:
Price: $50-100

RC2010-225
Title / English: Green 50-year stamp 1775 - 1975
Designed by: Kai Lange
Theme: Stamp
Price: $50-100

RC2010-226
Title / English: Pink 90-year stamp 1775-1975
Designed by: Kai Lange
Theme: Stamp
Price: $50-100

RC2010-227
Title / English: Blue 130-year stamp 1775-1975
Designed by: Kai Lange
Theme: Stamp
Price: $50-100

RC2010-303
Title / English: Gavnø Castle
Title / Danish: Gavnø Slot
Designed by: Kai Lange
Price: $50-100

RC2010-304
Title / English: Danish Windmill, Solvang
Title / Danish: Dansk Vindmølle, Solvang
Designed by: Kai Lange
Price: $50-100

RC2010-305
Title / English: Mulberry Hall, York
Title / Danish: Mullberry Hall, York

Designed by: Kai Lange
Price: $50-100

RC2010-306
Title / English: Aalholm Castle
Title / Danish: Aalholm Slot
Designed by: Kai Lange
Price: $50-100

RC2010-307
Title / English: Gisselfeld Castle
Title / Danish: Gisselfeld Slot
Designed by: Kai Lange
Price: $50-100

RC2010-310
Title / English: Kong Håkon's Church
Title / Danish: Kong Håkon's Kirke
Designed by: Kai Lange
Price: $50-100

RC2010-312
Title / English: The Freedom Museum, Denmark
Title / Danish: Museet for Danmarks Frihedskamp
Designed by: Kai Lange
Price: $50-100

RC2010-327
Title / English: Karnan Helsingborg, Sweden
Title / Danish: Karnan Helsingborg, Sweden
Designed by: Kai Lange
Price: $50-100

RC2010-328
Title / English: The Helsingbord Town Hall, Sweden
Title / Danish: Raadhuset Helsingborg, Sweden
Designed by: Kai Lange
Price: $50-100

RC2010-329
Title / English: Lion & Lamb House, Biggs of Farnham
Title / Danish: Lion & Lamb House, Biggs of Farnham
Designed by: Kai Lange
Price: $50-100

RC2010-331
Title / English: Scout Camp 1979, Holstebro
Title / Danish: Nordlek 79 Holstebro
Designed by: Kai Lange
Price: $50-100

RC2010-332
Title / English: Bluck's Bermuda (Traffic cop)
Title / Danish: Traffik Betjent
Designed by: Kai Lange
Price: $50-100

RC2010-333
Title / English: Bluebeard's Castle
Title / Danish: Blåskægs Slot
Designed by: Kai Lange
Price: $50-100

RC2010-334
Title / English: Bluck's Bermuda, Gibbs Hill Lighthouse
Designed by: Kai Lange
Price: $50-100

RC2010-344
Title / English: Golden Gate Bridge
Title / Danish: Golden Gate Bro
Designed by: Kai Lange
Price: $50-100

RC2010-345
Title / English: Danish Windmill in Elk Horn, Iowa
Title / Danish: Den Danske Vindmølle i Elk Horn, Iowa
Price: $50-100

RC2010-sas1
Title / English: The Town Hall Copenhagen
Price: $50-100

RC2010-sas2
Title / English: The King's Lifeguard
Price: $50-100

RC2010-sas3
Title / English: Hans Christian Andersen's House
Price: $50-100

RC2010-sas4
Title / English: Danish Windmill
Price: $50-100

RC2010-sas5
Title / English: Tivoli Copenhagen
Price: $50-100

RC2010-sas6
Title / English: Kronborg Castle, Elsinore
Price: $50-100

RC2010-sas7
Title / English: Frederiksborg Castle, Hillerod
Price: $50-100

RC2010-sas8
Title / English: The Little Mermaid
Price: $50-100

RC2010-sas9
Title / English: Stork's Nest
Price: $50-100

RC2010-sas10
Title / English: Roskilde Cathedral
Price: $50-100

Royal Copenhagen Annual Mug Series / RC-Mug

The Royal Copenhagen Annual Mug series includes both large (4 1/2") and small (3") versions. The larger version features a sterling silver disk on the bottom of the cup for engraving. Both series have been made since 1967.

RC-Mug 1967
Designed by: Niels Thorson
Price: $200-300

RC-Mug 1968
Designed by: Ellen Malmer
Price: $80-120

RC-Mug 1969
Designed by: Niels Thorson
Price: $80-120

RC-Mug 1970
Designed by: Dorthe Schierup
Price: $40-60

RC-Mug 1971
Designed by: Hans Andersen
Price: $40-60

RC-Mug 1972
Desgined by: Bodil Buch
Price: $40-60

RC-Mug 1973
Designed by: Gerd Hiort Petersen
Price: $40-60
No picture available

RC-Mug 1974
Designed by: Ellen Malmer
Price: $40-60

RC-Mug 1975
Designed by: Bodil Buch
Price: $40-60

RC-Mug 1976
Designed by: Anne Marie Trolle
Price: $40-60

RC-Mug 1977
Designed by: Inge Lise Kofoed
Price: $40-60

RC-Mug 1978
Designed by: Bo Kristiansen
Price: $40-60

RC-Mug 1979
Designed by: Ivan Weiss
Price: $40-60

RC-Mug 1980
Designed by: Anne Marie
Price: $40-60

RC-Mug 1981
Designed by: Ellen Malmer
Price: $40-60

RC-Mug 1982
Designed by: Inge Lise Kofoed
Price: $40-60

RC-Mug 1983
Designed by: Jens Windfeld-Hansen
Price: $40-60

RC-Mug 1984
Designed: Ivan Weiss
Price: $40-60

RC-Mug 1985
Designed by: Ivan Weiss
Price: $40-60

RC-Mug 1986
Designed by: Inge Lise Kofoed
Price: $40-60

RC-Mug 1987
Designed by: Mogens Andersen
Price: $40-60

RC-Mug 1988
Designed by: Jens Birkemose
Price: $40-60
No picture available

RC-Mug 1989
Designed by: Wilhem Freddie
Price: $40-60

RC-Mug 1990
Designed by: Egill Jacobsen
Price: $80-100

RC-Mug 1991
Designed by: Inger Hanmann
Price: $80-100

RC-Mug 1992
Designed by: Lin Utzon
Price: $80-100

RC-Mug 1993
Designed by: Ivan Weiss
Price: $80-100

RC-Mug 1994
Designed by: Bodil Kiaalund
Price: $80-100

RC-Mug 1995
Designed by: Peter Brandes
Price: $80-100

RC-Mug 1996
Designed by: Jørn Larsen
Price: $80-100

RC-Mug 1997
Designed by: Bjørn Nørgaard
Price: $80-100
No picture available

RC-Mug 1998
Designed by: Arne Haugen Sørensen
Price: $80-100

RC-Mug 1999
Designed by: Maja Lisa Engelhardt
Price: $80-100

RC-Mug 2000
Designed by: Flemming Brylle
Price: $100-120

RC-Mug 2001
Designed by: Ivan Weiss
Price: $100-120

RC-Mug 2002
Designed by: Sten Lykke Madsen
Price: $100-120

RC-Mug 2003
Designed by: Doris Bloom
Price: $100-120

RC-Mug 2004
Designed by: Lisa Malinowsky
Price: $100-120
No picture available

Royal Copenhagen Dealer Signs

Dealer signs are found in numerous different designs, ages, and languages. A wide range of them are shown here. Though the production of dealer signs started very early, it was not until the late 19th century, when the products were being marketed through a larger number of retail outlets in Denmark and across the world, that the wider use of them began. The earlier signs can be found hand painted in overglaze and underglaze techniques. Most of the newer signs are done as transferware.

RC-Sign1

RC-Sign2

RC-Sign3

RC-Sign4

RC-Sign5

RC-Sign6

Rc-Sign7

RC-Sign9

RC-Sign8

RC-Sign10

RC-Sign11

RC-Sign12

RC-Sign14

RC-Sign13

RC-Sign15

RC-Sign16

RC-Sign18

RC-Sign17

RC-Sign19

RC-Sign20

RC-Sign22

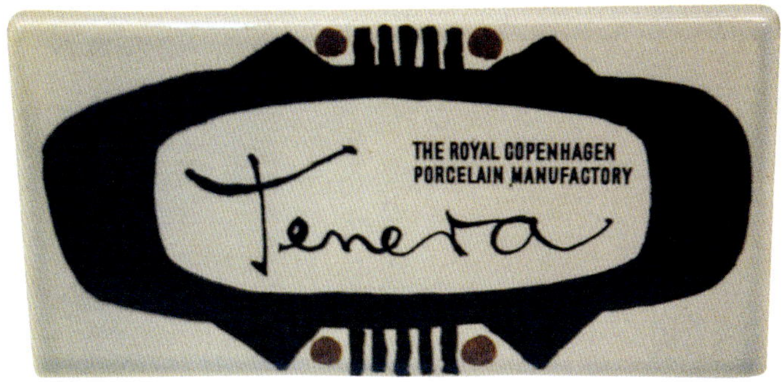

RC-Sign21

RC-Sign23

RC-Sign24

Other Royal Copenhagen Collectibles

Besides being known for its collector plates, Royal Copenhagen is also known for its vases, figurines and other collectibles. Here we show just a small selection.

RC-O-1
Title / English: Monkey - trio
Designed by: Knud Kyhn 1908
Size: 7" by 11"

RC-O-2
Title / English: Royal Copenhagen Lidded Vase
Title / Danish: Lågvase
Designed by: Unkown 1931
Size: 17"

RC-O-5
Title / English: Blue Crystaline Vase
Title / Danish: Vase med blå crystal glasur
Designed by:
Glaze by Poul M.Proschowsky 9-11-1924
Size: ca 7"

RC-O-6
Title / English: Bowl carried by angel sitting on a dolphin - Bisque and porcelain
Designed by: Unknown pre-1898
Size: 6.5" by 5.5

RC-O-7
Title / English: Aalborg Portland ink set
Size: 4.5" by 10"

RC-O-8
Title / English: Silver mounted Margrethe cup
Designed by:
Silver by Anthon Michelsen
Size: 4.75"

RC-O-9
Different types of vases and trays

RC-O-10
Different types of vases and trays

RC-O-12
Title / English: Clock

RC-O-11
Title / English: Wallpocket vase
Designed by: Christian Thomsen

RC-O-13
Title / English: Pharmacy jar

RC-O-15
Title / English: Charger with landscape
Designed by: Andy CT

RC-O-14
Title / English: Commemorative cup, "Belle Colle"

RC-O-16
Title / English: Blue crystaline cod tray
Designed by: Glaze by Poul M.Proschowsky 9-11-1924

RC-O-17
Title / English: Artichoke vase
Designed by: Arno Malinowski
Size:

RC-O-19
Title / English: Collie figurine
Designed by: Christian Thomsen

RC-O-18
Title / English: Georg Thylstrup figurine, Artist signed by Oluf Jensen
Designed by: Georg Thylstrup

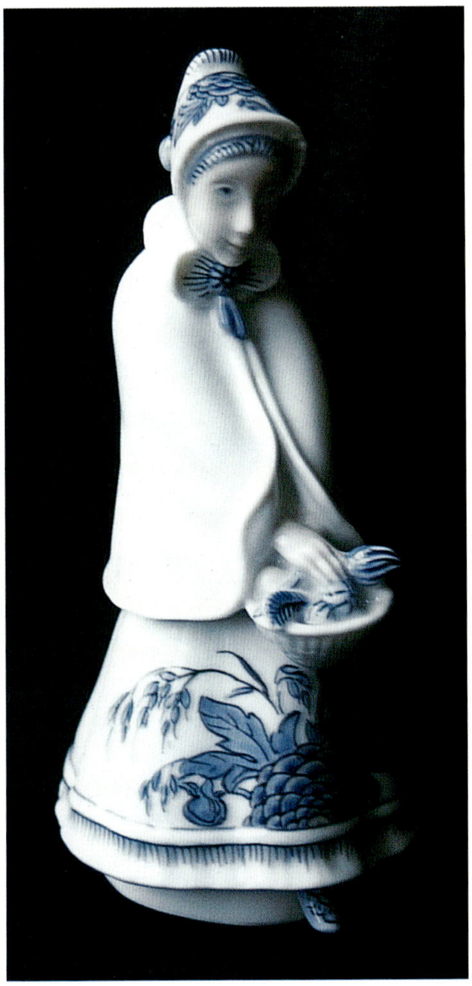

RC-O-20
Title / English: Early Bird vase

RC-O-21
Title / English: Vase with gold and silver

Designed by: around 1880-1890's.

RC-O-22
Title / English: Butterfly vase

RC-O-23
Title / English: Rundskue vases made from 1906 to at least 1941. We also know of one from 1952

RC-O-24
Title / English: Christmas vases made from 1917 to 1932

RC-O-25
Title / English: Easter vases. Made from 1917 to 1932

RC-O-26
Title / English: Commemorative vases, made for various occasions.

Chapter 4.

Aluminia and Anton Michelsen Collections

Aluminia

Small Christmas Plates / A-S

The small Aluminia Christmas plate series is rather strange, as the size of the plate varies from 7" to 7 1/3", and slightly more at times. Many of the plates feature almost the same motif, since only a handful of artists designed this series. These Christmas plates, just like the Royal Copenhagen Christmas plates, were done in different languages. The picture below is shown with German text, but they were also done in English and Czechoslovakian.

A-S1904
Title / English: Christmas Wreath
Title / Danish: Juleneg
Designed by: H. Slott-Møller
Price: $100-200

A-S1905
Title / English: Church and Christmas Roses
Title / Danish: Kirke og juleroser
Designed by: Chr. Joachim
Price: $100-200

A-S1906
Title / English: Bird and Christmas Roses
Title / Danish: Fugl og juleroser
Designed by: Chr. Joachim
Price: $100-200

A-S1907
Title / English: Evergreen branch
Title / Danish: Grangren
Designed by: Chr. Joachim
Price: $100-200

A-S1908
Title / English: Star over Church and Christmas Roses
Title / Danish: Stjerne over kirke og juleroser
Designed by: Chr. Joachim
Price: $100-200

A-S1909
Title / English: Three Lights and Christmas Roses
Title / Danish: Tre lys og juleroser
Designed by: Chr. Joachim
Price: $100-200

A-S1910
Title / English: Pinecones
Title / Danish: Grankogler
Designed by: Chr. Joachim
Price: $100-200

A-S1911
Title / English: Bell
Title / Danish: Klokke
Designed by: Chr. Joachim
Price: $100-200

A-S1912
Title / English: Christmas Light
Title / Danish: Julelys
Designed by: Chr. Joachim
Price: $100-200

A-S1913
Title / English: Star
Title / Danish: Stjerne
Designed by: Chr. Joachim
Price: $100-200

A-S1914
Title / English: Christmas Rose
Title / Danish: Juleroser
Designed by: Chr. Joachim
Price: $100-200

A-S1915
Title / English: Star outside Window
Title / Danish: Stjerne udenfor vindue
Designed by: Chr. Joachim
Price: $100-200

A-S1916
Title / English: Christmas Rose
Title / Danish: Julerose
Designed by: Chr. Joachim
Price: $100-200

A-S1917
Title / English: Flower
Title / Danish: Blomst
Designed by: Chr. Joachim
Price: $100-200

A-S1918
Title / English: Flower and Stars
Title / Danish: Blomster og stjerner
Designed by: Chr. Joachim
Price: $100-200

A-S1919
Title / English: Angel
Title / Danish: Engel
Designed by: J.M. Heiberg
Price: $100-200

A-S1920
Title / English: Two Angels
Title / Danish: To engle
Designed by: J.M. Heiberg
Price: $100-200

A-S1921
Title / English: Flowers
Title / Danish: Blomster
Designed by: J.M. Heiberg
Price: $100-200

A-S1922
Title / English: Flower
Title / Danish: Blomst
Designed by: J.M. Heiberg
Price: $100-200

A-S1923
Title / English: Flower
Title / Danish: Blomst
Designed by: Chr. Joachim
Price: $100-200

A-S1924
Title / English: Church and Roses
Title / Danish: Kirke og roser
Designed by: Nils Thorsson
Price: $100-200

A-S1925
Title / English: Bell
Title / Danish: Klokke
Designed by: Nils Thorsson
Price: $100-200

A-S1926
Title / English: Christmas Rose and Crown
Title / Danish: Julerose og krone
Designed by: Nils Thorsson
Price: $100-200

A-S1927
Title / English: Star and Church
Title / Danish: Stjerne og kirke
Designed by: Nils Thorsson
Price: $100-200

A-S1928
Title / English: Three Bells
Title / Danish: Tre klokker
Designed by: Nils Thorsson
Price: $100-200

A-S1929
Title / English: Evergreen and Christmas Roses
Title / Danish: Gran og juleroser
Designed by: Nils Thorsson
Price: $100-200

A-S1930
Title / English: Church and Star
Title / Danish: Kirke og stjerne
Designed by: Nils Thorsson
Price: $100-200

A-S1931
Title / English: Boy on Goose
Title / Danish: Dreng på gås
Designed by: H. H. Hansen
Price: $100-200

A-S1932
Title / English: Angel with Lights
Title / Danish: Engel med lys
Designed by: H. H. Hansen
Price: $100-200

A-S1933
Title / English: Angel with Hearts
Title / Danish: Engel med hjerter
Designed by: H. H. Hansen
Price: $100-200

A-S1934
Title / English: Angels with Evergreen Garland
Title / Danish: Engle med granguirlande
Designed by: H. H. Hansen
Price: $200-300

A-S1935
Title / English: Crowned Baby Jesus
Title / Danish: Kronet Jesusbarn
Designed by: H. H. Hansen
Price: $200-300

A-S1936
Title / English: Baby Jesus with Shepherds, Staff and Lamb
Title / Danish: Jesusbarn med hyrdestav og lam
Designed by: H. H. Hansen
Price: $200-300

A-S1937
Title / English: Angel with Trumpet
Title / Danish: Engel med trompet
Designed by: H. H. Hansen
Price: $200-300

A-S1938
Title / English: Angel with Censer
Title / Danish: Engel med røgelseskar
Designed by: H. H. Hansen
Price: $200-300

Aluminia Large Christmas Plates / A-L

These large Aluminia Christmas plates are nearly 13" in diameter, except for 1904, 1905, and 1908.

A-L1904
Title / English: Mary with Baby, Joseph and the Animals in the Stable
Title / Danish: Maria m. barnet, Josef og dyr i stalden
Designed by: H. Slott-Møller
Price: $400-600

A-L1905
Title / English: Star of Bethlehem and the Three Kings
Title / Danish: Ledestjernen og de hellige tre konger til hest
Designed by: H. Slott-Møller
Price: $400-600

A-L1906
Title / English: Flight to Egypt
Title / Danish: Flugten til Ægypten
Designed by: H. Slott-Møller
Price: $400-600

A-L1907
Title / English: Angel and Shepherd in the Field
Title / Danish: Engel og hyrder på marken
Designed by: R. Harboe
Price: $400-600

A-L1908
Title / English: Manger and Animals
Title / Danish: Julekrybbe og dyr
Designed by: R. Harboe
Price: $400-600

A-L1909
Title / English: The Annunciation of the Virgin Mary
Title / Danish: Bebudelsen
Designed by: R. Harboe
Price: $400-600

A-L1910
Title / English: Angel Ringing Bells
Title / Danish: Engle ringer med klokker
Designed by: R. Harboe
Price: $400-600

A-L1911
Title / English: Santa Claus and Children
Title / Danish: Julemand og børn
Designed by: R. Harboe
Price: $400-600

A-L1912
Title / English: Mary Worshiping the Baby
Title / Danish: Maria tilbeder barnet
Designed by: R. Harboe
Price: $400-600

A-L1913
Title / English: Angel and Star
Title / Danish: Engel og stjerne
Designed by: R. Harboe
Price: $400-600

A-L1914
Title / English: Angel and Candlelabrum
Title / Danish: Engel og armstage
Designed by: R. Harboe
Price: $400-600

A-L1915
Title / English: Four Bells Ringing
Title / Danish: Ringer med fire klokker
Designed by: R. Harboe
Price: $400-600

A-L1916
Title / English: Swaddled Child
Title / Danish: Barn i svøb
Designed by: R. Harboe
Price: $400-600

A-L1917
Title / English: Christmas Angel with Ribbon
Title / Danish: Jule engel med bånd
Designed by: R. Harboe
Price: $400-600

A-L1918
Title / English: Angel with Chimes
Title / Danish: Engel med klokkespil
Designed by: R. Harboe
Price: $400-600

A-L1919
Title / English: Angel with Flag
Title / Danish: Engel med flag
Designed by: R. Harboe
Price: $400-600

A-L1920
Title / English: The Crowned Baby Jesus
Title / Danish: Kronet Jesusbarn
Designed by: R. Harboe
Price: $400-600

A-L1921
Title / English: Angel with String Instrument
Title / Danish: Engel med strengeinstrument
Designed by: R. Harboe
Price: $400-600

A-L1922
Title / English: Angel with Chandelier
Title / Danish: Engel med lys-krone
Designed by: R. Harboe
Price: $400-600

A-L1923
Title / English: Angel with Music
Title / Danish: Engel med nodebånd
Designed by: R. Harboe
Price: $400-600

A-L1924
Title / English: Mary with Child
Title / Danish: Den tronende Maria med barnet
Designed by: R. Harboe
Price: $400-600

A-L1925
Title / English: Angel with Cymbal
Title / Danish: Engel med bækkener
Designed by: R. Harboe
Price: $400-600

A-L1926
Title / English: Angel in Starlight
Title / Danish: Engel i stråleglans
Designed by: R. Harboe
Price: $400-600

A-L1927
Title / English: Angel with Music
Title / Danish: Engel med nodebånd
Designed by: R. Harboe
Price: $400-600

A-L1928
Title / English: Mary with Child
Title / Danish: Maria med barnet
Designed by: R. Harboe
Price: $400-600

A-L1929
Title / English: Angel
Title / Danish: Engel
Designed by: R. Harboe
Price: $400-600

A-L1930
Title / English: The Crowned Baby Jesus
Title / Danish: Kronet Jesusbarn
Designed by: R. Harboe
Price: $400-600

Aluminia Childrens Help Day Series / A-CH

The Alumina Children's Help Day plates are 4 1/3" in diameter. The first five were hand painted and numbered. From 1914 on, they were airbrushed, and during the years 1915 through 1918, two separate pictures were produced for each year, one featuring a boy and the other featuring a girl.

A-CH9
Title / English: Girl with Basket
Title / Danish: Pige med kurv
Designed by: Chr. Joachim
Price: $100-200

A-CH10
Title / English: Boy with Wreath and Bouquet
Title / Danish: Dreng med krans og buket
Designed by: Rasmus Harboe
Price: $100-200

A-CH11
Title / English: Stork with Baby
Title / Danish: Stork med barn
Designed by: Chr. Joachim
Price: $100-200

A-CH12
Title / English: Boy with Trumpet
Title / Danish: Dreng med trompet
Designed by: Rasmus Harboe
Price: $100-200

A-CH13
Title / English: Boy in Boat
Title / Danish: Dreng i båd
Designed by: Rasmus Harboe
Price: $100-200

A-CH14
Title / English: Boy with a Wooden Horn
Title / Danish: Dreng med traetudehorn i træ
Designed by: Oscar Willerup
Price: $100-200

A-CH15
Title / English: Girl Lifting Baby Girl / Swaddled Baby
Title / Danish: Pige løfter lille pige / Barn i svøb
Designed by: Louis Moe
Price: $100-200

A-CH16
Title / English: Girl Picking Flowers / Children Sitting
Title / Danish: Pige plukker blomster / Siddende barn
Designed by: Oscar Willerup
Price: $100-200

A-CH17
Title / English: Girl in Wagon / Boy with Flower
Title / Danish: Dreng i legevogn / Dreng med blomst
Designed by: Louis Moe
Price: $100-200

A-CH18
Title / English: Girl with Doll / Boy with Flower in Silhouette
Title / Danish: Pige med duke / Dreng med blomst i silhuet
Designed by: Else Hasselriis
Price: $100-200

A-CH19
Title / English: Girl with Flower Basket on Her Head
Title / Danish: Pige med blomsterkurv på hovedet
Designed by: Oscar Willerup
Price: $100-200

A-CH20
Title / English: Child in Playpen
Title / Danish: Barn i kravlegård
Designed by: Oscar Willerup
Price: $100-200

A-CH21
Title / English: Boy with Teddybear
Title / Danish: Dreng med teddybjørn
Designed by: Oscar Willerup
Price: $100-200

A-CH22
Title / English: Boy with Ball
Title / Danish: Dreng med bold
Designed by: Oscar Willerup
Price: $100-200

A-CH23
Title / English: Boy Eating Porridge
Title / Danish: Barn spiser grød
Designed by: Oscar Willerup
Price: $100-200

A-CH24
Title / English: Girl with Doll
Title / Danish: Pige med dukke
Designed by: Oscar Willerup
Price: $100-200

A-CH25
Title / English: Boy Reading Book
Title / Danish: Barn læser i bog
Designed by: Oscar Willerup
Price: $100-200

A-CH26
Title / English: Child with Birds
Title / Danish: Barn med fugle
Designed by: Oscar Willerup
Price: $100-200

A-CH27
Title / English: Child Pulling Off Sock
Title / Danish: Barn trækker strømpe af
Designed by: Oscar Willerup
Price: $100-200

A-CH28
Title / English: Child with Flower
Title / Danish: Barn med blomst
Designed by: Oscar Willerup
Price: $100-200

A-CH29
Title / English: Boy with Mushrooms
Title / Danish: Dreng med svampe
Designed by: Oscar Willerup
Price: $100-200

A-CH30
Title / English: Girl with Picnic Basket
Title / Danish: Pige me madkurv
Designed by: Oscar Willerup
Price: $100-200

Anton Michelsen

A. Michelsen Christmas Spoons and Forks / M

The Michelsen Christmas Spoon series began in 1910 as simply "gilded" sterling silver spoons with a design. It was not until the middle 1920s that the first forks were produced. This series varies from everything else we have in this book, as each piece was made for more than one year and many of them for as many as ten years after the year marked on the piece. This makes collecting them easier as more pieces are available. Because of improvement in craftsmanship, the later pieces are of higher quality than the earlier productions. Pieces that have an "R" in a circle, stamped on the reverse side of the spoon or fork, are reproductions. These were not made in the year that is stated on the front of the piece.

M-1910
Title / English: Star of Bethlehem
Title / Danish: Bethlehems Stjernen
Designed by: N. C. Dyrlund

M-1911
Title / English: The Infant Christ
Title / Danish: Jesus Barnet
Designed by: Gudmund Hentze

M-1912
Title / English: Christmas Bells
Title / Danish: Juleklokker
Designed by: Poul U. Michelsen

M-1913
Title / English: Christmas Scenery
Title / Danish: Julescenning
Designed by: Poul U. Michelsen

M-1914
Title / English: Christmas Angel
Title / Danish: Juleenglen
Designed by: H. Slott-Møller

M-1915
Title / English: The Three Kings of Cologne
Title / Danish: Hellige tre konger
Designed by: H. Slott-Møller

M-1916
Title / English: The Madonna
Title / Danish: Madonna og barnet
Designed by: Marie Henriques

M-1917
Title / English: Epiphany
Title / Danish: Helligtrekongerlyset
Designed by: Kay Bojesen

M-1918
Title / English: Mistletoe
Title / Danish: Mistleten
Designed by: Gustav Lorenzen

M-1919
Title / English: Peace on Earth
Title / Danish: Fred på jorden
Designed by: Gudmund Hentze

M-1920
Title / English: The Dybbøl Mill
Title / Danish: Denforeningen
Designed by: H. Slott-Møller

M-1921
Title / English: Christmas Boat
Title / Danish: Jule båden
Designed by: Kay Bojesen

M-1922
Title / English: Holly
Title / Danish: Kristtjørn
Designed by: Bertha Dorph

M-1923
Title / English: The Cathedral of Copenhagen
Title / Danish: Vor frue kirke
Designed by: Anton Rosen

M-1924
Title / English: Sheaf of Grain
Title / Danish: Julenget
Designed by: Bertha Dorph

M-1925
Title / English: Poinsettia
Title / Danish: Julestjernen
Designed by: Ellen Michelsen

M-1926
Title / English: Organ Pipes
Title / Danish: Orgelpiper
Designed by: Hans Tegner

M-1927
Title / English: Spire of Our Saviors Church in Copenhagen
Title / Danish: Vor Frelfers Kirkespir
Designed by: Hans Tegner

M-1928
Title / English: Epiphyllum
Title / Danish: Julekaktus
Designed by: Thorkild Olsen, Spoon signed

M-1929
Title / English: Christmas Rose
Title / Danish: Juleroser
Designed by: Ebba Holm, signed EH

M-1930
Title / English: Christmas in Port
Title / Danish: Jul i havnen
Designed by: Arne Bang

M-1931
Title / English: Star of Bethlehem (with a map of Denmark)
Title / Danish: Bethlehemsstjernen
Designed by: Ebbe Sadolin

M-1932
Title / English: Children around the Christmas Tree
Title / Danish: Børn rundt om Juletræet
Designed by: Ebba Holm

M-1933
Title / English: The Little Match Girl
Title / Danish: Den lille pige med svovlstikkerne
Designed by: Ib Lunding

M-1934
Title / English: Holy Night
Title / Danish: Altertable
Designed by: Olaf Stæhr-Nielsen

M-1935
Title / English: Kneeling Shepherd
Title / Danish: Hyrden og julestjernen
Designed by: Jais Nielsen

M-1936
Title / English: Christmas Candle
Title / Danish: Julelys
Designed by: Arno Malinowski

M-1937
Title / English: Birds in the Christmas Sheaf
Title / Danish: Juleneget
Designed by: Palle Suenson

M-1938
Title / English: Snow Berries
Title / Danish: Snebær
Designed by: Ebbe Sadolin

M-1939
Title / English: The Gift Laden Christmas Tree
Title / Danish: Jule træet med pakker
Designed by: Olaf Stæhr-Nielsen

M-1940
Title / English: The Star of Bethlehem
Title / Danish: Hyrderne p marken
Designed by: Paul Erlinger

M-1941
Title / English: Mistletoe
Title / Danish: Mistletenen
Designed by: Ole Hagen, Signed OH

M-1942
Title / English: Madonna and Child
Title / Danish: Madonna med barnet
Designed by: Ib Lunding

M-1943
Title / English: The Dove of Peace
Title / Danish: Fredsdue
Designed by: Olaf Stæhr- Nielsen

M-1944
Title / English: The Hearty Holiday spirit
Title / Danish: Julens hjearter
Designed by: Ole Hagen

M-1945
Title / English: Snow Crystals
Title / Danish: Snekrystaller
Designed by: Erik Herløw

M-1946
Title / English: Holly
Title / Danish: Kristtjørn
Designed by: Johan Pedersen

M-1947
Title / English: Falling Snowflakes
Title / Danish: Snedolde
Designed by: Ibi Trier Mørch

M-1948
Title / English: Christmas Ram
Title / Danish: Jule bukken
Designed by: Ilse Nalbandian

M-1949
Title / English: Candles of Advent
Title / Danish: Adventskransen
Designed by: Mogens Nilsson

M-1950
Title / English: Winter Forest
Title / Danish: Juletræet
Designed by: Poul Høyrup

M-1951
Title / English: Colorful Christmas
Title / Danish: Julenjerte
Designed by: Eigil Jensen

M-1952
Title / English: Santa and the Reindeer
Title / Danish: Julemanden med rensdyr
Designed by: Arne Ungermann

M-1953
Title / English: The Herald Angels
Title / Danish: Juleengle
Designed by: Ebbe and Karen Clemmenson

M-1954
Title / English: Cornets
Title / Danish: Kræmmerhuse
Designed by: Søren Sass

M-1955
Title / English: Poinsettia
Title / Danish: Julestjerne
Designed by: Palle Pio

M-1956
Title / English: Snow Flowers
Title / Danish: Julebegonea
Designed by: Jørgen Michelsen

M-1957
Title / English: Danish Pixie
Title / Danish: Danske Uldgarnsnisser
Designed by: Erik Ellegaard Frederiksen

M-1958
Title / English: The Wise Men from the East
Title / Danish: Hellig Tre Konger
Designed by: Karl Gustav Hansen

M-1959
Title / English: The Lucia Bride
Title / Danish: Skt. Lucia brud
Designed by: Henry Thelander, signed

M-1960
Title / English: The Winter Solstice
Title / Danish: Vinter Solhverv
Designed by: Rolf Middelboe, signed RM

M-1961
Title / English: Organ Pipes
Title / Danish: Orgelpiper
Designed by: Arne L. Hansen

M-1962
Title / English: Madonna and Child
Title / Danish: JMadonna og barnet
Designed by: Carl R. Frederiksen

M-1963
Title / English: Santa's Village
Title / Danish: Nordlys
Designed by: Carsten Frölich, signed

M-1964
Title / English: Orion
Title / Danish: Orion
Designed by: Inger Hanmann

M-1965
Title / English: The Christmas Tree
Title / Danish: Juletræet
Designed by: Theresia Hvorslev, signed TH

M-1966
Title / English: The Flight into Egypt
Title / Danish: Flugten til ægypten
Designed by: Jørgen Dahlerup, signed JD

M-1967
Title / English: Splendor of Yule
Title / Danish: Juleglansen
Designed by: Paul Rene Gauguin

M-1968
Title / English: A Mother's Heart
Title / Danish: Moders hjerte
Designed by: Henry Heerup, signed Heerup

M-1969
Title / English: Greenlander (set includes one of each color)
Title / Danish: Grønlænder
Designed by: Ib Antoni, signed Antoni

M-1970
Title / English: Mr. Snowman's Christmas Tree
Title / Danish: Snemandens jule træ
Designed by: Mogens Zieler

M-1971
Title / English: Golden Universe
Title / Danish: Gyldent univers
Designed by: Else Alfelt

M-1972
Title / English: Herald
Title / Danish: Herold
Designed by: Bjorn Wiinblad

M-1973
Title / English: Solstice and Family
Title / Danish: Solhverv og familie
Designed by: Ib Spang Olsen

M-1974
Title / English: The Blue Bird
Title / Danish: Blå fugl
Designed by: Carl-Henning Pedersen

M-1975
Title / English: Shooting Star
Title / Danish: Stjerneskud
Designed by: Per Arnoldi

M-1976
Title / English: Snow Crystal
Title / Danish: Snekrystal
Designed by: Gudmund Olsen

M-1977
Title / English: Winter Rose
Title / Danish: Vinter rose
Designed by: Poul Hanmann

M-1978
Title / English: Solstice
Title / Danish: Solhverv
Designed by: Vibeke Alfelt

M-1979
Title / English: The Sun Kingdom
Title / Danish: Solriget
Designed by: Lars Aakirke

M-1980
Title / English: The Mask
Title / Danish: Masken
Designed by: Egill Jacobsen

M-1981
Title / English: Red Robin
Title / Danish: Rødkælk
Designed by: Falke Bang

M-1982
Title / English: Queen of Sheba
Title / Danish: Dronningen af Sheba
Designed by: Kamma Svensson

M-1983
Title / English: The Snow Queen
Title / Danish: Snedronningen
Designed by: Lars Bo

M-1984
Title / English: Her Majesty (The Queen of Denmark, Margrethe II, created the design for this Christmas set)
Title / Danish:

M-1985
Title / English: The Bird Sheaf
Title / Danish: Juleneget
Designed by: Naja Salto

M-1986
Title / English: The Tree of Life
Title / Danish: Livetstræ
Designed by: Bent Karl Jacobson

M-1987
Title / English: Festival of Light
Title / Danish: Livetstræ fest
Designed by: Mogens Andersen

M-1988
Title / English: The Town
Title / Danish: Byen
Designed by: Knud Erik Færgemann

M-1989
Title / English: The Angel
Title / Danish: Englen
Designed by: Hans Voigt Steffensen

M-1990
Title / English: Potsherd
Title / Danish: Potteskår
Designed by: Pia Schutzmann

M-1991
Title / English: Northern Lights
Title / Danish: Nordlys
Designed by: Lin Utzon

M-1992
Title / English: Harmony
Title / Danish: Harmoni
Designed by: Tom Krøjer

M-1993
Title / English: Winter Stars
Title / Danish: Vinterstjerner
Designed by: Ivan Weiss

M-1994
Title / English: Christmas Cactus
Title / Danish: Julekaktus
Designed by: Poul Janus Ipsen

M-1995
Title / English: Winter Solstice
Title / Danish: Vinter Solhverv
Designed by: Ole Kortzau

M-1996
Title / English: Seraphs
Title / Danish: Seraf
Designed by: Bjorn Norgaard

M-1997
Title / English: Burning Bush
Title / Danish: Den Brandenebusk
Designed by: Maja Lisa Engelhardt

M-1998
Title / English: Three Suns
Title / Danish: Tresole
Designed by: Carl-Henning Pedersen

M-1999
Title / English: The Star's Light
Title / Danish: Stjernelyset
Designed by: Peter Brandes

M-2000
Title / English: Heart Bud
Title / Danish: Hjerteknop
Designed by: Doris Bloom

M-2001
Title / English: Heart
Title / Danish: Hjerte
Designed by: Lisa Malinowsky

M-2002
Title / English: Snow Drop
Title / Danish: Snedråbe
Designed by: John Mortensen

M-2003
Title / English: Glowing Heart
Title / Danish: Die Glut des Herzens
Designed by: Esben Hanefelt Krisensen

M-2004
Title / English: Heavenly Spoon
Title / Danish: Himmelskeen
Designed by: Anne Tholstrup

Appendix A:

Artist List

Aamodt, Worked for Bing and Grøndahl. Designed commemorative plate number 16.
Agergaard Jensen, Merete (1937) Sculptor. B&G and RC
Ahlmann, Michaela B&G figurines
Albertsen, Tova (1945 - *), Illustrator. Designed bowls and vases for RC
Amberg, Hans Christian (1837-1919) Architect. Com. #49 Plate for RC
Andersen, Mogens Helge Thestrup (1916 -*) Painter. Decoration for RC of the Annual egg 1975, vases and jars in bisquit with transfer print 1977-1978
Andersen, Anders Valdemar Peter (1875-1928) Painter and illustrator. At B&G about 1909-1912
Miss Andresen (-1902 -), Sculptor for RC. Model 1902
Arnoldi, Per (1941 -) Illustrator. Decoration of Annual Egg for RC 1980

Benter, Lotte (- 1911-1914 -). Sculptor. Figurines in national dresses for RC 1911-1914
Berg, Søren (1897-1978) Chemistry ingeneur. At RC 1923-1933
Bindesbøal, Thorwald, Designed for Bing and Grøndahl, designed commemorative plate number 7.
Bing, Harriet (1863-1919) Painter. At B&G 1887-1919
Bjerg, Johannes Clausen (1886-1955) Sculptor. Danaide head in blanc de chine for RC 1947
Bjergborg, Anders Holme (1928) Ceramicist. AT Bing & Grøndahl 1949-1963
Blache, Vigilius Christian (1838-1920) Marine Painter. RC Plate Frigate Jutland 1909
Blom, H. () Painter. At RC 1913 - 1918
Blom (Holm), Karin Anna Katharina (1881-1951). Ceramicist at RC from 1942
Boesen, Nicolai Arthur (1870-1949) Painter. Three years at Bing & Grøndahl. At RC Factory 1912-1926. Signing master painter at Dahl Jensen Porcelain Factory from 1926
Bonfils, Ada (Adda) Andrea Elisabeth (1883-1943) Sculptor. Figurines. At RC Factory 1915-1941
Bonfils, Kjeld
Bonnesen, Carl Johan (1868-1933) Sculptor. Models for RC: French Workhorse 1895 and "Northpoole" 1900. Made figurines for Dahl Jensen Porcelain
Borlwyich, Jessie Figurine for RC
Bovenschulte, Mogens (1920 -) Sculptor Models for RC 1961-62
Brandstrup, Ludvig (1861-1935) Sculptor. RC: Child bust 1891 - decorated in underglaze by C.F.Liisberg 1893. Worked at B&G
Bregnø, Jens Jacob Nielsen (1877-1946) Sculptor. At Bing & Grøndahl
Broekoe, Gitte works for Bing and Grøndahl. Artist of the Snow Fairies collection
Brunø, Søren. B&G figurine
Bruun, Edith Sonne (1910-1993) Ceramicist. Worked at Saxbo 1938-1939 and 1946-1961. AT B&G from 1962
Bruun, Palle () Sculptor. At B&G
Brüel, Axel (1900-1977). Sculptor. AT B&G
Buch, Bodil (1945 -) Ceramicist. Associated with the Royal Copenhagen factory 1969-1974. Designed vases and jewelry together with Jens Windfeld Hansen
Busch-Jensen, H. O. (1887-1972) Ceramicist. At B&G 1910-1916 and after 1930
Bussenius. Figurine for RC
Bæch, Gudrun Meedom (1915) B&G
Bøcher, Karl Peter (Ricard) Richard (1887-1953) Painter. At RC Factory 1912 - 1953. Director for underglaze department from 1934. Signing artist. Børnehjælpsdag 1924-1940
Bogelund, Gerd (1923-1987) Ceramicist. An artist-in-residence at RC Factory since 1946. Worked a couple of years with Nathalie Krebs at Saxbo 1943. Most of her works is stoneware - but she also did porcelain pieces.
Bøggild, Mogens Kruse (1901-1987) Sculptor. Associated with B&G during 1943-1959

Cadavius, Ludvig Rudolf (1890-1966) Sculptor. Worked with plaster 1914-1966 at RC factory. Eskimo model 1939
Carl-Nielsen, Anne Marie (1890-1966) At B&G
CF
Christensen, Leo Emanuel Holger (1890-1966) Sculptor and designer at RC Factory 1910-1960. Figurines
Christoffersen, Djalmar
Christoffersen, Helge (1925-1965) Sculptor. AT RC Factory 1948-1954. Figurines and vases
Clausen, Poul Finn (1932 -) Painter and **grafic** artist - At RC Factory from 1964
Clément, Charles Adolphe Antione (1860-1933) Chemical engineer. At RC 1883-1891

Dahl Jensen, Jense Peter (1874-1960) Sculptor. At Bing & Grøndahl from 1897-1917. Director Norden Porce-

lain factory 1917-1925. Had his own factory Dahl Jensen Porcelain from 1925 - carried on by the family until 1985
Daneskjold-Samsoe, Count Adam Sofus (1874-1961), painter, sculptor. Figurine group. In the field (Roemarken) 1924
Didier, Les (1930 -) US artist working for Bing & Grøndahl
MDJ (Martha Dahl Jensen??
Drewes-Kofoed, Elizabeth (1877-1948) Painter. Signing artist for B&G 1895-1912

Ellison, Pauline
Engelhardt, Valdemar (1860-1915) Chemistry At RC 1891-1915
Erhard, Jens Aage (1898 - *) Sculptor. AT RC Factory 1923-1955
Eriksen, Christian Johannes Edvard (1876-1959) Sculptor. Model for RC of the Little Mermaid from 1913 - 1954
Ersgaard, C.

Fischer, Vilhelm Theodor (1857-1928) Painter and sculptor. At RC Factory 1894-1928 signing underglaze painter 1894-1928. Sea eagle 1919.
Flygenring, Hans (1881-1958). Painter. At the RC factory from 1902-1917. Overglaze painter 1902-1912. Signing underglaze painter 1912-1917. Artistic director at the Porsgrund Porcelain factory Norway 1920-1927
Fog, Astrid (1907-) Designer. Jewelry 1974 for RC
Fog Rostrup, Ester (Tut) (1907) Ceramicist. At B&G from 1947
Friis, Johannes Achton (1871-1939) Painter and illustrator. Bing & Grøndahl factory 1912-1925
Frimodt, Charlotte (1862 -1950) Painter at RC 1904 - 1905
Fristrup, Nilaus (1836-1909) Painter. Designer at Aluminia from 1868
Fritsch, Elisabeth (1940) At B&G

Galster, Johan Georg Castonier (1910 -) Sculptor. Figurines At RC factory 1961-1972. Figurines for B&G
Garde, Suzanne (Susanne) Fanny (1855-1928) Painter. At Bing & Grøndahl Factory 1886-1928. Designer of the Seagull pattern
Gauguin, Jean René (1881 Paris - 1961) Sculptor. Signing artist at B&G 1923-1961
Gelert, Johannes (1852-1923) Sculptor. Bust of Ludvig Holberg 1881 in Bisquit 1884 at Royal Copenhagen
Griegst, Arje (1938 -) Goldsmith, Sculptor. Designed Jewlry 1975. "Havterrin" and "Konkylie (conch)" for RC
Grut, Vivian Jeanne (1927 -) Sculptor. At RC Factory from 1950 Animal Figurines
Guldberg, Frk.
Guldbrandsen, Julius Vilhelm (1869 - 1908) Painter. Signing underglaze artist at RC Factory 1902-1908.

Hallier, Carl (1873-1948). Ceramicist. At RC 1913-1948
Hallin, Frederik August (1865-1947) Signing underglaze painter at RC factory 1885-1895. At Bing & Grøndahl 1895-1935
Hammeleff, Frederik (1847-1916) Sculptor. Shield with portraits of the Royal Family 1887 at the RC Factory
Hammershøj, Svend (1873 - 1948) Painter and ceramicist. Signing underglaze painter at RC Factory 1891-1894. AT B&G from 1898 - 1900
Hansen, Vilhelm (1824-1898) Painter. 1839 -1894 at RC Factory. Decorating vases and dinnerware.
Hansen, Aksel (Axel) Christian Henrik (1853-1933) Sculptor. RC: Bust in underglaze 1887,
Hansen, Bente Vita (1941) Ceramicist. AT B&G 1964-1970
Hansen, Einar
Hansen, Hans Henrik (1894-1965) Sculptor, From 1908 at RC. Design master at the RC Factory from 1926 -1965
Hansen-Reistrup, Frederik Karl Kristian (1863-1929) Painter and Sculptor. 1882-1885; 1887 and 1893 at RC factory. Blueprint for decoratiions and a few unica vases. Artistic Director at the Kahler Art Pottery. Postplate 1909
Harboe, Rasmus (1868-1912) Aluminia
Hasselriis, Kathrine Antoinette Else (1878-1943) Painter and silhuettør at RC Factory 1904 - 1949. 121 H.C. Andersen motives 1938
Hasted, Martha (1888 -1992) Sculptor. Designer at RC Factory 1911-1920. Figurines
Hatting, M.
Hedegaard, Johannes (1915 -) Sculptor. At the RC factory 1948 - 1967. Figurines Vases Bowls. Dinnerware pattern "Rimmon" and "Sheba" 1965-1966
Heerup, Henry (1907) Painter and sculptor. Royal Copenhagen decoration of annual egg 1976 and WNF plates 1979-1981
Heesen Cooper, Addie Works for Bing and Grøndahl. Designed the Gentle Love Collection
Hegermann-Lindencrone, Effie Frederikke Nicoline Octavia (1860-1945). At Bing & Grøndahl Factory 1886-1942
Heiberg
Heilmann, Gerhard (1859-1946) Painter. Signing underglaze painter at Royal Copenhagen 1890-1902
Hein, Piet (1905) Designer. Salt and pepper shaker Royal Copenhagen
Helweg-Møller, Bent (1883-1956) architect. At RC Factory 1910-1914. Vases, bowls and plates. Child Welfare 1910-1914. Carlsberg 1911
Henning, Gerhard (1880-1967) Sculptor. Figurines for Royal Copenhagen 1908-1914 and 1920-1925
Henriksen, Nikolaj Kampmann Harald (1883-1960) Painter. At Royal Copenhagen 1912-1930. Signing underglaze painter.
Henriksen, Niels Georg (1855-1922). Sculptor. At RC Factory 1876-
Herløw, Erik (1913 -) Architect and designer. AT Royal Copenhagen 1956-1961
Herold, Christian Peter (1879 - 1920) Sculptor. Animal figurines for Royal Copenhagen 1908-1909
Hetting, Willy Georg (1920). Ceramicist. At B&G 1950-1960

Heuch, Jacob Aall Bonevie (1862-1913) Sculptor. Figurines, inkset, vases and the Tulip patern for Royal Copenhagen 1895-1912

Hjuler, Charlotte Frederikke Marie (1894-1986) Illustrator. H.C. Andersen figurines for Royal Copenhagen 1975

Hoffmann, Anker (1904-1985) Sculptor. Figurine for Royal Copenhagen 1928

Holten (Skovgaard), Suzette Cathrine (1863 -1937) Signing underglaze painter RC Factory 1910 - 1914

Hyldahl, Margrethe Artist at Bing & Grøndahl factory 1909-1963

Høst, Marianne Mathea (1863-1929) Painter. Started at Royal Copenhagen as blue painter # 46 later signing underglaze painter 1885-1904

Haack, Eva () Painter at RC

Irminger, Engeborg Plockross (1872-1962) Bing & Grøndahl 1897-1960

Jacobsen, C. ( ) Sculptor. At B&G 1896-1898

Jacobsen, Carl Ludvig (1835-1923) Nowegian painter and sculptor. Statue in bisquit for Royal Copenhagen 1888

Jacobsen, Robert (1912) Decoration of Royal Copenhagen Annual Egg 1978

Jahn, Adolf (1858) German sculptor. Designed "Nathan the wise" in 1913 for Royal Copenhagen

Jais-Nielsen, Johannes Knud Ove (1885-1961). Sculptor and painter. At RC 1920-1961

Jensen, Edvard ( ) Bing & Grøndahl RC Factory

Jensen, Freddy (1935 -) Illustrator. Trained painter at Royal Copenhagen. Designing utilian items 1970

Jensen, Laurids (Lauritz) (1859-1935), Sculptor. Animal figurines for Royal Copenhagen 1906-1916. Worked for B&G and Dahl Jensen Porcelain

Jensen, Carl Christian Oluf (1871-1934) Painter. At RC Factory 1885-1934. Educated at Royal Copenhagen as a blue painer 1885. Signing underglaze painter until 1934. Decoration of Gray Porcelain, Vases and bowls. Christmas Plates 1911, 1917, 1918, 1919, 1921, 1923, 1925, 1929, 1932 and 1934. Signed works in Crackle

Jensen, Søren Georg (1917-1982) Ceramicist. At B&G 1962 -

Jensen-Klint, Peder Vilhelm (1853-1930) Architect. Blueprint to pharmacy Jars for Royal Copenhagen 1909

Jensen-Kromand, Sophus ( ) Painter. Signing artist at B&G 1910-1947

Jeppesen, Anni Rigmor (f. 1922 -). Ceramicist. At Royal Copenhagen 1953-1958 and 1961 - 1965. Works in blanc de Chine

Jespersen, Svend Olfert Neumann (1895-1985) Sculptor. B&G

Joachim, Hans Christian (1870 -1943) Painter and ceramic artist. The widdow of P.Ipsen art pottery in the 1890s. Aluminia 1901 where he became Artistic director 1911. Artistic director at RC Factory 1922-33.

Johansen, Karl Otto (1918) Sculptor. At B&G 1960 -

Jørgensen, J. Block

Jørgensen, Alma Agnethe (1918 -) Ceramicist and sculptor. AT B&G 1967-1976

Jørgensen, Anna Birgitte (1870 -) Painter. At RC 1887 - 1892

Jørgensen, Poul Christian (1882-1941)

Jørgensen, Axel Valdemar (1879-1929) Painter. At RC 1911 - 1912

Kelsey, Sterett RC figurines and Bronze

Kinck, Agnete Helvig (1872 - 1956), painter and sculptor at Royal Copenhagen

Kinstler, Calvin Roy ( ) Sculptor. At Bing & Grøndahl

Kiærschou, Paul Andrreas (1900-1933). Dog figurines for Royal Copenhagen 1921-1927

Kjærgaard, Richard (1919) Ceramicist. At B&G 1958-1962

Kjølner, Theodor Balduin (1886 -1972) Signing painter at RC Factory 1913 -1933 and 1936-1972

Klein, Christian Leonhart (d) (1810-1891) Painter. At RC Factory 1824-1891

Klyde, Henry worked for Bing and Grøndahl

Koefoed (Sørensen), Inge-Lise Ceramicist at Royal Copenhagen 1976-1978

Kofoed, Hans Peter (1868 - 1908) Painter. At B&G 1898-1908

Kondrup, Miss J. () Painter. AT RC 1885 - 1890

Kongsbøll, Emma Sofie (1880-1944) Painter. At B&G

Koppel, Henning (1918-1981) Designer. Associated with B&G since 1961

Kortzau, Ole (1939 -) Architect and designer. At Royal Copenhagen 1978

Krebs, Johanne Nathalie (1895-1978) Chemical Engineer. AT B&G 1920-1928. Founded Saxbo 1931-1968

Kristiansen, Bop (1944-1991) Ceramicist. AT RC from 1974

Kristoffersen, Karl Inuit figurines for B&G

Krog, Arnold Emil (1856-1931) Architect and painter, Architect Director of Royal Copenhagen 1885-1916, then artistic adviser to 1931

Krogh, Christian Worked for Bing and Grøndahl. Designed commemorative plate number 26.

Krohn, Pietro Købke (1840-1905) Ceramicist, Painter and illustrator. Artisitic Director of Bing & Grøndahl 1885-1890

Kyhn, Carl Edward Knud (1880-1969), painter and sculptor, RC Factory in periods: 1903-1910; 1924-1932 and 1936- 1967. Herman A Kahler, Naestved 1920-1924. Bing & Grøndahl 1908-1915 and 1933-1935.

Køje, Valdemar Ernst (1872- 1960), Painter. Brogetmaler 1903-08 at Royal Copenhagen.

Lange, Kai (1905 - 1987) illustrator and designer. At RC Factory in periods 1919 -1983. Christmasplates, lamps and vases

Langelund, Pia (1960-) At the RC Factory 1991

Larsen, Jenny ( ) Painter. At B&G 1901-1922

Larsen, Ove Julius (1889-1945) At Bing & Grøndahl 1918-1922 and 1927-1945

Larsen, Peter Thorvald Kristiansen (1881-1947) At Bing & Grøndahl factory 1903-1918

Larson, Carl (1853 - 1919) Swedish artist. Decoration on plates for B&G

Lautrup (Willumsen), Edith Wessel (1875-1963) AT B&G

Lehmann (Westring), Jenny (1869 -) Sculptor at RC 1911-1913

Leonhardt, Harry Axel Eduard (1879-1963) Painter. At B&G 1910-1915 and 1920-1925

Liisberg, Carl Frederik (1860-1909). Sculptor and painter. At RC Factory 1885-1909

Liisberg, Carl Hugo (1896-1958) Sculptor. Animal figures. At Royal Copenhagen 1918 - 1921

Lindahl, Lotte () Ceramicist and painter. At B&G 1902-1946

Lindhart, Svend Villiam Peder (1898-1989) Sculptor. At B&G

Lindstrøm, Svend Aage Robert (1902) RC

Locher, Axel Thilson (1879-1941) Sculptor. At B&G 1897 - 1900. Figurines to Royal Copenhagen in 1913.

Locher, Jo(hanne) Hahn (1876-1961) Painter. Signing artist at Bing & Grøndahl 1898-1940

Loon, Johan van (1934 -) Dutch ceramicist. One-of-a-kind works 1977 at Royal Copenhagen

Lucheschitz Jensen. Therese Maria (1896-1985) Sculptor. At B&G from 1946

Ludvigsen, Carl Frederik (1883-1958) Chemical engineer At RC 1911-1922 and 1947-1953

Lund, Carl Ove Julian (1852 - 1936), painter at Royal Copenhagen 1872 -1886 and 1893 - 1995

Lundberg, Theodor (1852-1926) Swedish Sculptor. Designed "The wave and rock" for Royal Copenhagen 1897

Madsen, Sten Lykke (1937) Ceramicist. Associated with B&G since 1962. Modern sculptures

Madsen, Svejstup (1883 - 1946) Sculptor. Figurins for B&G and Royal Copenhagen

Madsen, Theodor (1880-1965) Sculptor. At Royal Copenhagen 1896 - 1936. Designed more than 61 animal figurines.

Madslund, H.A.L. (1888-1947) Ceramicist. AT B&G 1916-1930

Magadini, Christopher Bing and Grøndahl artist and designer of the American Heritage plate series

Magnussen, Erik (1940) Ceramicist. Associated with B&G since 1962

Malinowski, Johannes Franz Arno (1899-1976) Sculptor. At Royal Copenhagen from 1921 - 1936.

Malmer, Ellen (1942) Ceramicist. Since 1965 at Royal Copenhagen Alluminia

Princess Marie-Amélie-Francoise-Hélène, Princess of Denmark (1865-1909) Painter Sculptor. Hippos for Royal Copenhagen 1901 - 1902

Martin-Hansen, Mads Christian Carl (1877-1941) Sculptor. Overglaze figurines 1904 - 1912 at Royal Copenhagen

Mathiesen, Olaf (1876 -1953) Ceramicist and sculptor. At Royal Copenhagen from ? 1904

McPailey, Roger () British artist - made models for Royal Copenhagen 1978

Meyer, Grethe (1918 -) Architect and designer. Dinnerware pattern "Hvidpot" 1972

Meyer, Jenny Sophie (1866-1927) Painter. Signing underglaze artist at Royal Copenhagen 1892 - 1927

Mezger, Gerda (1885 - 1964) Painter. Signing underglaze painter under the name Gerda von Kohl at Royal Copenhagen 1911-1913

Middelboe, Doreen ( ) Ceramicist. Associated with RC from 1968

Mitchell, James E. (b.1926) US Marine Painter

Moe, Louis (1857 - 1945) Painter and illustrator. War and peace plate for Royal Copenhagen 1915

Mogensen, Jørgen (1927) Chemical engener. At RC 1949-1964

Moltke, Count Harold (1971-1960) Painter. Designed Greenland motives plates for RC Factory 1907 -1908. At Bing & Grøndahl 1908-1914

Mortensen, Carl (1861-1945). Sculptor and Painter. Signing underglaze painter at Royal Copenhagen from 1887-1901. Figurines for B&G

Mourier-Petersen, Christian Vilhelm (1858-1945) Painter. Signing underglaze painter at Royal Copenhagen 1894 - 1895

Munck Andersen, Hans Erik (1943) Annual mug for RC

Munch-Petersen, Lisbet (1909 - 1997) Ceramicist. Associated with B&G 1961-1966

Munch-Petersen, Ursula Birgitte (1937) Ceramicist. At B&G 1961-1968

Musse, Malene Müllertz (1949) Ceramicist. AT B&G 1970-1973. AT RC from 1977

Møller, Knud Max (1879-1965) Sculptor. At B&G 1909-1912 and 1914-1921

Nathanielsen, Miss Bertha (1869-1914) Painter. At RC 1893-1906

Nielsen (Petersen), Andrea (1872-1936) Sculptor. Designed animal figurines for Royal Copenhagen 1897-1919

Nielsen, Clara ( ) Painter. AT B&G 1896 - 1948

Nielsen, Erik (1857-1947) Sculptor. At Royal Copenhagen from 1887-1926

Nielsen, Herne (1912 -) Designer & ceramicist. At RC Factory 1928-1945. Christmas plate 1938

Nielsen, Ingeborg (1879 -) Sculptor. AT Royal Copenhagen 1904

Nielsen, Jørgen (1942 -) Painter. Design of jewelry for RC 1977

Nielsen, Kai (1882-1924) Sculptor. Did work for both RC and B&G

Nielsen, Niels (1872 - 1921) Sculptor. Polar bear for Royal Copenhagen in 1911

Nielsen, Otto (1877-1959) Painter. Underglaze painter at RC from 1913 - 1932

Nielsen, Poul Jacob (1917) Ceramicist. At RC

Nielsen, Svend Nicolai (1899-) Ceramicist. AT RC

Nissen, John Meiniche (1931 -) Sculptor. Designing for RC 1957-1958

Nordstrøm, Patrick (1870 -1929). Sculptor. At RC 1911 - 1923

Nylund, Felix ( ) Finish sculptor and painter. Worked at B&G

Nylund, Gunnar Åge Felix David (1904-1996) Ceramicist. Worked at B&G 1937- 1938

Nyrop, Martin (1849-1921) Architect. Designing Pharmacy Jars for RC 1913

Nørretranders, Johs. () Paintter. At RC 1902 - 1905

Obel, Nils (1937 -) Painter. RC 1976 - 1978

Olsen, Cathinka Wilhelmine (1868-1947) Ceramicist. At Bing & Grøndahl factory 1896 -1947

Olsen, Christian Benjamin (1875-1935) Marine painter. At Bing & Grøndahl 1906- 1913. Signing underglaze painter at RC Factory 1913-1935

Olsen, John (1938 -) Sculptor - bisquit works 1977 for RC

Olsen, Thorkild (1890-1973), Painter. AT RC 1908-1968. Dinnerware: "Dagmar"; "Qaker Grass";"Hvedekorn" Vases poupre de Chine and bleu royal

Olsen, Viggo (1885-1955) Painter RC Factory (1913 -1955) Christmas plates 1944 and 1950

Oppenheim, Johanne Louise (1860-1939) Painter. Signing underglaze painter at RC 1889-1895

Oppenheim Jais-Nielsen, Ville (1886 - 1949) Sculptor. Model for RC 1913

Orth, Emil Cordius Heinrich (1833-1919). Painter. At RC Factory 1869-1902

Overgaard, Regitze (1946) Designer. Jewelry 1977 for RC

Pedersen, Michael (1882-1918) Sculptor. Models for RC 1913 - 1918

Pedersen (Petersen), Knud Valdemar (1906-1981) Ceramicist. At B&G from 1931

Petersen, Armand ( ) Sculptor. At B&G

Petersen, Johan Carl Christian (1874-1923) Architect and ceramicist. At B&G 1910 - 1912

Petersen, Peter Elias (1859-1950) Painter. 1892 -1996 at Royal Copenhagen

Petersen, Rita Byrge (1944 -) Illustrator - RC 1974

Petersen, Åge Emanuel (1894-1948) Painter - marinemotives for RC 1918-1922

Platen-Hallermund, Count Francis Valdemark (1875-1965). Sculptor. Fish, dogs and animals for RC 1918-1931

Plockross, E. Worked for Bing and Grøndahl, designed the 1907 Christmas plate

Plum, Niels Munk (1878-1959) Painter. Signing underglaze painter at RC 1912 - 1931

Poulsen, Christian Theodor (1911-1991) Ceramicist. At B&G 1940 - 1945

Pramvig, Børge

Printz Mogensen, Ursula (1920) Ceramicist. One-of-a-kind works for Rc 1951-1953

Proschowsky, Poul M. (1893-1968), Cheical Engener at RC 1918-1925

Quistgaard, Erik Einar Harald (1887-1979) Sculptor. 5 soldier figurines in overglaze for RC 1935

Rasmussen, Peder (1929-1964) Ceramicist. At Bing & Grøndahl 1959 - 1964

Refsgaard, Niels (1934 -) Ceramicist. Dinnerware "Noblesse" 1980-1982 for RC

Reiff, Erik (1923 -) Ceramicist. At RC from 1977

Ring, Svend (1893-1933), Painter. Signing underglaze painter at RC 1919-1922

Rode, Aksel (1905-1988) Painter. Signing artist B&G

Rode, Gotfred Andrew Anderson (1862 -1937) Painter. Signing artist at RC Factory 1896-1933

Rosing, Jens Christian (1925) Greenland

Sabra, S. B&G 1901 Christmas Plate

Sadolin, Ebbe (1900 -), Maler. At B&G from 1926

Sadolin, Else ( )

Salto, Axel (1889-1961), Painter; Sculptor and Ceramicist. At B&G 1923-1925. Dinnerware, Vases, Stoneware for RC 1931-1961

Samsung, Dag (1949 -) Painter. Design of plates.

Sandholt (Bluhme), Else Marie (1872-1942) Painter. Child figurines for RC 1913-1918

Schou, Johanne Amalie (- 1966). Painter. At B&G 1907 - 1966

Schou, Hans Henrik (1884 - 1949) Painter. Signing artist at RC 1912-1913

Schou, Helen (1905 -) Sculptor. Models for RC 1959 and B&G

Schwalpe, Ole (1929 -) Painter. Decoration of Annual egg for RC 1977

Seeberg, Kirsten works for Bing and Grøndahl. Artist of the Snow Fairies collection

Seidelin, Henning (1904-1987) Sculptor. At B&G 1943 -1951

Selchau, Ellinor (1899 -) Ceramic artist. Com. Plates fro RC

Sinding, Stephan Worked for Bing and Grøndahl. Designed the first two commemorative plates.

Skrydstrup, Ingeborg () Painter. At B&G 1903-1957

Slott-Moeller, Georg Harald (1864-1937) Painter. Artistic director Aluminia 1902 -1906

Smidth, Anna (1861-1951) Painter. Signing underglaze painter 1885-1915 at RC

Smidth, Marie Margrethe (1877-1978) Painter. AT B&G 1900 -1957

Spang Olsen, Ib Otto (1922) Author and artist

Spies, Sophie (1858-1934) Sculptor. Figurine for RC 1911

Stage, Mads Gerhard (1922) Danish illustrator. Plate decoration at RC from 1956

Stenstrup, Gert. Johannes Resen (1898 - 1921)

Stephensen, Magnus Læssøe (1903 -1984) Architect and designer. Dinnerware "Patella" 1957

Stephensen, Snorre (1943 -) Ceramicist. Models and glaze for vases, lamps and more at Royal Copenhagen 1970

Strand, George Kofød (1895 - 1930) Sculptor. Models for RC 1919-1927

Stæhr-Nielsen (Vilhjelm), Eva (1911-1976) Ceramicist. AT RC from 1968. At Saxbo from 1932 - 1968

Sternow, Worked for Bing and Grøndahl designed commemorative plate number 36

Svensson, Karen Margrethe (Kamma) (1908-1988) Illustrator. Mother´s days plates 1971 og 1972

Swane, Lars (1913 -) Painter. Signing underglaze painter at Royal Copenhagen 1954 - 1959

Syberg, Hans Peter (1895-1979) Sculptor. AT B&G 1920 - 1922

Søe (Howitzz), Mrs. I. H. (1885) Sculptor. At RC 1913 -

Sørensen, Karl (1896 - 1947) Painter. Signing underglaze artist at RC 1923 - 1927

Tegner, Hans Christian Harald (1853-1932) Artist & Ceramicist. At Bing & Grøndahl 1912-1932

Thejll, Andreas (1852 - 1908) Architect. Com. Plate for RC

Thelander, Henry

Therkelsen, Allan Jochum (1960) Sculptor RC Factory 1990 -

Thomsen, Christian (1860 -1921) Sculptor and modeller. At RC Factory 1898 - 1920. Christmas plates, figurines and vases

Thorsson, Nils Johan Thorvald (1898 - 1975) Ceramic artist. Worked at RC from 1912 - 1975). Artistic director at Royal Copenhagen from 1949

Thylstrup, Georg Christian Peter (1884 - 1930) Sculptor. Made models for RC from 1911 -1923. Signed One-of-a-kind charger and vases

Thymann, Vita Birgitte (1925) Figurines for B&G

Tidemand, Nicolai (1888- 1975) Painter. Overglaze decoration crackle on vases and chargers. Signing artist at RC 1918 - 1943

Timyn, William () British Sculptor. Figurines for RC 1976

Tjerne, Hans Frithjof Immanuel (1899-1968) Painter and ceramicist. At Bing & Grøndahl 1927-1940

Trap, Anna (1877 - 1943) Sculptor. Made birds for RC 1909-1910

Trolle (Oxmund), Anne Marie (1944 -) Ceramicist. AT RC since 1960

Ungermann, Arne (1902-1981) Illustrator.Mother's days plates for RC 1973 - 1975

Ussing, Stephan Peter Johannes Hjort (1868 - 1958) Painter. At RC Factory 1894 - 1930. Signing artist

Utzon, Lin (1946 -) Designer. Dinnerware decoration for RC 1975

Utzon-Frank, Einar (1888-1955) Sculptor. Models for RC 1939

Varming, Hanne (1939) Sculptor. Models for RC 1968

Vasegaard (Hjorth), Gertrud (1913) Ceramicist. Dinnerware for RC: "Gemina" 1960, "Gemma" 1961, "Capella" 1975

Vasegaard, Marie Myre (1936) Ceramicist. At Bing & Grøndahl 1955-1959.

Vestergaard, Sven (1932 -) Illustrator. RC Factory 1965 -

Wagner, Olga (1873 - 1963) Sculptor. Models for RC 1913. Mermaid

Wagner, Seigfried (1874 - 1952). Sculptor. Models of chess figurines for RC 1913

Waldorff, Vilhelm (1877-1935) Sculptor. Models for RC 1923 - 1925

Warberg, Alhed (1872-1927) Painter. Signing artist for RC 1890-1893

Weiss, Claire (1906) Sculptor. AT B&G

Weiss, Ivan (1946) RC

Wieben, Anthon Christian (1894 - 1947) Painter. At RC 1918 -1931

Windfeld-Hansen, Jens (1944) Silversmith. At RC from 1970. Jewelry

Wilhjelm, Edith Fransiska (1893-1919) Painter. At B&G 1916 - 1919

Willerup, Peter Oscar (1864-1931) Painter. Aluminia from 1910

Willumsen, Bode (1895 -1987) Sculptor, Ceramicist. Signing artist at RC 1941 - 1947

Willumsewn, Jens-Ferdinand (1863-1958). Designer. Artistic Director for B&G 1897-1900

Witter, Anna Deborine Dorthea Kristine (1884 - 1938), Sculptor. Models for RC 1913 - 1918

Wolffsen, Hans Ancher (1870-1924) Painter. AT B&G 1910-1928

Woodson, Jack American artist and designer of the Bing and Grøndahl Christmas in America Plate Series

Zernichow, Catherine Helene (1864 - 1942) Painter. Signing artist at RC 1905-1926

Appendix B:

Factory Date Marks

Bing & Grøndahl

Date Marks

1853-1894

1899-1901 (and/or 1923-1934)

1914

1895-1897

1902-1913

1915-1947

1948-1951

1952-1957

1958-1961

1962-1969

1970 to merger with Royal Copenhagen

Royal Copenhagen Date Marks

1870-1893

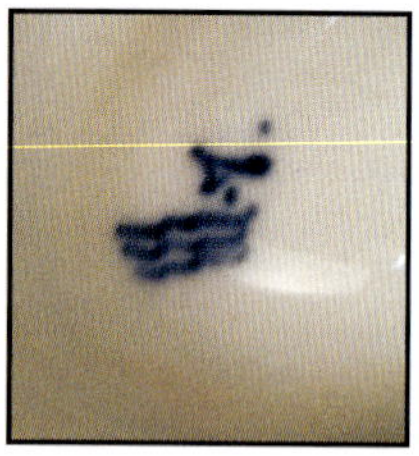

1894-1900

1898-1923

1923-1934

1935 to present

Specific Date Marks from 1935 to present

Underglaze			Year
Strike Over letter	R	ROYAL	1935
	O		1936
	Y		1937
	A		1938
	L		1939
Strike over letter	C	COPENHAGEN	1940
	O		1941
	P		1942
	E		1943
	N		1944
	H		1945
	A		1946
	G		1947
	E		1948
	N		1949
Strike under letter	R	ROYAL	1950
	O		1951
	Y		1952
	A		1953
	L		1954

Strike under letter	D	DENMARK	1955
	E		1956
	N		1957
	M		1958
	A		1959
	R		1960
	K		1961
Strike under letter	C	COPENHAGEN	1962
	0		1963
	P		1964
	E		1965
	N		1966
	H		1967
	A		1968
	G		1969-1974
	E		1975-1979
	N		1980-1984
Strike over both letters	R O	ROYAL	1985-1993
	R Y		1994-1999
	R A		2000-2004